Illustrated Buyer's Guide
PORSCHE

BY DEAN BATCHELOR
REVISED AND UPDATED BY RANDY LEFFINGWELL

motorbooks

First published in 1983 by Motorbooks, an imprint of MBI Publishing Company, 400 First Avenue North, Suite 300, Minneapolis, MN 55401 USA

Motorbooks titles are also available at discounts in bulk quantity for industrial or sales-promotional use. For details write to Special Sales Manager at MBI Publishing Company, 400 First Avenue North, Suite 300, Minneapolis, MN 55401 USA.

To find out more about our books, visit us online at www.motorbooks.com.

Library of Congress Cataloging-in-Publication Data

Batchelor, Dean.
  Illustrated Porsche buyer's guide / Dean Batchelor; revised and updated by Randy Leffingwell. — 5th ed.
    p. cm.
  Includes index.
  ISBN 978-0-7603-3606-9 (softback)
  1. Porsche automobiles—Purchasing. I. Leffingwell, Randy, 1948- II. Title.
  TL215.P75B37 2010
  629.222'2—dc22
                                    2010012157

Front cover: © Ron Kimball/Kimball Stock

Title page: Porsche's newest model, the four-passenger sedan Panamera, provides occupants an exciting driving and riding experience. Engineers developed handling in the base model rear-drive Panamera S that strongly resembles two-door rear-engined 911 models. Acceleration and handling in the all-wheel drive Turbo S are on a par with the best high-performance two seaters, adding the luxury of comfortable rear seats and a large rear storage area.

Back cover: The importation saga for hopeful American buyers was stormy at best. Soon after assembly began, Porsche decided not to bother federalizing 959s for U.S. customers. Only a few cars filtered into the country until laws changed in the early 2000s, allowing their use in the States.

Editor: Peter Schletty
Design Manager: Kou Lor
Cover designed by: Pauline Molinari

Printed in China

Contents

Credits and Acknowledgments

I want to express my sincere and grateful thanks to those who gave time, information, technical assistance, or furnished photos, to aid in the creation of this book: Argus Publishers Corporation; Frank Barrett; Tom Birch; Greg Brown, *European Car* (formerly *VW & Porsche*); Larry Brown, Porsche+Audi; Gary Emory, Porsche Parts Obsolete; Brett Johnson, PB Tweeks; Bill Jones, Jones' Autowerkes; Fred Heyler, Porsche+Audi; Martha McKinley, PCNA; Don Orosco; Jim Perrin; Rudi Spielberger, Porsche+Audi; Chuck Stoddard, Stoddard Imported Cars, Inc.; Vic Skirmants; Betty Jo Turner, *Porsche Panorama*; Dr. Leonard Turner; Robert Wood, Robert W. Wood, Inc.; *Road & Track* library.

And to those who allowed me to photograph their cars: Gene Gilpin, Harrah's Automobile Collection, Brian Kleeman, Bill Motta, Bob Racher, Carter Robinson, Steve Sailors, Dean Watts.

—Dean Batchelor

I wish to express my sincere thanks to those who contributed time, photos, information, automobiles or philosophy to this 4th edition. Foremost, I thank the late Dean Batchelor, who inspired and encouraged me to do my first book and whose deep footsteps have directed my own path.

For this new revised edition, I am most grateful to Porsche Cars North America for permission to reproduce their photographs of current and recent Porsche production automobiles. In addition, I wish to thank Bob Carlson, General Manager, Public Relations; Barbara Manha, Media Relations Manager, and Dan Hopper, Public Relations, Porsche Cars North America, Reno, Nevada, for their generous assistance.

In addition, I want to convey my gratitude to several individuals for their efforts on this new edition: Bruce Anderson, BookWorks, Clark Anderson, San Jose, California; Sunnyvale, California; Jaime Arias, Steve Taub Porsche, Santa Monica, California; Otis Chandler, Ojai, California; Warren Eads, Palos Verdes Estates, California; Matt Harrington, Chatsworth, California; Prescott Kelly, West Redding, Connecticut; Dirk Layer, Vail, Colorado; Kent Morgan, Montebello, California; Dave Morse, Campbell, California; Kerry Morse, Tustin, California; John and Ray Paterek, Paterek Brothers, Chatham, New Jersey; Gerry Reilly, Hardwick, Massachusetts; Steve Sailors, Huntington Beach, California; and Carl Thompson, Torrance, California.

—Randy Leffingwell

Introduction

by Dean Batchelor

Porsche fever has got you, right? You see the beautiful people zipping around in those squat, racy-looking coupes with five-thousand-dollar paint jobs and raucous exhausts that make them sound like they've just finished twenty-four hours at Le Mans. Maybe you've been passed on a winding road by a road-hugging coupe that has wheels and tires that look too big for the car, and on the rear sloping deck is a strange-looking device (looks sort of like the tail of a whale) that's large enough to be a picnic table.

Or you're sitting in your car at a stop signal and a low-slung coupe pulls alongside. You can't decide which to admire first, the car or the driver. (Porsches always seem to be driven by, or have as a passenger, a beautiful woman—they go together somehow.)

Maybe you've been to Sebring, Riverside, Elkhart Lake, Road Atlanta, Le Mans, or the Nürburgring and seen Porsches in action—very often in the winner's circle.

Nevermind what prompted you, you're finally ready to make your move, but you aren't 100 percent sure you know the best way to do it. I'm not sure there is a "best way" but I'll do what I can to help you make the right decision.

One thing to get straight right at the start is that even though you may have located a car you want—through a friend or an advertisement in a magazine or newspaper—you don't have to be in a hurry. That car you've located may not still be available next month, next week, or even tomorrow, but that doesn't mean you have to buy it today either. It is possible you would miss the greatest bargain of all time, but it's also possible (and may even be probable) the car is a disaster and to jump into the deal without sufficient knowledge could be the costliest automotive investment mistake you'll ever make.

Porsche A. G. has been building cars since 1949 and in mid-July 1996, it produced its one millionth automobile. Of those, more than 700,000 are still on the road. Half of its total production was sold in European, United Kingdom, Australian, and Asian markets. The other half came to the United States. Of those, half came to West Coast, primarily to southern California. This distribution is beneficial to Americans looking for a used Porsche; the climate in California is so mild that automobiles live longer, and there are a greater number of serviceable, more readily enjoyable, and more economically restorable Porsches available, which is important because the earlier models have severe rust problems (more about this later).

At this point I should say that research and thorough preparation will be your biggest assets (along with money) in buying the right car. At the back of this book are lists of Porsche clubs, magazines that carry features about Porsches on a regular basis, selected books about Porsches, and sources for service and hard-to-get parts.

A tremendous cottage industry has sprung up in the last few years with persons specializing in certain models: 356, 911/912, 914, or the later front-engined, water-cooled models. The specialization goes even further with those who work only on the four-cam, four-cylinder engines, or do only upholstery, or only metal work, or painting. There are stores that have bought up all the old stocks of Porsche parts they can get their hands on, and a few of them are manufacturing repro parts and accessories.

Finding a used Porsche to buy is not difficult. Finding a rare or special model probably will be difficult. The major newspapers in the larger U.S. cities such as New York, Los Angeles, Houston, Dallas, Atlanta, Miami, San Francisco, Boston, Chicago, or Detroit should all have Porsches offered through their classified advertising section. Specialty automotive publications such as *Road & Track, AutoWeek, Hemmings Motor News*, or *Old Cars Weekly*, in the United States, or *Autocar, Autosport, Motor, Motor Sport, Motoring News, Classic and Sports Cars*, or *Thoroughbred and Classic Cars*, in England, are all excellent sources. *Das Auto Motor und Sport* in Germany, *l'Auto Journal* and *le Fanatique de l'Automobile* in France should also be good sources (Porsche-produced cars for the British and Australasian markets, so don't fail to find out which side the steering wheel is on).

The ads placed in these publications may or may not be accurate, and you're at their mercy (caveat emptor) unless you've done your homework. Ads in Porsche club publications, and they all carry ads for cars or parts for sale, are better in many ways. The car may not be priced right, but it should be pretty much described because the seller is reaching a knowledgeable audience (one which may know more about the car than he does), many of whom are his friends and acquaintances.

You can just about forget the "bargain" Porsche, or the one you think you can "steal" from some pigeon who doesn't know what he or she has. It still happens, but it's so rare that you can safely discount the probability

of it happening to you. Apocryphal stories such as the one about the divorcee who's advertised a low-mileage 911SC in mint condition for $100 (because her ex-husband told her to sell the car and send him half the money) abound; and if you believe that nonsense, I have a "waterfront" lot in Florida I'd like to sell you. . . .

So, to acquire the Porsche of your dreams, you must learn as much as you can about Porsches—particularly the years and models that are close to the one you want. If your heart is set on an early 356, there's no reason to go overboard researching the 900 series cars. And if you prefer a later model then you can skip research on the earlier cars. All that can come later if you decide you want to know all there is to know about the company and its cars. Save yourself time and money by pinpointing your research toward the model you want. If you don't want, then read on. The *Illustrated Porsche Buyer's Guide* can be considered a primer, as you'll get the basic information about each model built, and you can then zero in on your target car.

Even limiting the research to one model or one type can be time-consuming, and you can count on spending $1,000 or more on books and other literature, just on a limited area of Porsche information. But this is a drop in the bucket when compared to what you'll spend on the car, and thorough research can save you far more money than the research material cost you. If you bought every book, brochure or magazine with Porsche features you could spend in the neighborhood of $10,000.

That's the good news about Porsche books. Now for the bad news. You'll note that my recommended list of Porsche books isn't very long, considering the number of books that has been published about the marque. This is because I've found, while doing research for this book, that the vast majority of Porsche books are not accurate enough to use for research. They all contain some good information, and some good-to-excellent photos or artwork, but forget most of them for total accuracy.

I invested a great deal of money and time buying and reading some of the books left off my list when I started research for this book, before I discovered them to be worthless for my purposes. If you find a book you think you want to buy but aren't sure about, ask a member of one of the Porsche clubs. Chances are he or she has at least seen them all, if not actually read them all. The avid car nut, no matter what make he likes, will often buy every book published about his favorite cars simply to have that photo or bit of information he didn't see elsewhere. He'll know the right books to buy.

Unfortunately, some of the information published by the Porsche factory or the distributor is confusing because it contradicts some other bit of information also published by the company.

Like many other car companies, Porsche may designate its components for a particular model year, but the parts may appear on an earlier or later car because they were on the shelf when a particular car went through the assembly process. This is not a prevalent situation, and the quantity of "odd" bits on a car is low, but it did happen often enough to cause argument among Porsche "experts" about a certain part being right or wrong. These odd parts don't make the particular vehicle any better or any worse, just different. And they don't make it any less desirable.

One of the major problems I've had in researching this book was to determine just when a certain mechanical change was made. Many of the sources you'll find won't tell you if they're using the calendar year or the model year.

This particular type of information is all academic to the buyer who simply wants to drive the car and enjoy it, with no intention of attempting to restore it to factory original or to show it at a Concours d'Elegance. Enthusiasts are strongly divided on this and there are good points to be made for either side.

There are enough Porsches of all years, all models, and all body styles left in the world so that I don't see anything wrong with installing disc brakes on a non-disc-brake-model, or later wheels, or even a different engine. If there were only three of a certain model left, and two were in museums and you had the third, then you would probably want to keep it original. it would be worth more, and should be preserved anyway.

Along with deciding which year, model, and body style you want, and whether the car is to be for driving or for show, you will need to know who is going to work on it. Will you do it, or take it to someone else? Unless you already know quite a bit about the mechanical makeup of a Porsche, you should probably join a club. I am not a "joiner" but in this case it makes sense, because if you need to find a mechanic, painter, upholsterer, or simply a good place to have the car serviced, chances are pretty good the members of a Porsche club will know all the good, and bad, mechanics in the area. And if you plan to work on the car yourself, these same clubs will also have members who have done a lot of their own work and can help you.

Porsches, Ferraris, Maseratis, and the like seem intimidating to the uninitiated, but if you have the right tools, a place to work on the car, and have a basic understanding of an automobile's components, you can do it. I have friends who have overhauled a Porsche or Ferrari engine with excellent results, due in part to being very careful when they dismantled and then reassembled the engine. I also know some professional mechanics whom I wouldn't take a car to—any car, never mind something a bit out of the ordinary.

If you have owned Porsches, or some other sports-type car, you will probably understand the advantages and disadvantages of owning and maintaining a car that is a bit out of the norm for parts, service, and driving.

Anyone who buys a Porsche should understand that it is a car that needs constant care and attention, and if properly maintained will be a joy to drive and probably as reliable as anything else on the road. Without this attention and careful maintenance, a Porsche could strand you in a terribly inconvenient spot, and then cost a bundle to fix once it's in the shop. But then, so could a lot of other cars that wouldn't be half as much fun to drive.

There's also the investment angle. Porsches are becoming more valuable and, although the early Porsches haven't caught up to early Ferraris for cost or value, they are therefore easier to buy, and still less expensive to restore than the Italian V-12.

And now a few words about a subject that is important to anyone considering the purchase of a used Porsche—rust and corrosion.

The unique design and unusual method of construction that make a Porsche a great automobile are also factors that may cause certain areas of the vehicle to be extremely susceptible to rust and deterioration. Obviously, older cars, and ones that live in areas where salt air and humidity are prevalent, are top candidates for rust. Also, those cars driven in areas where salt is used to melt ice from the roads in winter should be suspect, although most Porsche owners I know won't take their cars out in the winter in those areas.

On all 356 series cars, give the underside a very careful inspection. Start at the rear suspension torsion bar support tube that's attached to the floor or chassis pan (it's located in front and to the inside of each rear wheel). Inspect the box section where the tube is attached and move forward observing the floor from both under and inside the car. Lift up or remove the front and rear floor mats. Inspect carefully in the areas where the floor pan meets the vertical bulkheads, and also where the pan is spot-welded to the outer thresholds and the center tunnel. It is important to know:

1. Is the floor pan original, solid, and intact?
2. Or has it been replaced?
3. Will it need to be replaced or repaired?

Next, look at the longitudinal panels and jacking point spurs. These are the long panels that run along the outside of the floor pan between the front and rear wheels. They house the heating tubes that conduct warm air from the engine heat exchangers to the inside of the car, and support the jack points; two on each side of the car. These panels must be in excellent condition to do their job, which provides much of the car's rigidity.

Next, open the front hood and remove the spare tire so you can inspect the front battery pan. Look at it from both inside and under the nose. Even though this area is not as critical as the floor pan, it is important that you check for the same three points listed above.

Directly behind the battery pan are the front suspension torsion bar tubes. These were jig-welded in a fabricated box section. Close inspection for rust, corrosion, and previous accident damage is extremely important in this area.

Now open each door and inspect its bottom. If you don't have the car on a hoist, this will mean getting down on your knees; so, unless you're wearing your grubbies, bring along a cloth or piece of paper to kneel on. This area is important because rust repair on a 356 is very time consuming (read expensive) if done properly. I emphasize this on the 356 because all cars of this series were virtually handmade and each hinged panel (doors, front and rear lids) was hand-fitted and leaded to fit its own opening, then serial numbered to that particular body.

In other words, interchangeability with another 356 is almost impossible (without more hand-fitting and leading) if you want to maintain correct fit—gaps and contours—between body and hinged panel. This also means that even a brand new door or hood panel, if you're fortunate enough to find one, probably won't fit properly until it has been fit to the body.

All production Porsches of the 356 series were given a factory undercoating treatment that served as a sound deadener and protective undercoat over the bare metal. Unfortunately, it did a better job of dampening sound than of protecting the metal from rust. I urge you to be very careful while inspecting any area of a 356 where undercoating has been applied, especially fresh undercoat, as it could be a coating over good solid metal or it could be covering and hiding rusty metal.

The same areas need to be inspected on 900 series Porsches as on the 356 series. It will probably be easier to spot a rusty area on a 911 than it is on a 356 series car, and repairs are easier to make because the 900 series cars have some removable and interchangeable body panels. The 900 doors are still gapped by leading, but the front and rear hoods are not, and it is possible to interchange 911 panels from one car to another of the same year and model and still achieve a good fit. This applies to the removable front fenders of all 900 series cars.

Once you've found the Porsche you think you want to buy, try to find a similar car in either original or excellent restored condition to examine so you'll have something to compare your prize to. If that can't be done, try to take a knowledgeable Porsche enthusiast with you to examine your "new" car.

Better yet, insist on taking the car to a good mechanic for a thorough checkup. If the seller is convinced you're sincere, he shouldn't object to an inspection unless he has something to hide. It's your money, and it'll be your car to live with, good or bad.

At this point I can probably alienate most avid Porsche fanatics, but at the risk of being the target of the tar-and-feather brigade I may also save you some time and money. If you're undecided about what year Porsche to buy, consider an older one for investment or for show, and a newer one for driving. When I say older, I'm talking about road cars, not race cars (those are almost always good investments). A race car will be far more costly to buy, and may be more costly to restore, but it'll also be worth more in the end.

Porsches have mystique (as do Ferraris, Bugattis, pre-World War II Alfa Romeos, pre-Rolls-Royce Bentleys, and Mercedes-Benz SS, SSK, and SSKL), But not all Porsches are great cars. All the 356 series were ill-handling beasts in my opinion (the older they are, the worse they are), and have few qualities that recommend them for everyday driving. Wider-based wheels help, as do higher tire pressures at the back than at the front. And a camber compensator at the rear is a good addition; but no matter what is done to a 356, 356A, 356B, 356C, or 356 Carrera—particularly a Carrera 2—it will not give you the handling, safety, or comfort of the later Porsches.

The next question from the audience is: "If the early Porsches were really that bad, how did they achieve such a great reputation?" The answer is by comparison to their contemporaries. When the first Porsches were built, the buyer of a sports car had few choices: MG TC and later the TD and TF, Singer, Triumph TR-2 and 3, Jaguar XK-120, Jowett Jupiter or . . . Porsche. A few buyers were aware of Ferraris and Aston Martins, but most had never heard of those marques, let alone seen or driven one.

When an early Porsche, as poor a handling car as it was, is compared to its contemporaries it comes off pretty well. It cost more than all but the Jaguar, Aston Martin, or Ferrari, but it delivered performance that made it outstanding at the time. The speed, comfort, silence (once under way), and passenger room were unobtainable elsewhere at the price, and the Porsche was a gas miser compared to anything else—with or without the performance. But all these attributes have since been surpassed by most other cars, particularly by Porsche itself, and the early Porsche ride and handling simply are not satisfactory by today's standards.

This is not to say that an early 356 would be unbearable, but the potential buyer must understand that he or she would be getting a rather crude automobile by today's Porsche standards, If this is acceptable, and you can live with it, go for it. But you should drive one before you pay your money. Actually, one should drive any car before buying it.

Investment Rating

At this writing, prices have begun a slow, steady climb from the reaction to speculators earlier in the decade. Prices hit a bottom during the mid-1990s for all collectible automobiles and what is apparent now is slow, sensible growth, driven by serious collectors and wise enthusiasts. Educated, experienced market observers predict a snail's pace increase instead of the jack-rabbit run of the late 1980s and early 1990s. Finally, because the investment market is less consequential, this book—and these stars—may be taken more as a guide to driving enjoyment than as retirement fund planning.

In many cases, older cars have been refitted or retrofitted with large proportions of aftermarket parts. These ratings apply to cars as they would have left the factory, not those heavily modified. Porsche parts are generally expensive; aftermarket makers usually charge considerably less. Buyers should be aware that, with high performance driving capabilities, buyers get what they pay for.

★★★★★ The best. Highest values, both in financial and driving pleasure terms. These cars have the best probability of further appreciation. Generally, you will not find these advertised in magazines or newspapers. Most Porsches in this group are sold (or traded back and forth) from one knowledgeable enthusiast or collector to another. Prices can be in the six-to-seven figure brackets.

★★★★ Almost the best. Investment potential and driving excitement are very good, and these cars are more easily obtainable than the five-star cars. Some of these will be like five-star cars in that you may choose not to drive them regularly on the street because of their value or vulnerability. At the time of writing, these cars may reach very high-five figure prices.

★★★ Excellent value. These Porsches are highly desirable for being a very enjoyable driving experience and yet they will also not lose value. The investment value increase will be much slower than the higher two groups. Because these are more affordable, there will always be a reasonably good selection from which to choose.

★★ Good cars to drive and enjoy. They are more common because more were produced, thereby making them less likely to be a good financial investment. These, however, even make greater sense as regular drivers. They are, after all, Porsches.

★ Cars in this category are here for a number of reasons. In some cases, they represent years when Porsche, like all other car manufacturers, struggled mightily to meet U.S. emissions and safety standards but had to compromise performance so much in comparison to their European models that these cars are simply not desirable from either an enjoyment or investment point of view. Careful study of the star boxes at the beginning of each chapter, and of the text as well, will explain these situations and point out more desirable vintages or versions of the same models.

Chapter 1

How it All Began

The first car to bear the Porsche name, a two-passenger sports car, came about as much by chance as by some great plan.

In 1947, Porsche Konstruktionen GmbH, in Gmünd, Austria, was being run by Ferry Porsche, his sister Louise Piech, Karl Rabe and Hans Kern—the latter two, longtime associates of Ferry's father, Dr. Prof. Ferdinand Porsche. The firm's primary business was technical design and consultation.

Carlo Abarth, an Austrian former-motorcycle racer then living in Merano, Italy, began corresponding with Louise Piech (Abarth's wife had been Louise's husband Anton's secretary before World War II). Soon Ferry Porsche was drawn into the correspondence, as was another Austrian living in Merano, Rudolph Hruska, who had been involved with Dr. Porsche and Karl Rabe on the Volkswagen project from 1939 to 1941.

Ferry Porsche and Karl Rabe were unable to travel outside Germany or Austria at that time due to postwar restrictions, and Ferdinand Porsche and Louise's husband Anton were still in prison because of alleged "war crimes." Ferry Porsche suggested that Abarth and Hruska, who were both free to travel, might like to act as Porsche's agents to sell the company's design services in Italy.

Hruska and Abarth had other things on their minds, though, and, at the instigation of Tazio Nuvolari and with the assistance of Corrado Millanta and Johnny Lurani, they approached Porsche to design a new Grand Prix car to be built in Italy under Porsche supervision. Porsche agreed to do it, and backing for the project was obtained from Piero Dusio, owner of the Cisitalia company in Torino.

Porsche subsequently entered into an agreement to design a Grand Prix car, a small tractor, a sports car, and a water turbine for Cisitalia. Part of the money (1,000,000 French francs) advanced for the work was turned over to the French authorities to get Dr. Porsche and Anton Piech out of prison. This was accomplished on August 1, 1947.

A visit by Ferry Porsche and Karl Rabe to Torino in mid-1947 (one of their first trips outside Germany after the war) was to see the progress being made on the Type 360—the Cisitalia GP car. This visit proved to be a pivotal point in Porsche history. What interested Porsche and Rabe even more than the Grand Prix car was the fact that Dusio had not gone ahead with the Porsche-designed sports car because he was having so much success with his Fiat-based cars.

The Cisitalia coupes and cabriolets, with their beautiful Pinin Farina bodywork were light, and fast, but expensive to build because of their hand-built tubular space frames. Despite this, Dusio had plans to build 500 cars—coupes and convertibles—which were to sell for $5,000 in Italy, and $7,000 in export markets. This was a tremendous price for a car with a Fiat 1100 engine,

The first Porsche, as it looked when completed in Gmünd, Austria, in May 1948. It was a mid-engined car with an aluminum body designed by Erwin Komenda.

Porsche number 1; the matriarch—or patriarch, depending on your perspective—of all Porsches. The aluminum body covered a Volkswagen suspension and modified VW engine, held together by

a space frame. Unlike future road-going Porsches, the engine was ahead of the rear axle. It has been recently restored by the factory. *Dean Batchelor*

transmission, and rear axle; no matter how good-looking it was.

When Porsche and Rabe returned to their offices in Gmünd, they immediately revived a previously conceived plan for a Porsche-designed, Porsche-built sports car, with the design number 356.

Unlike Dusio's expensive and time-consuming method of building cars, they wanted a car based on a production chassis and running gear. For this project they had chosen the Volkswagen, which not only served their purpose admirably but also was the product of the elder Porsche's inventive mind more than a decade earlier.

Despite their belief that a hand-built space frame was uneconomical for mass production, Porsche's first car was built with inexpensive Volkswagen components—but held together by a space frame. The engine was in front of the rear axle; a position not to be duplicated by another Porsche until the 550 Spyder in 1953. Erwin Komenda designed a simple roadster body, fabricated from aluminum, to clothe the Volkswagen mechanical components. The car was driven to Switzerland in June 1948, and was the subject of tests by automotive journalists at the time of the Swiss Grand Prix at Bern on July 4.

On July 11, the roadster, driven by Prof. Porsche's nephew, Herbert Kaes, won a "round the houses" race in Innsbruck, Austria—the first-ever Porsche racing victory. Ferry Porsche, in the meantime, had been planning a car that would be more practical, both for manufacturing and sales, to replace the original car.

The new design, 356/2, placed the engine behind the rear axle, as it had been in the Volkswagen. This design simplified manufacturing and allowed considerably more luggage space. The frame, in effect a unibody and no longer a space frame, was built up from sheet steel into a platform with welded box-section side sills and a central "tunnel," which added chassis stiffness and provided a space for wiring and controls to run from the front to the back of the car. A coupe and cabriolet were planned.

Production of the Austrian-built 356/2 reached only four cars in 1948, twenty-five cars in 1949 and eighteen cars in 1950. The major problem was body construction, as they were built by hand in Gmünd. By spring of 1951, Porsche had sold only fifty-one cars of the 356/2 type; forty-three coupes and eight cabriolets—six of the latter were bodied by Beutler, in Switzerland, and the other two by Porsche, as were the coupes.

Volkswagen, meanwhile, was rising from the ashes of World War II, under the direction of Heinz Nordhoff and, in September 1948, Porsche became a design consultant to Volkswagenwerk. This arrangement benefited VW not only from the engineering side, but also effectively kept Porsche from working for a competing car company.

Members of the Porsche family had been wanting to move their operation back to Stuttgart, and reached this goal in two stages in 1950. First, they rented a bit more than 5,000 square feet of space in Reutter's body plant to perform final assembly of the cars, and soon afterward an 1,100-square-foot building was purchased to serve as office and design space.

It was on the day before Good Friday of 1950 when the first German-built Porsche made its debut, which was only one of several events that year which were of utmost importance to Porsche. Professor Porsche's seventy-fifth birthday was celebrated on September 3, and a month later Porsche's small exhibit of two cars at the Paris Auto Salon marked the fiftieth anniversary of the first Porsche-designed car's exhibit—the electric Lohner-Porsche—at the Universal Exposition in Paris in 1900.

Professor Porsche suffered a stroke in November 1950, and he succumbed to his illness on January 30, 1951.

Many automobile companies have started as family-owned and operated businesses, but Porsche remains unique in that after 49 years as a builder of fine cars, the company is still fifty percent family owned.

Because of sibling rivalry, and the fear of nepotism hurting the company, management was turned over to trusted employees in 1972, and the families became stockholders only. Ferry Porsche, his sister Louise Piech, and their eight children each held ten percent of the company. Since 1972, management had been by someone other than a Porsche or Piech family member. In 1984, a major change took place when one third of the company's capital stock was offered on the German stock exchange in the form of nonvoting preferred shares and made available to family members for additional liquidity at their discretion.

The bank had planned to take three days to sell the 420,000 shares offered, but the offering, with a DM 50 book value, which went out at DM 780 and quickly rose to 1,000, was sold out in three hours! It had been planned to limit individuals to 100 shares and institutions to 2,000 shares, but this was quickly reduced to 10 and 200 limits.

As this update is being written, in the spring of 1997, Porsche production for the 1997 model year for the U.S. market includes the 911 Carrera S Coupe ($63,750); 911 Carrera Targa ($70,750); 911 Carrera Cabriolet ($73,000); 911 Carrera 4S (also $73,000); 911 Carrera 4 Cabriolet ($78,350); 911 Turbo coupe ($105,000); and the new Boxster ($39,980). The 911 Carrera Coupe, Targa, and Cabriolet, and the Boxster, are all available with the latest Tiptronic S transmission.

Porsches represent a superb balance of extremely high-quality assembly and high-

Anton Piech with the first Porsche coupe, completed in July 1948 in Gmünd, Austria. It was also the first rear-engined Porsche; the type 356/2. Also a Komenda design, the body was aluminum, and it had opening quarter windows. The subsequent Gmünd-built coupes had curved plexiglass fixed quarter windows. *Porsche A. G.*

Early VW engine with Porsche modifications was used in early Porsches. It produced 40 horsepower at a time when the stock VW unit had 25 horsepower. *Dean Batchelor*

performance machinery, at a price commensurate with what you get. The nearest automobile in price that is also handmade is Ferrari's F355, at nearly twice the price of the 911 Carrera. Porsches have never been meant for those drivers wanting simple transportation from point A to point B. They are certainly reliable enough to accomplish even those mundane driving chores, yet they are not cars for those who don't appreciate what they have. During the late 1980s, there were buyers who acquired Porsches (or Ferraris, Lamborghinis, Aston Martins, or other exotics) because "it was the thing to do" to be recognized in their crowd.

Many of them spent a lot of money for the best that was available but they didn't know (or perhaps even care) why. They would have been better off driving something else—and many did sell or trade away nearly new Porsches after a brief ownership. Still, their patronage helped keep Porsche in business building cars for those who *do* know and care.

Maybe we should be grateful. Many of those low-mileage, one-owner cars are some of the best road-going vehicles Porsche ever produced and, as barely used cars, they fall much closer to the dreams of many more of us.

Chapter 2

356

★★	**Coupe**
★★★	**Cabriolet**
★★★ 1/2	**Speedster**
★★★★★	**Gmünd-built Cars**
★★★★★	**America Roadster**

Late in 1949, Porsche, then operating under the official name of "Dr.-Ing.h.c.F. Porsche KG," in Stuttgart-Zuffenhausen, ordered 500 bodies from Reutter Karozzerie. The bodies were to be delivered at the rate of eight or nine per month.

Based on reaction from potential dealers and customers, Porsche management believed that it could sell 500 cars of this design, but wasn't sure how long it might take.

Original projections were abandoned by mid-1950 as sales accelerated beyond Porsche's wildest dreams. Deliveries actually started in April 1950, and by the end of the year 298 cars had been built and sold—an average rate of thirty-three per month.

The "chassis" consisted of a boxed, pressed-steel assembly in unit with the floor pan, full independent suspension with parallel trailing arms on each side in front and swing-axle rear with the wheels located by a single, flexible trailing arm on each side. Transverse torsion bars (laminated into a square section in front, round at the rear) supplied the spring medium. The shock absorbers were hydraulic; tubular in front and lever-type at the rear. Brakes on the Gmünd-built cars were cable-operated mechanical units from the Volkswagen, but VW switched to hydraulic brakes in 1950, and these were incorporated into the Stuttgart-built Porsches.

The engine, at the back, was a Porsche-modified Volkswagen unit of 1,131 cubic

centimeters displacement, although many of the cars built at Gmünd during 1949 had 73.5 instead of 75 mm bores, which resulted in 1086 cc—allowing them to run in the 1100 cc competition classes. Either engine drove through a VW four-speed nonsynchromesh transmission. Two Solex 26 VFJ carburetors were used on the Gmünd cars, but Solex 32 PBI carburetors were used on the Stuttgart cars. Each engine was assembled by one workman who took twenty-five hours to do the job.

Flat glass was used for the side windows, and the two-piece vee windshield was flat from the center to the outer three to four inches which was curved.

Interiors were Spartan by any standards, and particularly so compared to today's Porsches. Some literature lists a bench seat as standard for the early 1949 Gmünd-built cars, with bucket seats optional (no rear seats were provided), but there is little evidence that many were built this way. A bench seat was later listed as an option on 356 A and B cars but, again, there can't be more than a handful built with that option.

1951

For 1951, the Porsche 356 remained visually almost the same as the 1950 model; but underneath, it got two leading-shoe Lockheed-type hydraulic brakes from Ate, and tubular shock absorbers replaced the lever-arm type at the rear during the model run.

Beutler, in Switzerland, built six of the eight Cabriolet bodies for the Gmünd 356/2 series cars. They had two-piece flat-glass vee windshields and full-wheel discs. The Porsche lettering was on the front lid, unlike later models on which it appeared below the opening.

A 1286 cc engine was added, by enlarging the bore to 80 mm. It produced 44 hp, four more than the 1100 engine, at 4200 rpm. In October, the 1488 cc engine became the top option, with roller-bearing rod journals and two Solex 40 PBIC carburetors. This engine was actually a 1952 model power plant.

Many myths surrounded the "roller-bearing engine" then, and still do. Low friction and high revs were the most commonly stated reasons for this expensive and complicated assembly. Generally speaking, the primary reasons for a roller-bearing rod journal are to obtain a one-piece connecting rod, which is inherently stronger than a two-piece rod, and to eliminate the necessity for high oil pressure at high rpm. Porsche's reason for adopting this design was simpler. According to Karl Ludvigsen in *Porsche: Excellence Was Expected*, the absence of rod bolts at the lower end allowed an increase of 5 mm on the crank throw radius, which resulted in a stroke increase of 10 mm. The longer stroke, of 74 mm, brought the engine displacement up to 1488 cc. All other considerations, according to Ludvigsen, were secondary.

The roller-bearing-crank engines acquired a reputation of fragility that was not entirely deserved. In the hands of customers who drove these cars on the road, the engine needed an expensive overhaul more often than a plain-bearing engine would have. But this type of engine installed in a racing car proved extremely reliable—probably because the engine was set up and maintained properly, and the car was driven in the manner for which it was intended. An engine with a roller-bearing crank did not respond kindly to lugging, and customers were admonished to "keep the revs up or you'll hammer the roller bearings flat." This was probably good advice as far as it went, but the philosophy rubbed off on the drivers of Porsches with plain-bearing engines, and the sound of Porsches on the streets in the early 1950s was always on of "two gears too low, and 2,000 revs too high."

1952

Important changes were made in 1952: A one-piece windshield was adopted (two flat sections, with a "fold" at the vertical center line); a folding rear seat was added; the spare wheel was moved farther to the front in a near-vertical position, allowing more luggage space; brake drum diameter was increased from 230 to 280 mm (from nine to eleven inches), width from 30 to 40 mm; and a fully synchronized transmission with the patented Porsche split-ring synchromesh became standard on all models. Stronger bumpers were set out from the body.

At the suggestion of U.S. Porsche distributor Max Hoffman, a lightweight roadster—the America—was built. Of the sixteen Americas, fifteen came to the United Stated where most were raced successfully by private owners on both coasts.

Possibly the most significant, and lasting, change for 1952 was the creation of the Porsche emblem. Taken from a sketch drawn by Ferry Porsche on a napkin, while lunching with Max Hoffman, the final design was the work of Porsche publicity chief Lepper, and Porsche engineer Reimspiess.

This emblem, which is so well known today, is made of a background of the crest of the State of Baden-Wurttemburg, with it six staghorns. In the center is the coat of arms of Stuttgart-a rampant black horse on a yellow shield. The horse represents the old area of Stuttgart which had been a stud farm (Stuotgarten).

Ferry Porsche has alluded to a historical tie between the prancing horse of Stuttgart and the prancing horse of Ferrari—both of which are black on a yellow shield.

1953

Visually, the 1953 Porsches were much like the late 1952s, but improvements were made in soundproofing and general equipment. In November a roller-bearing 1300S engine was introduced as a 1954 model.

1954

Five engines were offered during the 1954 model year—1100, 1300, 1300S, 1500, and 1500S—but only the 1500 and 1500S were exported to the United States. American importer Max Hoffman didn't accept the smaller-displacement models for sale in the United States. He thought, and was probably right, that Americans wouldn't buy the smaller engine sizes at the price the cars would have to be sold for in the United States. Further, he made the 1500S his "top of the line" and the 1500 Normal the standard model.

Aside from the engine differences, the lower-priced version had no radio, aluminum wheel trim rings, passenger's sun visor, adjustable passenger's seatback, or the folding rear seatback—all of which were standard on the 1500 Super.

On March 15, 1954, the five-thousandth Porsche was driven off the line in Stuttgart— a production figure no one at Porsche would have dreamed possible four years earlier when they talked bravely of eight or nine cars per month.

The heater control was moved from the dashboard to the floor " tunnel" and a windshield washer became standard equipment. In September the Speedster was added to the line for export to the United States only. Like the 1954 models, the Speedster was equipped with 406 mm (sixteen-inch) wheels until the 356A models were introduced in October 1955.

1955

Production started on the 1955 models in November 1954. The major changes were

An aluminum frame around the license plate area and valances off to each side were designed for the Gmünd coupe, but fortunately left off later Porsches. The windshield wipers parked in the upright position for unknown reasons (this, too, was later changed). The first Gmünd-built coupe had two-piece vee windshields and flat plexiglass side windows with opening vent wings. Subsequent cars (this is number 17 built in 1949) had non-opening curved quarter windows in an early search for better aerodynamics. Curved windshields came late. *Dean Batchelor*

The rear of the Gmünd-built coupe was about as barren of decoration as you'll find on a Porsche; the need for license-plate light, back-up light, bumper uprights, and the mandatory reflectors came later. Even the bumper, though, was more for looks than it was for practical work. *Dean Batchelor*

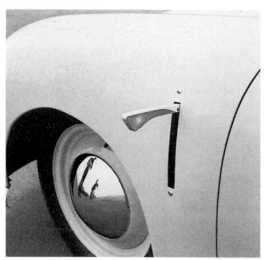

Turn indicators, or "trafficators," as the British called them, were of the swing-arm type in the late forties. A light in the end went on when the arm was raised, day or night, and could be seen from both front and rear through the plastic sides of the arm. *Dean Batchelor*

A 160 km/h speedometer was set behind a "banjo" type steering wheel reminiscent of many late-thirties American cars (Ford and Buick come to mind). The interior was not as complete or as elegant as later Porsches, but the developing style was already evident. *Dean Batchelor*

mechanical: engines had a three-piece aluminum crankcase instead of the previous two-piece magnesium case. Oil capacity increased from 3.5 to 4.5 liters. Many of the engine's dimensions and its general layout were similar to the earlier engine but new parts were not interchangeable. Porsche thus moved further away from dependency on Volkswagen parts.

After Max Hoffmann's successful America Roadster, he wanted another U.S.-only model. Porsche produced the "Continental" for a year until Ford Motor Company claimed it owned the name and announced plans to reintroduce its own in 1956.

Early in 1950, the first Reutter-built Cabriolets appeared. The Reutter emblem on the side has been seen with a height-placement variation of almost three inches. *Kurt Worner/*Road & Track

Pre-1952 Porsche 356 models had the spare tire mounted almost horizontally in the front compartment, leaving little space for anything but the gas tank and windshield washer fluid reservoir just behind the tire. Road & Track

Another significant change in November 1954 was the addition of a front anti-roll bar, which was accompanied by a change in front spring rate—the lower laminated bar retained its original five leaves, but the upper bar now had six.

Because of the availability of Speedster bodies, and the start of its own total engine production, Porsche production reached as many as twelve cars per day, and 2,952 Porsches—Coupe, Cabriolet, and Speedster—were built during the 1955 model run. A new model, the 356A, would be started in October 1955, as a 1956 model; but what were the 356s like?

Early driver reports, road impressions, and road tests can give us a clue. In England's *Light Car* of September 1951, it was reported that "If the steering has a 'different' feel at cruising speeds of 70 mph it is completely accurate, high-geared, light and free from wander. The comfort of one's ride over all types of surface is one of the delights of the car. Pot-holed roads, adverse cambers hump-backed bridges, can all be taken with confidence at a fast cruising speed."

And, the writer continued, "The Porsche engine . . . is mounted behind the rear axle, a

In 1950, production started in Stuttgart and the cars acquired windshields with the ends rounded for better airflow to the body sides. The bodies were made by Reutter (note the unusual Reutter emblem on the side). *Kurt Worner/*Road & Track

Stuttgart-built coupe of 1950 had the form that would continue through the 1955 model year; steel body by Reutter, with two-piece windshield (flat in the center and curved at the outer edges), two round and two rectangular lights flanking the light

bar over the rear plate and a single round parking/turn signal lens under each headlight. The Porsche lettering was now standardized in design and mounted front and rear under the opening lids. *Dean Batchelor*

position which creates marked oversteer characteristics. This is by no means a fault of design but is something which the new owner must learn before the combination of wet road and over-enthusiastic right foot induces the Dreaded Spin."

These last words were repeated many times in many ways during the lifetime of the 356 models.

John Bentley, writing in the January 1952 edition of *Auto* (Petersen Publishing Company), said: ". . . the first things that impressed

Several removable hardtops were available for the Speedster. Glasspar made one, illustrated, of fiberglass, and the factory also offered one in fiberglass. *Ralph Poole*

The stock top, only for late-1955 Speedsters like this one, was the "high bow" version. Compare this crude roof line to the more attractive Cabriolet top at right or the "low bow" top on page 24. *Ralph Poole/Dean Batchelor*

Unlike the thin Speedster top, the Cabriolet top was padded, which gave it a smoother look and made the interior quieter. With its roll-up windows, the Porsche Cabrio was one of the most weather proof of convertibles.

me were the high grade detail workmanship and the amazing amount of front seat room," and "Steering is so light that despite its fairly high gearing I got the deceptive impression of steering wheel 'play' when in fact, there is none . . . Steering response is so quick that I had to accustom myself to 'wishing' the car through turns, the slightest wheel movement being enough when used in conjunction with the throttle."

Further into the report, Bentley wrote: "Should the sporting purist take the car out

for the sheer fun of driving, mastery of the gearbox offers a stimulating challenge rewarded by a sense of achievement. . . . In the near future the Porsche will be coming out with synchromesh and one serious criticism of this outstanding car will be eliminated."

The writer was right on target with his remarks about space, handling and the as-yet nonsynchromesh transmission, but his conclusion to the article was a bit faulty, in retrospect: "Porsche production is rising toward 100 cars a month, but is unlikely ever

The 1955 Speedster interior displayed the functionally stark design. The Cabriolet and Coupe still had the "bent in the center" flat vee windshield with curved outer edges but the Speedster had a fully curved windshield—a style that would be adopted by all Porsche models late in the year when the 356A was announced. *Ralph Poole*

A 1955 356 Cabriolet. This radio is a Telefunken. A special floor mat has been fitted over the stock rubber mat.

A 1955 356 Coupe interior. Fuel reserve handle and fuel filter were under dash. The radio is an aftermarket unit made by Motorola. *Dean Batchelor*

to exceed this figure, no matter how great the backlog of orders." Well, John, you can't win 'em all.

A year later in the January 1953 issue of *Auto*, Dick van Osten wrote: "This is not the type of car that Mr. Average Man can hurl around the first time he steps behind the wheel. The Porsche requires a different technique that

is alien to most of us; but, once mastered, the car will do your bidding with an absolute minimum of effort. The basic key to success in handling a Porsche is to use about half the effort you usually use in driving." Commenting on the mechanical design, van Osten said, "The argument of front vs. rear engine location will go on forever, but here is some food

Side-by-side comparison of a 1955 Continental Coupe and Speedster shows the similarity in body design, but difference in windshields. The striper's brush has, unfortunately, been applied to the Coupe. Porsche dropped the Continental name in 1956, in deference to Lincoln when it brought out the Continental Mark II. *Ralph Poole*

23

The Coupe style lent itself to a rear-engined design because it easily covered the vertical fan, but the Speedster and Cabriolet required more "hump" in the back than might otherwise be used for a notchback design. *Ralph Poole*

Extras—factory or aftermarket—have always been popular with Porsche owners. This 1955 Continental has a luggage rack attached to the air intake grille (no self-respecting Porsche owner would drill holes in the body to attach one), chrome wheels, and an Abarth exhaust system. *Ralph Poole*

Speedsters were often referred to as "inverted bathtubs" or as "upside-down soap dishes." Owners loved their "bathtubs." The cloth top was not one of the car's strong points. This low-bow version is more visually appealing than the high-bow (on page 22), but neither one shed water very well. The desirability of Speedsters prompted at least one kit builder to offer a reproduction of the 1957–1958 body. *Ralph Poole*

This 1955 Continental Coupe—the script logo is on the fender—is original except for its 4 1/2x15-inch wheels. Original wheels for the 1955 models were 3 1/4x16. This particular car was purchased from the Los Angeles auto show in October 1954. Unless a car is to be used now only for shows where authenticity is critical, this change to wider wheels is sensible and safer. Wet and dry handling is much improved by the lower, wider tires. *Dean Batchelor*

for thought. Dr. Porsche once said that it does not make any difference where the engine is located as long as it is light. The Porsche engine weighs 160 lbs!"

In the March 1953 *Autosport,* John Gott was impressed with the performance of the new Porsches: "The Tulip Rally, in which Ray Brookes and I drove my 1947 H.R.G., gave me a chance to meet the Porsches in di-rect competition for the first time. Nine Porsches started in the 1500cc sports class. . . . On the run from Brussels to Rheims, whilst cruising at around 75 mph, I was startled to be passed by a Porsche which had left Brussels 28 minutes behind me. However, I was not therefore unduly shocked when Porsches took eight of the 10 class placings on the timed climb on the Ballon d'Alsace."

---

356 (1950–1955)

Engine

Design: ....Air-cooled flat (opposed) four
Type:
  1100 (April 1950–mid-1954) ....369, 2-piece crankcase, plain-bearing crank
  1300 (Jan. 1951–May 1955)..........506, 2-piece crankcase, plain-bearing crank
  1500 (Oct. 1951–Sept. 1952)........527, 2-piece crankcase, roller-bearing crank
  1500 (Sept. 1952–Nov. 1954)........546, 2-piece crankcase, plain-bearing crank
  1500S (Oct. 1952–Nov. 1954) ....528, 2-piece crankcase, roller-bearing crank
  1300S (Nov. 1953–May 1954) ....589, 2-piece crankcase, roller-bearing crank
  1300A (June 1954–Nov. 1954)....................506/1, 2-piece crankcase, plain-bearing crank
  1300 (Nov. 1954–Oct. 1955) ....506/2, 3-piece crankcase, plain-bearing crank
  1300S (Nov. 1954–Oct. 1955) ....589/2, 3-piece crankcase, roller-bearing crank
  1500 (Nov. 1954–Oct. 1955) ....546/2, 3-piece crankcase, plain-bearing crank
  1500S (Nov. 1954–Oct. 1955) ....528/2, 3-piece crankcase, roller-bearing crank
Bore x stroke, mm/inches:
  1100 ....73.5x64/2.89x2.52
  1300 (Jan. 1951–May 1954) 80x64/3.15x2.52
  1300S, 1300A................................74.5x74/2.93x2.91
  1500, 1500S....................................80x74/3.15x2.91
  1300 (Nov. 1954–Oct. 1955) 74.5x74/2.93x2.91
Displacement, cc/cubic inches:
  1100...1086/66.7
  1300...1286/78.4
  1300S, 1300A (1300 Nov. 1954–Oct. 1955) 1290/78.7
  1500, 1500S..1488/90.6
Valve operation: ....Single camshaft with pushrods and rocker arms; inclined exhaust valves
Compression ratio:
  1100, 1500...7:1
  1300, 1300A..6.5:1
  1300S, 1500S..8.2:1
Carburetion:
  1100, 1300, 1300S,1300A, 1500............Two Solex 32 PBI
  1300S (1955–56)...............Two Solex 32 PBIC or 40 PBIC
  1500S (till Nov. 1954)..............Two Solex 40 PBIC (Town)
  1500S (Nov. 1954–Oct. 1955) ....Two Solex 40 PICB (Sport)
BHP (Mfr.):
  1100 ....40 DIN/46 SAE @ 4200
  1300, 1300 ....44 DIN/50 SAE @ 4200
  1500 (Oct. 1951–Sept. 1952) ....60 DIN/70 SAE @ 5000
  1500 (Sept. 1952–Nov. 1954) ....55 DIN/64 SAE @ 4400
  1300S..60 DIN/70 SAE @ 5500
  1500S..70 DIN/82 SAE @ 5000

Chassis & Drivetrain

Frame: ....Boxed-section pressed steel in unit with floor pan
Component layout: ....Rear engine, rear drive
Clutch: ....Fichtel & Sachs single dry-plate
Transmission:
  1100 (through 1952) ....VW four-speed (all gears indirect)
  1300 (through 1951) ....VW four-speed (all gears indirect)
  1100 (1953–1954) ....Porsche four-speed, all-synchromesh (all gears indirect)
  All others.................Porsche four-speed, all-synchromesh (all gears indirect)
Axle ratio: 4.43:1
Rear suspension:...........................Independent (swing axle) with transverse torsion bars & lever-action shock absorbers (changed to telescopic during 1951 model run)
Front suspension: ....Independent, with parallel trailing arms, transverse laminated torsion bars, telescopic shock absorbers (anti-roll bar added in 1954)

General

Wheelbase, mm/inches 2100/82.7
Track: front, mm/inches 1290/50.8
  rear, mm/inches 1250/49.2
Brakes: 1100 (first cars)....................Mechanical, drum-type
  All others..Hydraulic, drum-type
Tire size, front and rear: 5.00–16
Wheels: ....Bolt-on, steel disc
Body builder: ....Reutter (1952 American roadsters were built by Glaser, and some Cabriolets in 1950, 1951, and 1952 were build by Heuer)

Later in his report, Gott commented: "I counted myself extremely lucky to finish fourth at Zandvoort, behind Van der Lof and Porsches of Van der Muhle and Nathan, and certainly would not have done this had not three Porsches displayed a defect in road holding and crashed into the sand dunes. Observing these unpleasing sights from the immediate rear, I came to the conclusion that when driven into corners at the extreme high speeds of which the cars are capable, the combination of swing axle, rear mounted engine and low general weight caused a breakaway at racing speeds to come without warning and some violence."

After the Liege-Rome-Liege rally, writer/competitor Gott had more observations about the Porsches: "The 'works' drivers stressed that not only was competition found to be the best test bed, but that the successes gained in competitions all over the world were invaluable publicity."

A different observation of the early Porsches came from Maurice Gatsonides, writing in the June 5, 1953, *Autosport*: "The lights, possibly adequate for other types, are certainly not strong enough for the speeds possible with the Super."

The British magazine *Autocar* tested a 1954 Porsche coupe for the November 1953 edition and was exceedingly charitable in its report of a non-British design, saying, among other things: "The gear change, operated by a short, slender central lever with a large knob, is one of the most pleasant and certainly one of the fastest manually operated changes experienced. It is possible to make noiseless changes just as fast as the driver can move the lever." And, "The brakes are in keeping with the performance, the car pulling up straight even with all wheels locked. The pedal pressure required for an emergency stop is fairly heavy, but at no time was any tendency to fade noticed."

All magazines that reported on the early Porsches were in general agreement on all aspects of the cars: excellent quality, lack of wind noise, superb synchromesh transmission (after the development for the Porsche synchromesh system), abundant space for large drivers, excellent brakes, and superior handling—for an expert or skilled driver.

But, in the hands of an incautious, inexperienced, or less-than-skillful driver, the car could be treacherous.

A thinking Porsche salesman would warn his customers that a few months and several thousand miles of experience would be gained before playing "boy racer"; particularly on a back country road with curves, some of which might be off-camber, or have drop-offs. A 356 Porsche could be driven exceedingly fast—if the driver had the right feel for the car, but it could also get a driver into trouble faster than almost anything on the road if the driver was over his head. A tail-heavy car with swing-axle independent rear suspension is not forgiving, and is quick to let the less-than-prudent driver know that he has gone beyond his limit.

Chapter 3

★★	**Coupe**
★★★	**Cabriolet**
★★★★	**Speedster**
★★★★	**Carrera**

356A

Production for the first 356A, a 1956 model, started in October 1955. Five engines were offered: 1300, 1300S, 1600, 1600S, and 1500GS. Only the latter three were exported to America. The car looked little different, but it had a new windshield and dash, and significant suspension modifications.

The engines were still air-cooled flat-fours, and all but the 1500GS Carrera were the standard Porsche pushrod-and-rocker-arm ohv design. The Type 547 1500GS engine, a detuned version of the four-cam (double overhead on each bank) 550 Spyder engine, had a Hirth roller-bearing crankshaft (rollers on both mains and rods), 8.7:1 compression ratio, dry-sump lubrication, and produced 100 DIN horsepower at 6200 rpm.

All 356A engines had warm air directed from the cylinders to the carburetors for quicker warm-up. This air supply was thermostatically controlled by a bellows near the fan housing. Catering to a broader spectrum of customers, the flywheel was made heavier—to smooth out the idle and to allow smoother starts.

A new transmission, the Type 644, was used. This unit had a one-piece housing (previous gearboxes were split along the centerline) with the gear shafts installed through the front. At the same time, the front transmission mounting was changed from a single rubber pad to twin circular rubber mounts.

Suspension had been "softened" at the front by eliminating leaves from the laminated torsion bars from 21.8 to 24.7 inches, and reducing the bar diameter from 25 to 24 mm.

Wheels of the 356A were of fifteen-inch diameter with 4.5-inch-wide rims, compared to the sixteen-inch by 3.25 rims of the 356.

Body styles for the 1956 356A were Coupe, Cabriolet and Speedster, each available with all engine options (1300 not available in Speedster). All three body types were built by Reutter in Stuttgart. The windshield was now a one-piece curved glass unit, and the dash was padded and upholstered in either leather or imitation leather. Both front seats were fully reclining, and the rear seatbacks could be folded down to carry more luggage.

A new instrument panel carried three large, round instrument dials: speedometer, tachometer, and combined fuel level and oil temperature gauges. Headlight flashers were now standard equipment—except on Speedsters.

1957
Body design remained unchanged from 1956, but minor cosmetic changes were made in the spring of 1957: Padded sun visors became standard, the speedometer was moved from the left to the right side of the panel, and the dial for the fuel/oil temperature gauge was moved to the left. Outside, "teardrop" taillights (mounted horizontally)

This 1956 Porsche 356A/1600 Super was equipped for German delivery. Rudge chrome-plated wheels and center-lock hubs were optional equipment. The hub nuts had no "wings" or "ears" because German law eliminated projections that might harm pedestrians. (Projecting radiator ornaments were outlawed at the same time.) *Dean Batchelor*

replaced the twin round lights of previous models, and the license plate/backup light bar was moved from above the plate to a position below the license plate. The exhaust tips were routed through the bumper guards on the late 1957 cars. Raising them provided better ground clearance for steep driveways but they also got the bumpers dirty.

Several running changes were made to the engine during 1957: Offset piston wrist pins were adapted to the 1600 engine to counteract piston "slap" in a cold engine (inherent with air-cooled engines), and the normal 356 engines were given the aluminum camshaft gear, which was already used on the 1600 Super, to replace the fiber-toothed gear.

1958

To the uninitiated, the 1958 Porsche 356A was visually like its predecessors. While retaining the basic shape, the T-2 body (an internal Porsche designation for the mid-1957 body that would be carried through subsequent model years) had optional vent wings

in the door glass of the Cabriolet. (The Coupe also offered wind wings but this rarely seen option mounted on the door frame, outside the window.) The Speedster and Cabriolet had larger rear windows and the factory offered a removable fiberglass hardtop, made by Brendel, for the Cabriolet as an option. Glasspar in Santa Ana, California, produced an aftermarket fiberglass top.

Under the skin, more changes were made: Cast-iron cylinders were used in the 1600 Normal engine, which was standard practice for Volkswagen but the first for Porsche since the early 356 1100. The results, for this primarily touring car, were lower manufacturing cost and a quieter engine, with only minimal weight increase.

The 1300 engine was dropped. All Porsche pushrod engines ran in plain bearings. (Carrera and Spyder four-cam engines kept the roller bearing cranks.) Zenith NDIX carburetors and a new carburetor linkage were used. A Haussermann diaphragm spring clutch replaced the Fichtel & Sachs coil-spring unit.

The 1956 356A Speedster panel: stark but functional. Instruments included, center 6000 rpm tach; left, 120 mph speedometer; right, fuel level and oil temperature gauges.

A new steering box, a Ross-type worm-and-stud design made by ZF, replaced the VW worm-and-nut steering design. The steering ratios increased from 14.15:1 to 16:1. At the same time, a larger—16 3/4-inch diameter—steering wheel (already used on the Carreras) became standard on all Porsches, further reducing steering effort because of better leverage.

This 1957 1600 engine has the Solex carburetors. Porsche replaced these in mid-model year with Zenith NDIXs. *Ralph Poole*

1959

In August 1958, Porsche started production of its Speedster replacement, the 1959 Convertible D. These bodies, with a higher windshield and chrome frame, were built by Drauz, from which came the "D." While the Speedsters had only side curtains, the new car had roll-up windows. The top, however, was an uninsulated shell similar to the one on the Speedsters, and it fit in height somewhere between low- and high-bow versions. The body resembled the Speedster and carried over its chrome side trim strip. With its coupe seats, it is more comfortable and a bit more practical than the "bathtubs." The Coupe and Cabriolet, built by Reutter, continued as before.

Later in 1958, single, progressively wound valve springs replaced the dual springs in all Porsche pushrod engines.

Production of the 356A ended in September 1959, when the 356B was introduced.

Going back to magazine road tests and owner comments, we can find out what was thought of the "A" model.

One of the first road reports on the 356A appeared in the November 18, 1955, issue of the *Autocar*, and the writer caught the spirit of the car just as I imagine the designers had

This 356A 1600 has the standard one-piece front bumper "bow" connected to the tall uprights. It is also fitted with "turbo rings," the wheel trim rings that were introduced in 1952 as standard equipment. While they were common on 356 pre-A series cars, they were uncommon on production 356As. *Ralph Poole*

planned it: "Thus we find the 1956 Porsche almost in a class by itself for the combination it offers of high cruising and maximum speeds without mechanical fuss, coupled with real economy in fuel consumption and, for a sporting vehicle, excellent comfort for two." Later in the same article, the writer commented on the displacement increase to 1582 cc: "The effect of this has been to improve the low speed torque characteristics, so that the Porsche is a little more tractable and less dependent on the gear lever; at the same time it possesses an increased ability to maintain speed on its very high top gear when confronted with a long gradient." And, this: ". . . to drive a Porsche is to experience a new form of motoring, so refreshingly different is it from the usual run of vehicles."

Across London, in the offices of *The Motor*, Joseph Lowrey wrote in the January 18, 1956, edition: "Having quite a personal liking for cars which can be 'wished' around corners without appreciable physical 'steering,' my first reaction was to prefer the handling of the 1955 car to the slightly more 'Americanized' controls of the 1956 model." Lowrey later in the same piece said: "I soon forgot my reactionary ideas."

Continuing, Lowrey dwelt on the greater flexibility of the new 1600 engine compared

Even with the spare tire mounted more vertically in the front, the huge square gas tank kept the usable space to a minimum. Most Porsche travelers utilized the space behind the front seats for larger luggage pieces, putting things they wanted to hide in the front. *Ralph Poole*

The late 1957 Coupe, left, shows the light above the plate, one-piece upper bumper bow, moon caps, and four taillights. *Ralph Poole*

1957, right, has light below plate, two-piece upper bumper, teardrop taillights, and crested protruding hubcaps.

This early 1957 Speedster has the heater control behind the shift lever, which was standard for that time. In mid-model run positions were switched—shift lever behind the heater control. *Dean Batchelor*

Other than the steering wheel, this early 1957 Speedster interior is very much like the 1956 model. *Dean Batchelor*

to the previous 1500, and hit upon a significant point with this observation: "My impression, incidentally, was that it was not really the engine which was in any way inflexible, but that the use of a short and 'solid' transmission line was probably making the use of low rpm a jerky business. A spring center clutch, long propeller shaft and axle mounted on 'cart' springs together provide flexibility which if cleverly used can reduce the 'resonant' speed of a transmission to a very low figure." This latter was in reference to front-engined cars with rear drive being generally less critical of engine rpm for driving smoothness.

In a full-scale road test of the 1600, *The Autocar* writer said, in the May 4, 1956, issue: ". . . the handling has less 'rear engine feel' to it." And, later, ". . . these cobbled downhill curves can be negotiated with an absolute stability that flatters any driver who has a light

Speedster seats (these are early 1957) were simple buckets with little padding, which were both comfortable and supportive for fast driving. *Dean Batchelor*

Both the similarities and the differences between this 1959 Convertible D and the 1957 Speedster, opposite page, can be seen; the bodies and trim are identical, but the Convertible D top is higher and includes roll-up windows. *Ralph Poole*

Speedsters, like this early 1957 1600 Normal, always looked better with their tops down. "Moon" hubcaps were standard issue on Normal models while Supers and Carreras got protruding center caps with the Porsche crest. Competition models used aluminum "moon" disks. High bumper uprights protected the delicate bodies.

All 356 and 356A Porsches had the "five-bolt" door striker plates set high on the door jamb through 1957, as shown in this early 1957 Speedster (left). In 1958 the striker plate was moved to the center of the door jamb where it remained through the B and C series 356s, as shown on the 1959 1600 Coupe (at right). At the same time, the shift lever and heater control swapped places. Porsche replaced the four round taillights with two teardrop-shaped lights. The rear upper bumper bow became a two-piece unit. Inside, the door handle moved from the center of the door to the front. Rear lights, bumpers, and hubcaps often were changed by owners; striker plates, heater control/gearshift lever, and door handle locations are permanent clues to the year the car was built. *Dean Batchelor*

touch." Not all comments were laudatory in the report, for the driver noted: "When a window is open, discomfort is caused at high speed by reverberation of the air in the car which hurts the ears; because it is desirable to keep the window closed, some improvement in ventilation in warm weather is desirable."

Motor Trend editor Walt Woron and writer Bob Rolofson commented favorably about putting the Cabriolet or Speedster tops up and down, saying that even without power assist they were "one man" tops. The heavily padded Cabriolet top made the car as quiet as the Coupe, and the Speedster top was claustrophobic. They were impressed with the quality—from overall fit and finish to the "magnificent adjustable seats."

In 1958, when the hardtop became available, *Sports Cars Illustrated* (now *Car and Driver*) drove one in Europe. The writer liked the vision ("Rearward vision is better than in the Coupe.") and the ventilation ("Ventilation in the hardtop is improved by two wind wings—optional on coupes and Cabri-

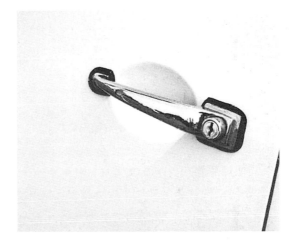

The 356A Normal came equipped with the moon-type hubcaps, while the 1600S and Carrera GS had the deluxe caps, which proved popular enough that they started to appear on many other Porsche models—either ordered when new, or added later. *Dean Batchelor*

Square-end door handles, as on this 1955 Continental Coupe (top), were used until mid-1957, when they were changed to the somewhat more rounded design as on this 1959 1600 Coupe (bottom). *Dean Batchelor*

Early 1957 356A Porsches had the speedometer on the left, as on this 1600 Coupe (top), but later in the year the speedometer was on the right, as seen in this European delivery Cabriolet with a 200 km/h speedometer (bottom). Both cars have the standard rubber floor mats and carpeted kick panels. *Coupe photo, Ralph Poole; Cabriolet photo, Zwietason*

olets but standard here."), but didn't like other aspects of the removable hardtop: "When cracked open to allow the heater-ventilation system to operate efficiently, the wind noise is considerably louder than with the regular coupe's trailing quarter windows." The magazine staffers also like the steering, saying: "The latest Porsche steering is a real improvement over the first 356As. Considerably lighter and with quicker return, we found the Ross box to be most satisfactory." The steering was a Ross design, but was made by ZF.

The Autocar, October 10, 1958, carried a test report on the Porsche 1600 "Damen," a nickname given to the most docile of the 1958 356As, and waxed eloquent about the car: "As soon as one moves off from rest, it is clear that the Porsche's individual character is not confined to its design alone. One quickly begins to feel a part of it—as though one were wearing, rather than sitting in the car. Acceleration is impressive, particularly so because of the seemingly effortless way in which the car gathers speed, the almost complete absence of transmission noise, and the low level of road-

A 1958 356A 1600 European delivery model, with no upper bumper bows. The wire screen over the headlights was an optional item used originally by rallyists, to protect the lens from gravel thrown up by other cars, but adopted by enthusiast drivers as an indication of serious intentions. *Dean Batchelor*

induced body noise." And, later: "Somehow the car seems to slip through traffic, eagerly taking advantage of every gap that presents itself; the impressive performance in first and second in part accounts for this."

Perhaps John Jerome explained the Porsche owner's philosophy best. Writing in the September 1967 *Car and Driver* about his own 356A Speedster, John said: "The car oversteered like crazy until you started fiddling with it. Clutch cables broke occasionally, clutches burned out regularly and throttle linkages fell off often (at any one of at least 12 different connection points that I can remember offhand). The oil radiator, hidden inside the fan shrouding, would sometimes develop copious leaks, and it was easier but messier to keep adding oil than to tear the engine apart to get to the oil cooler. . . . You overlooked those things. You liked the way the doors and hinges worked. You liked the way the car was so all-of-a-piece that nothing ever rattled. you liked the screwball handling, so easy to dirt-track around . . . and so capable of convincing you that you were really pretty fast after all."

Early in 1958, Porsche introduced a new engine, the Type 692, intended to power the Carrera models in a manner that was more appealing to street drivers who had difficulties with the high revs required of roller-bearing engines. Displacement was increased to 1,587cc and it was referred to as the 1600GS. The slight increase added torque, and engineers replaced the delicate crankshaft roller bearings with

A 1958 356A 1600 Super engine. Zenith carburetors used the same wire-mesh air filters as T-1 Supers with 40 mm single-throat Solexes. Zenith-carbed T-5 and T-6 Bs and Cs used can-type filters with paper elements. *Ralph Poole*

more durable plain bearings. This increased oil temperatures, so they fitted two small oil radiators behind the horn grilles below the headlights at the front of the car. Two versions of the engine were developed. One, the 692/2 for the Carrera de Luxe, used Solex carburetors and developed 105hp; only 94 were produced. The 692/3, Gran Turismo (GT), introduced in February 1959, with Weber carburetors, 12-volt electrics yielded 114hp. Just 100 were built.x

From the side, 1957 Speedsters are almost identical to the 1958. This car has the "turbo rings" on the wheels. The instrument panel resembles the 1956 and 1957 cars; this one has a custom-installed radio in front of the passenger and uses a nonstandard steering wheel. The rear also resembles the 1956 and 1957 cars, with the low license plate light, teardrop taillights and two-piece upper bumper. However, the exhaust tips through the bumpers indicate that it is a 1958 model. *Ralph Poole*

This 1958 1600 Normal Cabriolet is the T-2 body. As a European car, it had no bumper bars. Yet it had standard quarter windows and a larger rear window. *Porsche A. G.*

A 1959 356A 1600 Coupe with all the extras, including an accessory luggage rack for the rear deck. The grille on the engine lid is for air intake, so the luggage doesn't get as much heat as one might expect from this location, but it does add weight in the wrong place: high and behind the rear axle. *Dean Batchelor*

The 1959 356A Convertible D carried over the side trim of the Speedster. It was fitted with a higher-profile top, like the Cabriolet, but still unpadded, like the Speedster. This Normal-engined car was fitted with standard "moon" hubcaps. *Dean Batchelor*

The 1959 Convertible D, with body by Drauz, was a continuation of the Speedster but with roll-up windows, higher top, coupe seats, and more luxurious trim. *Ralph Poole*

The 1959 Coupes, this one a 356A 1600, didn't have vent wings built into the door, but had a factory option pivoting wind wing on the outside. *Dean Batchelor*

The front bumper "bow" was raised during the 1959 model run to give a bit more protection.

The Convertible D, left, is an early 1959; the Coupe, right, is a late 1959. *Ralph Poole/Dean Batchelor*

356A (1956–1959)

Engine

Design: . . . . Air-cooled flat (opposed) four

Type:

1300 . . . . (Oct. 1955–Sept. 1957) 506/2,
three-piece crankcase, plain-bearing crank

1300S . . . . (Oct. 1955–Sept. 1957) 589/2,
three-piece crankcase, roller-bearing crank

1600 . . . . (Oct. 1955–Sept. 1959) 616/1,
three-piece crankcase, plain-bearing crank

1600S . . . . (Oct. 1955–Sept. 1957) 616/2, 3-piece
crankcase, roller-bearing crank

1600S . . . . (Oct. 1957–Sept. 1959) 616/2,
three-piece crankcase, plain-bearing crank

Bore x stroke, mm/inches:

1300, 1300S 74.5x74/1.93x2.91

1600, 1600S 82.5x74/3.25x2.91

Displacement, cc/cubic inches:

1300, 1300S 1290/78.7

1600, 1600S 1582/96.5

Valve operation: . . . . Single camshaft with pushrods
and rocker arms; inclined exhaust valves

Compression ratio:

1300 . . . . 6.5:1

1300S 8.2:1

1600 . . . . 7.5:1

1600S 8.5:1

Carburetion:

1300 . . . . Two Solex 32 PBI

1300S . . . . Two Solex 32 PBIC or 40 PICB

1600 . . . . 1958-1959: Two Zenith NDIX,
1956–1957: Two Solex 32 PBIC

1600S. . . . . 75 DIN/88 SAE @ 5000

Chassis & Drivetrain

Frame: . . . . Boxed-section pressed steel in
unit with floor pan

Component layout: . . . . Rear engine, rear drive

Clutch: . . . . . . 1956–57: Fichtel & Sachs single dry-plate,
1958–59: Haussermann single dry-plate

Transmission: . . . . Porsche four-speed, all-synchromesh
(all gears indirect)

Axle ratio: 4.43:1

Rear suspension: . . . . Independent (swing axle)
with transverse torsion bars and
telescopic shock absorbers

Front suspension: . . . . Independent, with parallel
trailing arms, transverse laminated torsion bars,
telescopic shock absorbers, & anti-roll bar

General

Wheelbase, mm/inches: 2100/82.7

Track: front, mm/inches. 1306/51.4

rear, mm/inches 1372/50.1

Brakes: . . . . Aluminum drums with iron liners

Tire size, front & rear: 5.60–15

Wheels: . . . . Bolt-on steel disc

Body builder: . . . . . Reutter (Coupe, Cabriolet, Speedster),
Convertible D (1959) Drauz

Interior of the 1959 356A 1600. A clock has been added to the center of the dash above the radio, the fuel reserve control can be seen just under the dash at right, the radio speakers mounted in the carpeted kick panels. The windshield washer was activated by the left foot (above brake and clutch pedals). *Dean Batchelor*

The 1959 1600 Coupe interior was superbly finished and, while very comfortable up front, was a bit tight in the back. The rear seat back folded flat to allow luggage to be placed on top—a necessary addition if traveling for any length of time. *Dean Batchelor*

Detail of the 1959 356A parking light and horn grille. *Dean Batchelor*

The serial number (107819) on the Reutter karosserie plate identifies the car as a 1959 356A/1600 Coupe with a Type 616/1, three-piece crankcase engine with two 32 NDIX Solex carburetors. The engine bore and stroke are 82.5x74 and with a 7.5:1 compression ratio the engine delivers 60 DIN horsepower at 4500 rpm. *Dean Batchelor*

Chapter 4

★★	**Coupe**
★★1/2	**Cabriolet**
★★★1/2	**Roadster**
★★★★	**Carrera**

356B

The most radical looking Porsche yet—the 1960 356B—made its public debut at the Frankfurt auto show in September 1959. The bumpers on this, the T-5, body were raised—3 3/4 inches in front, 4 1/8 inches at the rear to increase traffic and parking protection. Large, vertical bumper guards also helped in this respect. The headlights were raised so that the fender line went almost straight forward to the top edge of the chromed light frame. The parking lights protruded forward above the bumper, at the outboard edge of small twin grilles covering the horns. Air intakes, for brake cooling, were cut into the body on either side below the bumper.

Inside, the rear seats were lowered for more passenger head room, and the rear seat backs were split so three persons and some luggage could be carried; or two, and more luggage. The rear window could be defrosted from outlets below the window. Ventilation was aided by vent wings in the door glass, which were standard on all bodies except the Roadster.

Brake drums with circumferential fins were replaced by new cast-aluminum drums with seventy-two radial fins; the cast-iron liners being held in place by the Alfin process. At the same time, a new seal was incorporated into the design, between the edge of the drum and the backing plate, to help keep water out of the brakes.

Engines were almost unchanged from the last 356A, but the 1600 Super 90 engine announced at Frankfurt didn't appear in production until March 1960. A number of crankshaft failures in early 356Bs caused Porsche engineers to enlarge oil pump capacity (by lengthening the gears), and the new pump was fitted to all 616 engines during the 1960 model run. Stronger rods and larger main bearing journals became standard on the Super 90.

At first, the Type 741 transaxle had a single front mount, similar to the Type 519 used before the 356A. As before, Porsche engineers decided that the double mount of the Type 644 was better, so after 3,000 of the 356Bs were built, they went back to the Type 644 design.

1961

Dutch-made Koni shock absorbers were fitted as standard equipment on both the 1600S and Super 90. Simultaneously, the rear roll stiffness was reduced by the use of one-millimeter-smaller torsion bars (24 to 23 mm). The addition of a transverse leaf spring helped carry the weight of the rear of the car, but didn't affect body roll. This spsring was called a "camber compensator," which was standard on the S-90 and optional on all other models.

The Convertible D, built by Drauz, became the Roadster in 1960. About 230 were built through 1961 and into 1962. Early in 1961, D'Ieteren of Belgium joined Drauz building Roadster bodies. About this time, Karmann began producing the hardtop

The 356B, in 1960 and 1961 had the T-5 body with the high bumpers, raised-center hubcaps, and head-lights mounted higher on the front fenders, which made the fender line straighter from the windshield to the top of the light (when compared to the 356A). The front compartment opening was rounded at the leading edge. Shown is a standard Cabriolet. *Porsche Cars North America*

The 356B, in 1960 and 1961 had the T-5 body with the high bumpers, raised-center hubcaps, and headlights mounted higher on the front fenders, which made the fender line straighter from the windshield to the top of the light (when compared to the 356A). The front compartment opening was rounded at the leading edge. Shown is a standard Cabriolet. *Porsche Cars North America*

Coupe (also called the notchback), which resembled the removable hardtop Cabriolets; however this top was fixed permanently to the body shell, basically a Cabriolet body. The Karmann notchback Coupe continued through 1962.

1962

Once again the new Porsche was updated without losing its character and traditional appearance, although the changes were significant from both an esthetic and practical point. When the 1962 356B (T-6 body) was shown at the Frankfurt show in September 1961, it displayed twin air-intake grilles in the rear lid, a larger windshield and rear window on the Coupe, an outside gas filler under a door in the right front fender, a new cowl vent, and a "squared-off" lower edge of the front lid.

The battery moved to the right side of the front compartment and the optional gasoline heater nestled in the space formerly occupied by the battery. Fuel was put into the 13.2-gallon tank through a filler hidden under a door in the right front fender. This door was spring-loaded, and was opened from inside the car.

Each year and model has subtle differences from the next. This 1962 356B Super 90 had a Fram oil filter, Knecht air filter, and Bosch ignition. All this was standard Porsche equipment, but shapes and colors can make a difference. This engine has an aftermarket fuel filter. *Mike Parris/Argus*

The fuel tank itself was no longer the familiar box that had been used since the first 356 coupe, but was now flatter and spread out over the floor of the front compartment. At the

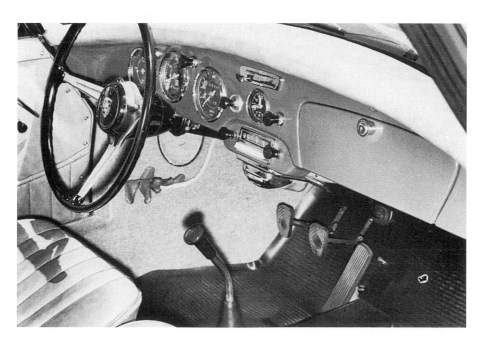

The 1962 T-6 body interior had the traditional Porsche look with rubber floor mats and carpeted kick panels. Three instruments were still grouped in front of the driver, but a VDO clock was placed in the center of the panel just below a heater/ventilation control. A second heater control to open or close the heater boxes by cables was still on the floor tunnel. *Mike Parris/Argus*

back of this compartment the fuse box was located, which had been inside the car, and a plastic container for windshield washer fluid.

A new fresh-air system was incorporated to allow better outside air intake to the occupants by means of an intake air grille located in the center of the cowl. It put fresh air under the front hood where it was picked up by two air regulators—one on the right and one on the left of the hood hinges. The occupants could regulate the forced air down under the dash. It was a far superior system to the one previously used and eliminated another customer complaint.

The Haussermann A-10 180 mm clutch was replaced by a larger A-12 200 mm model in the Super 90; and the 1600 Super engine had cast-iron instead of aluminum cylinders, as in the 1600.

Porsche transmissions were available with four different ratios for first, second, and fourth gears, and five ratios for third. These were referred to as A, B, C, D, and E gearing. Unless ordered otherwise, the 1962 Porsches came with a 7:31 axle (4.428:1 ratio) and BBBD transmission gearing. Also available for road cars were BBBC or BBAB gear sets. The seventeen transmission ratios and three axle ratios were mainly available to racers, who could change ratios to suit the course conditions, but there was really no reason for the average driver to need or want odd combinations of gearing; the factory did have it worked out pretty well for its road cars.

Also announced at the 1962 Porsche introduction, in September 1961, was the Carrera 2—still four cylinders with double overhead camshafts, but with a bore increase from 90 to 92 mm, and a stroke increase from 66 to 74 mm, resulting in a displacement of 1,966 cubic centimeters, the type 587.

The two-liter Carrera retained the plain rod bearings of the previous Carrera, but the bearing diameter was reduced from 55 to 52 mm so the longer-stroke rods could clear the sides of the crankcase.

The fuel-level sending unit had been installed in the bottom of the new tank in the 1962 cars, but it all too often leaked, and was difficult to repair, so in February of 1962 the unit went back to the top of the tank.

1963

It had taken Porsche four years—from April 1950 until March 1954—to build and deliver the first 5,000 cars, but during the production years of the 356B, sales exceeded that figure each year: 1960—7,598; 1961—7,664; 1962—8,205; 1963—9,692 (includes 356C).

Running minor modifications continued to make Porsches gradually better each year for comfort, handling, driveability, or ease of maintenance—sometimes in all areas.

Other changes were made, though, which would have a long-range effect on Porsche's design and production. In 1963, Porsche absorbed the Reutter body company, spinning off the seat-building division, which became Recaro (from *Reutter Carozzerie*, although it's not known why the original German spelling, Karozzerie, was not used). In July, production started on the last 356 model, the C type.

In its April 15, 1960, road test of a 356B, *The Autocar* characterized Porsche: "When first presented to the public it was not an altogether good car on the road; it called for more than average skill—even courage—to get the best out of it. Over the years, various modifications to the suspension and steering gear have given the car progressively more orthodox handling characteristics."

Magazine road test reports were generally enthusiastic, sometimes to the degree that they sounded almost like press releases from the factory, but occasional criticism did crop up, as in this May 1960 report in *Sports Cars Illustrated*: "At the back, the exhaust pipes joggle through S-bends to get to the exits, which are integrated with—and which quickly discolor—the rear bumper guards."

The magazine's staff liked the interior, particularly the seating, but prefaced those comments with this: "There are many more detail changes inside the 356B. To discuss them we have to step inside a process which, in itself, isn't easy."

Sports Cars Illustrated's European editor had purchased a new Super 90, and waxed eloquent about it: "But it's on the bumpy back roads that this car really performs wonders. You find yourself searching for serpentine, climbing, diving and winding byways just to exploit the astonishing agility of this car. The surface doesn't matter; the bumpier it is, the more the Porsche likes it."

In its May 3, 1962, issue *The Motor* testers said: "Thirteen years of development have left few if any of the original components unaltered but the general layout remains the same . . ." And, "The usual tendency for cars to grow in size and weight has been largely resisted and although increasing refinement has brought some weight penalty, the 17 1/2-cwt [1,960-pound] car is one of the very few machines available to a buyer who insists on luxury in a compact and agile form."

Car and Driver's October 1963 report of a 356B listed a few criticisms, but on the whole, it was an extremely complimentary report, saying, among other things: "The renovation brought about a car that has virtually neutral steering characteristics; handling so safe that

The 356B changed to the T-6 body for 1962, shown in the darker car at right. The T-6 featured a squared-off front hood for easier luggage access, dual rear-lid air intake grilles for improved breathing, and a larger rear window. These are preproduction prototypes. The reflectors mounted below the bumpers were placed above the taillights in regular production. *Porsche A. G.*

only the most hapless, witless, inept driver could let the car get away from him (or, significantly, her—the Normal is called the 'ladies' model in German)."

Finally, capping the report, the writer became positively eloquent: "A Porsche's excitement is as much intellectual as visceral; the pride and pleasure of ownership comes not only from its characteristic comfort, controllability and roadability but also its freedom from temperament. Simply: the absence of pain. Its dependability can be taken as much for granted as that of a Chevy station wagon—you can toss in a girl and some luggage and shove off, never having any trepidation about the romance of the car, the road, the girl, being punctured by mechanical disaster. It's that kind of car."

Others might express it differently, but most owners felt that way about the 356B; and justifiably so. There are Porsche owners, even today, who don't see the need for disc brakes, and who consider the 356B as the best of the last "real Porsches."

356B (1960-63)

Engine

Design: ....Air-cooled flat (opposed four)
Type:
1600 ......616/1, three-piece crankcase, plain-bearing crank
1600S 1960–1961: 616/2,
1962–1963: ....616/12,three-piece crankcase, plain-bearing crank
1600S–90 ....616/7, three-piece crankcase, plain-bearing crank
Bore x stroke, mm/inches:
1600, 1600S, 1600S–90 ....82.5x74 / 3.25x2.91
Displacement, cc/cubic inches:
1600, 1600S, 1600S–90 ....1582 / 96.5
Valve operation: ....Single camshaft with pushrods and rocker arms; inclined exhaust valves
Compression ratio:
1600...7.5:1
1600S..8.5:1
1600S–90..9:1
Carburetion:
1600, 1600S ....Two Zenith 32 NDIX
1600S–90 ....Two Solex 40 PII–4
BHP (Mfr.):
1600 ....60 DIN/70 SAE @ 4500
1600S ....75 DIN/88 SAE @ 5000
1600S–90 ....90 DIN/102 SAE @ 5500

Chassis & Drivetrain

Frame: ......Boxed-section pressed steel in unit with floor pan
Component layout: ....Rear engine, rear drive
Clutch: ....Haussermann single dry-plate (first cars), Fichtel & Sachs single dry-plate (from early 1960)
Transmission: ....Porsche four-speed, all-synchromesh (all gears indirect)
Axle ratio: 4.43:1
Rear suspension: ....Independent (swing axle) with transverse torsion bars and telescopic shock absorbers
Front suspension: ....Independent, with parallel trailing arms, transverse laminated torsion bars, telescopic shock absorbers, and anti-roll bar

General

Wheelbase, mm/inches ....2100 / 82.7
Track: front mm/inches: ....1306 / 51.4
  rear, mm/inches ....1272 / 50.1
Brakes: ....Aluminum drums with iron liners
Tire size, front & rear:
1600S–90:...5.90–15
1600 & 1600S: 5.60–15
Wheels: ....Bolt-on steel disc
Body builder: Coupe & Cabriolet: ....Reutter
Roadster: ....1960: Drauz, 1961–1962: d'leteren
Hardtop: ....1961–1962: Karmann
Coupe: ....1962–1963: Karmann

Chapter 5

356C

When production began on the 356C in July 1963, the car was visually little changed from the 356B of 1963. A close look, however, revealed a new wheel and hubcap design that covered four-wheel disc brakes—a Porsche first on a customer road car.

The Porsche company had been experimenting with disc brakes since 1958, testing two systems: Porsche's own design had the brake disc attached to the hub at its outer periphery (to utilize the open-center wheels carried over from Volkswagen) and the caliper was inside the disc. This assembly was light, weighing only a few ounces more per wheel than the older drum brake design. The Dunlop disc brakes, also being tested, were much heavier than either the Porsche disc or drum design; but when the decision was finally made to adopt disc brakes on the production cars, this was the system that won. The decision was primarily one based on cost and supply. Porsche would have been the only car company using its design, but most of the world's cars using disc brakes were utilizing the Dunlop design, made either by Dunlop or another company building them under license from Dunlop.

Porsche's disc brakes were supplied by Ate (Alfred Teves), manufactured under license from Dunlop. Some unique Porsche features were incorporated into the new brakes, the most significant being the mechanical parking brake working in a "hat section"

which created a seven-inch-diameter drum inside the rear brake disc on each side.

Three engines were available in the C model: the Carrera 2, the 1600C and 1600SC— the latter two being derived from the 1600S and the Super 90, respectively.

Under Ing. Hans Mezger's direction, some significant engine changes were made. Intake valve diameter on the Super 90 was reduced from 40 to 38 mm, and exhaust valve diameter was increased from 31 to 34 mm.

The SC utilized the camshaft from the Super 90, and a new camshaft was developed for the 1600C which was similar to the 1600 cam, but with lift increased from 8.5 to 10 mm. The intake and exhaust ports on both engines were reshaped to give better flow.

At the start of 356C production, the 1600C engine had cast-iron cylinders, while the SC had Ferral-coated aluminum cylinders (also a holdover from the Super 90). But later in the 1964 model year, the SC was given yet a different cylinder treatment called Biral, which consisted of a cast-iron sleeve around which a finned aluminum "muff" was cast. This system, similar to the Alfin brake process, allowed much better heat dissipation from cylinder to air. It was better than cast-iron, and less expensive than the Ferral process.

The two engines had identical crankcases, with main bearing journals of 50-55-55-40 mm diameter, from flywheel to cranknose.

While some purists hold that the 356A (T-2) is the best early Porsche, the 356C is the most enjoyable of them to drive. Fifteen years of development had made it into a great car. *Dean Batchelor*

The Super 90 crank was 55-55-55-40. The SC crankshaft had four integral counter-weights that gave smoother running and, as a result, the maximum horsepower of 95 DIN was obtained at 5800 rpm.

At the same time, both engines were "Americanized" by adding tubing for positive crankcase ventilation; with the unburned hydrocarbons being sucked into the carburetor inlets of the right bank of cylinders.

Production of the 356s stopped in September 1965 after 86,303 cars and 15 1/2 years. Factory records indicate that ten additional Cs were built for special customers in 1966. During the lifetime of the 356C, Porsche introduced the electronic tachometer. The C model was probably the best of the series. Continual development improved an already good car, and it was a more refined-looking Porsche than previous models.

Apparently magazine road testers agreed, because their comments and evaluations criticized less and less as time went on.

A 356C is distinguishable from the 356B by the flat hubcaps tha t go with the C's disc brakes. These were not only the best of the 356 series, but the best looking. *Porsche A. G.*

Car and Driver's staff presented a mixed review of the 356C in its 1965 Car and Driver Yearbook, on one hand accusing the company of needless cost cutting, while on the other heaping high praise on the Porsche engine and disc brakes. The testers lamented the loss of the camber compensator: "Again, Porsche says the cars don't 'need' it . . . and again, it's a patently transparent move to cut corners—in this instance, maybe $6 per car. Any individual buyer who feels he 'needs' a camber compensator may buy one as an after-market accessory . . . for about $65 plus installation (or less, with the car)." The C and SC could

A flat hubcap, this one with an enameled Porsche crest (some had metal crests and some had no embellishment on the cap—see opposite page), identified a disc-braked 356C. *Dean Batchelor*

This dash shot of an early 1964 356C shows the glovebox, grab handle, and padded sun visors available on the C series. On later 1964 models the handgrip was eliminated, and the light switch moved from behind the steering wheel to where it was easier to reach. *Porsche A. G.*

Disc brake and caliper for the 356C were made by Ate under license from Dunlop. The rear disc incorporated a small drum-type parking brake, which was operated mechanically. *Dean Batchelor*

Porsche's own disc brake design, sometimes referred to as a "annular" brake, had the caliper on the inside, with the disc and hub attached at their peripheries in order to utilize the wide bolt pattern of the early Porsche wheels. *Dean Batchelor*

The 3 1/4-inch-wide wheels of the 356 had the rim and wheel center welded together and carried the large-diameter bolt circle to match the Volkswagen brake drums used on the early cars. *Dean Batchelor*

The 4 1/2J-15 wheel for the 356C was all steel and welded together as with other Porsche steel wheels. The bolt circle was smaller than before due to the hubs used with the new disc brakes on the C models. *Dean Batchelor*

Alloy wheels, either 4 1/2- or 5-inch wide rims, were riveted together. They were made for Spyders, some Carreras, and the 904 and 906 race cars. They started at 3.25x16 and ultimately grew to at least 7x15. *Dean Batchelor*

Carrera wheel, left, has steel center and 4.5x15 alloy rim, while the 356A is a 4.25x15 all-steel wheel. The Carrera wheel has a different offset to allow for the 60 mm drums, compared to standard 40 mm drums. *Dean Batchelor*

be special-ordered with the camber compensator for about $30 extra.

The writer qualified his remarks by saying: "We feel that Porsche enthusiasts have no use for second rate equipment—at any price. They strike us as being that rare kind of consumer who knows exactly what he wants, and who is willing to pay the going price to get it."

But about the engine and brakes, *Car and Driver*'s minions had this to say: "With the 1964 models Porsche may have taken a step backwards in suspension equipment, but there has been a great leap forward in brakes, and the SC engine is unquestionably the best pushrod engine Porsche has ever built."

This would seem to be the consensus of most 356 enthusiasts, but there are those who disagree for some reason. Regardless of personal preference, the 356C was and is the most highly developed of the line, and with that development came a combination of more comfort and better and more effortless performance. The C model is the most refined looking and more mechanically "civilized" than its predecessors. It is the car that Dean Batchelor would have liked to own from this series. He believed that with it, you got more of the better Porsche qualities and fewer of the poorer ones.

356C (1964–65)

Engine

Design: ....Air-cooled flat (opposed) four
Type:
  1600C............................616/15, three-piece crankcase, plain-bearing crank
  1600SC..........................616/16, three-piece crankcase, plain-bearing crank
Bore x stroke, mm/inches:
  1600C, 1600SC ....82.5x74 / 3.25x2.91
Displacement, cc/cubic inches:
  1600C, 1600SC...1582 / 96.5
Valve operation: ....Single camshaft with pushrods and rocker arms; inclined exhaust valves
Compression ratio:
  1600C..8.5:1
  1600SC..9.5:1
Carburetion:
  1600C..Two Zenith 32 NDIX
  1600SC...Two Solex 40 PII-4
BHP (Mfr.):
  1600..75 DIN/88 SAE @ 5200
  1600SC ....95 DIN/107 SAE @ 5800

Chassis & Drivetrain

Frame: ....Boxed-section pressed steel in unit with floor pan
Component layout: ....Rear engine, rear drive
Clutch: ....Fichtel & Sachs single dry-plate
Transmission: ....Porsche four-speed, all-synchromesh (all gears indirect)
Axle ratio: 4.43:1
Rear suspension: ....Independent (swing axle) with transverse torsion bars and telescopic shock absorbers
Front suspension: ....Independent, with parallel trailing arms, transverse laminated torsion bars, telescopic shock absorbers, & anti-roll bar

General

Wheelbase, mm/inches:......................................2100/82.7
Track: front, mm/inches:......................................1306/51.4
  rear, mm/inches:...1272/50.1
Brakes: ....Ate disc
Tire size, front and rear.......................................5.60-15
Wheels:..Bolt-on steel disc
Body builder: ....Cabriolet: Reutter, Coupe: Reutter & Karmann

Squeaky-clean 356C being shown at a concours with all the original tools, spares, and owners manual—all rare items on a 32-year-old car. *Dean Batchelor*

No doubt about the year or type. *Dean Batchelor*

Chapter 6

356 Carrera

The first Porsche Carrera was introduced along with the 356A at the Frankfurt auto show in September 1955; but the concept of the car goes back to 1952. Ferry Porsche and his team of engineers had wondered what the potential of the air-cooled four-cylinder boxer engine might be, and Dr. Ernst (later to be Prof.) Fuhrmann was told to find out. A figure of 70 hp per liter had been spoken of, and Fuhrmann's calculations indicated the figure was possible—with four camshafts instead of the single camshaft and pushrod/ rocker-arm valve actuation.

The Fuhrmann design followed the basic configuration of the standard Porsche engine, but differed in almost every detail. It had four camshafts (two per side, called double overhead, or dohc), twin ignition, dual twin-choke Solex carburetors, dry-sump lubrication, and roller bearings on both mains and rods.

Engineers have debated over using roller bearings in racing engines for decades. There is still no clear answer to the questions of advantages versus disadvantages. Dr. Porsche had used them for the connecting rod big ends of the Auto Union Grand Prix cars of the 1930s. (The upper, small end of the rods rode on needle bearings around the wrist pins.) There was precedent within Porsche. Ernst Fuhrmann used rollers to get a stronger single-piece connecting rod and because there was no need for high oil pressure at high rpm in a four-cam engine. When Porsche engineers introduced roller bearings in their pushrod engine (see Chapter 1), they did it to achieve a longer stroke in an existing crankcase.

Fuhrmann's design, Type 547, was tested on Maundy Thursday, 1953. It was a happy day for several reasons: It was three years to the day after the first Stuttgart-built Porsche 356 (1100 cc and 38 hp) rolled out of the Porsche works, and the new engine produced 112 hp at 6400 rpm on the first test of this 1498 cc engine; 74 hp per liter.

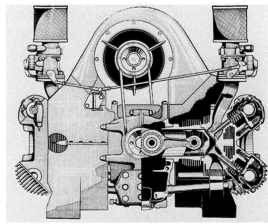

Basic layout of the Fuhrmann Type 547 Carrera engine, including the cams, valves and springs, pistons, roller-bearing rods, and crankshaft. Not shown here are the nine shafts, 14 bevel gears, and two spur wheels it took to drive the valve train. *Porsche A. G.*

The 1956 Carrera owned by John von Neumann was painted silver with a red stripe down the front hood and body. John's company, Competition Motors, was the Porsche/VW distributor for the Southwest, and John was a regular and successful racer in West Coast sports car events driving MG, Porsche, and Ferrari at various times. *Ralph Poole*

This von Neumann 1956 Carrera interior has a 160 mph speedometer, 8000 rpm tach, oil temperature and fuel gauges. Light-beam-change button is next to clutch pedal. *Ralph Poole*

Oil cooler mounted in the rear fender of this 1956 Carrera has a screen to let in air but keep out the larger pieces of gravel. *Ralph Poole*

You had *arrived* when your Porsche carried this gold script on the fender flank.

"These first four-cam engines took a skilled man 120 hours to assemble a complete engine, and the timing alone could take eight hours—sometimes fifteen," Fuhrmann recalled, "if tolerances weren't just right." The first few race engine builders trained another twenty to twenty-five mechanics from among Porsche's best to assemble four-cam engines when the Carrera came along.

The first competition appearance of the engine was at the Nürburgring in August 1953, where the car practiced but didn't race. A week later, the same car ran at the Freiburg hill climb and finished third, driven by Auto Union ace Hans Stuck. The engine was originally planned for the 550 Spyder (1500A/550RS); but in March 1954, one of the four-cam Type 547 engines was installed in Prof. Porsche's personal car, *Ferdinand*, to evaluate the engine/chassis combination.

In August 1954, a Le Mans-type four-cam was put in a Gmünd-built coupe for the Liege-Rome-Liege rally and, driven by Helmut Polensky and Herbert Linge, won outright victory. Porsche was still experimenting with this powerful engine and in the summer of 1955 installed a 547 engine in Ferdinand Porsche's gray Cabriolet. The enthusiasm was universal from Porsche personnel, only

Fuhrmann having had expectations of this possibility right from the start.

When the Carrera made its debut at Frankfurt in 1955, as the 1500GS, it had the 547/1 engine which was almost identical to the 1500RS Spyder power plant, with two Solex 40 PII carburetors, 8.7:1 compression ratio (it was raised to 9:1 by 1957) and produced 100 DIN horsepower.

The engine, unlike the pushrod 356, was dry-sumped, with the oil tank in the left rear fender. An 8000-rpm tach and a 250-km/h speedometer were fitted. Also included in the instrument panel were two switches that controlled the current to the dual coils. These switches were used mainly to check the ignition system as the engine normally ran on both coils and the two spark plugs per cylinder. The distributors were driven from the ends of the camshafts.

The four-cam engine was available in all three body styles, and the cars weighed a bit over 100 pounds more than the comparable car with a pushrod four. Weight distribution was forty-one percent front, fifty-nine percent rear.

Carrera owners were advised to keep the revs above 2500 and below 6500 for normal, or sustained, driving; but the engine would

Rear of the 1958 Carrera looked almost like the pushrod Porsches of the same period, but dual exhaust tips were under the bumper instead of through the lower end of the uprights. *Porsche A. G.*

Left, the 40 mm 356A brake shoe and drum is compared to the 60 mm Carrera shoe and drum. The Carrera drum is polished, not original. *Dean Batchelor*

run to 7500 and would accept full throttle at 1500 rpm.

The Carrera was distinguished from the normal Porsches by the gold Carrera script on the rear deck (and front fenders of the 356A), and the dual exhausts under the rear bumper. A close look would also reveal the screen in front of the dry-sump tank behind the left rear wheel.

In 1956 it was felt that the Carrera was neither luxurious enough for a comfortable road car nor light enough for a racer. In May 1957, the Carrera line was divided into Deluxe and GT (the latter available only as a stripped Coupe, or Speedster, with bucket seats, plastic windows, lighter bumpers, Nardi wood-rimmed aluminum steering wheels, and Spyder front brakes with 60-mm-wide drums instead of the normal 40 mm drums). No creature comforts were included in the GT, not even a heater. A GT Speedster was offered with Weber carburetors, twenty-one-gallon fuel tank, and an engine producing 110 DIN horsepower at 6400 rpm. Three axle ratios, 4.428, 4.85, or 5.167:1, were available.

1957-1958

In September 1957, the T-2 body became the standard Porsche configuration for all models, pushrod or four-cam, but the Carrera didn't have the exhaust through the rear bumper guards as did the pushrod cars. The removable hardtop version was available in Carrera Deluxe form and was continued until the phase-out of the 356A in 1959.

The 1958 Carrera GT had aluminum doors, and front and rear lids. The engine was now the Type 692, with plain bearings and two distributors driven from the front of the crank (actually, the rear of the car). A larger bore, of 87.5 mm, and a 66 mm stroke gave a displacement of 1587 cc. The engine in the Deluxe model had a compression ratio of 9.5:1 while the GT version had 9.8:1. The GT engine also had sodium-filled exhaust valves. Because of the plain bearings, oil pressure had to be raised over that of the roller-bearing engines and this was accomplished by widening the gears in the oil pump. To combat higher oil temperatures, two oil coolers, mounted in front behind the horn grilles, were incorporated into the dry-sump system.

The early 1958 Carrera engines were the Type 692/0 roller-bearing units which had 1500 cc and 110 hp at 6400 rpm. Twenty of these engines were made. Then came the 692/1 which also had 1500 cc, but plain bearings. It also developed 110 hp at 6400, and fourteen of these were built. The 692/2 was a 1600 cc engine which had "only" 105 hp at 6500.

1959

The 356B/1600 GS Carrera *de Luxe*, Porsche's most luxurious car to date, appeared in 1959. Its 692/2 engine developed 105 hp and the car weighed 2,100 pounds. Only 94 Type 692/2 engines were produced, from 1958 through 1960. Another 40 of the 356B/1600 GS *Carrera GTs*, the GS-GTs, with lightened body panels and 115 hp, were produced in 1959.

1960

Porsche Carreras were getting heavier while the competition was getting lighter. In 1960, to remain competitive, Porsche worked with Zagato (using friend Carlo Abarth as intermediary) to produce a series of lightweight Carreras. These Abarth Carrera GTLs were the fastest GT Porsches yet and were successful both in racing and rallying. Meanwhile, Porsche asked Reutter to bid on producing 40 bodies of the T-2 or T-5 configuration (contingent on which the Federation Internationale de l'Automobile [FIA] would approve for competition). As a result, Reutter built a series of T-5 bodies for the Carrera.

For the 1960 and 1961 model years, only lightweight GT Carrera Coupes were made with the Reutter bodywork. Outwardly these Reutter-bodied Carreras could be mistaken for production Porsches, but they had simpler, lighter bumpers without vertical guards, aluminum hubcaps, bucket seats, less interior trim, and aluminum doors and hood/deck lids.

These cars had the Type 692/3 engine in 1960, and the 692/3A engine in 1961. The 692/3 series had Weber 40 DCM2 carburetors, and a 12-volt electrical system—the first Carrera so equipped. The 692/3 engine produced 115 DIN/145 SAE horsepower at 6500 rpm. A total of 700 Carreras had been built up to January 1960.

With the advent of the 692/3A engine in 1961, the main bearing journals were enlarged from 55 to 60 mm in diameter, and the rod journals were left at 55 mm, but stronger rods were used.

When the 692 engine was first introduced, with its crank-driven distributors, a torsion vibration set in at about 7000 rpm and this was cured by the addition of six small flywheels on the 692/3A engine. Four of these flywheels, each about 45 mm in diameter, were attached to the exhaust camshafts, and two of about 75 mm diameter were attached to the inlet camshafts. The purpose was to dampen the harmonic vibration out of the valve train.

At the Frankfurt show in September 1961, the last 356 Carrera made its debut. This was the fastest Porsche 356 road car built, although the factory still claimed only a 125-mile-per-hour top speed. The Carrera 2000 GS went on sale in April 1962 as the Carrera 2.

It was often easier to remove the Carrera engine than it was to work on it in the car. This was a private entry at the Eberback hillclimb in 1962. *Kurt Worner/*Road & Track

A Carrera 356A Coupe, which the high front bumper "bow" identifies as a late 1959 unless the owner had added it later. The rear view mirrors are aftermarket items. The deluxe hubcaps were standard on the Carrera GS, but were often added to other models by owners.

The engine had 1966 cc and produced 130 bhp at 6200 rpm. It was not only the fastest road Porsche to date, but it was also the most demanding of the driver because of its extra power and the extremely tail-heavy weight distribution. It took an expert driver to realize the maximum potential from the Carrera 2.

A bit of aid in this area was provided by the addition of Porsche's first disc brakes on a road car. These were of Porsche design, and carried the cast-iron caliper (alloy on the racing cars) inside the ring disc, which carried the wheel bolted to its outer circumference to utilize the wide-spaced wheel attachments common to Porsches then. It was a carryover from Volkswagen that allowed a much lighter wheel (contributing to low unsprung weight), but heat transfer from the brake disc to the wheel after prolonged hard use—such as racing—caused fatigue cracks around the disc attachment holes.

The Carrera 2 won races and rallies, but was short-lived; the main reason for its existence seemed to be to legitimize a two-liter engine in the Abarth Carrera, which had started out as a 1600. So few Abarths were made, about twenty, that they were reengined as the factory or private owners deemed necessary to meet competition.

But by this time, racing had gotten so specialized that a dual-purpose car of this type was not a guaranteed race winner any longer. The Carrera in normal 356 body form gave way to specialized factory racers—first the 2000 GS/GT and then the 904 GTS.

Aside from driving skills necessary to achieve utmost performance from a four-cam Carrera, service and maintenance also became a problem. The first time the Porsche service chief looked into the engine compartment at the four-cam engine, he supposedly slammed the cover down with the comment "How can I change spark plugs I can't even find?" And there were eight to change! In Jerry Sloniger's fine book *Porsche: The 4-Cylinder, 4-Cam Sports & Racing Cars*, he says there was talk among Porsche people of hiring an asbestos octopus to change the plugs.

The Carrera 2 carried the same body configuration as other "B" series 356s, with the high front fenders and headlights, squared-off front and rear lids, wider front hood handle, twin air intake grilles, and raised bumpers at the back. The rear valence, which allowed the twin pipes to protrude through it, was unique to the Carrera 2. *Argus*

In its September 1956 road-test report on a 356A 1500 GS, *Road & Track's* writer said: "In addition, the Carreras appear to be coming through with a torsion bar setting which gives about one degree of negative camber at

the rear wheels, with no load. This, and the larger 5.90" section road racing tires give as close to neutral steering as is conceivable." But then: "High speed stability at over 100 mph in a cross wind still leaves something to be desired, in our opinion, but this applies to almost any well-streamlined coupe with preponderance of weight on the rear wheels."

Autocar, in a "used car" road test in June 1964, had this to say about the former Dick Stoop 1600 Carrera (a 1960 model): "It goes without saying for a Porsche that, although this car had traveled far and fast (the speedometer recorded just under 37,000 miles), there was not a creak, rattle or any sign of movement in the body structure." A great recommendation for a road/race car—or any sporting car for that matter.

Top Gear magazine (England) reported on the Carrera Speedster in a 1958 issue: "On the autobahn, which are not always smoothly surfaced, we discovered that bumps which would rock a more normally suspended sports car on its rebound stops became smoother as speed was increased. It was in

Carrera 2 Cabriolet and Coupe are rare and valuable cars, even more so today than when new. These are cars to be shown, treasured, and kept at home the rest of the time out of harm's way, unless you're the type who can stand the emotional trauma of a possible side-swipe or caved-in rear end from an inattentive driver.

fact possible to cruise this 1 1/2 liter motor car at a true 100 m.p.h. for long distances on the autobahn, and, the greater the speed, the smoother the ride."

John Bentley, writing in *Foreign Cars Illustrated*, October 1958, said: "I became convinced of one thing: any competition driver searching for the true all-purpose sports car—one that you could drive to the A & P and then race over the weekend—need not bother to look any further than the Carrera."

Bentley liked the Carrera so much that he bought a 1958 Carrera Speedster, but then trouble, rather than fun, began. After breaking

---

356-Based Carrera

Engine

Design: ....Air-cooled flat (opposed) four
Bore x stroke, mm/inches:
　356, 356A, 1500GS,
　　GS GT, and GS Deluxe............................85x66/3.35x2.60
　1600 GS GT, Abarth GTL I and II 87.5x66/3.45x2.60
　Carrera 2B, 2C, C-GT,
　　2000 GS-GT, and 904 GTS 92x74/3.62x2.92
Displacement, cc/cubic inches:
　356, 356A, 1500GS, GS-GT, and GS Deluxe 1498/91.4
　1600GS GT, Abarth GTL I and II..........................1587/96.8
　Carrera 2B, 2C, C-GT,
　　2000 GS-GT, and 904 GTS...........................1966/119.9
Valve operation: ....Gear and shaft-driven twin
　　　　camshafts on each bank; inclined valves
Compression ratio:
　356, 356A, 1500GS, GS-GT..............................9.0:1
　GS Deluxe, Carrera 2B and 2C, C-GT 9.5:1
　1600GS GT Abarth GTL I and II,
　　2000 GS-GT, 904 GTS..9.8:1
Carburetion:
　356, 365A, 1500GS, GS-GT....................Two Solex 40 PJJ
　356A GS Deluxe ....Two Solex 40 PJJ-4
　1600S GT, Abarth GTL I....................Two Weber 40 DCM 2
　Carrera 2B and 2C, Abarth GTL II........Two Solex 40 P-II-4
　C-GT, 2000 GS-GT, 904 GTS ....Two Weber 46 IDM 2
BHP (Mfr.):
　356, 356A 1500 GS ....100 DIN/115 SAE @ 6200
　356A GS-GT................................110 DIN/127 SAE @ 6400
　356A GS Deluxe.........................105 DIN/121 SAE @ 6500
　1600 GS-GT................................115 DIN/132 SAE @ 6500
　Carrera 2B and 2C ....130 DIN/150 SAE @ 6200
　356C-GT....................................160 DIN/184 SAE @ 6500
　Abarth GTL ....115 DIN/132 SAE @ 6500
　Abarth GTL I ....128 DIN/147 SAE @ 6700
　Abarth GTL II ....135 DIN/155 SAE @ 7400
　2000 GS GT ....155 DIN/178 SAE @ 7800
　904 GTS (road) ....155 DIN/178 SAE @ 6400
　904 GTS (race) ....180 DIN/207 SAE @ 7000

Chassis & Drivetrain

Frame:
　904.............................Boxed-section ladder-type frame
　　　　　　　　　　(bonded to fiberglass body)
　All others..............................Boxed-section pressed steel in
　　　　　　　　　　unit with floor pan
Component layout:
　904 ....Mid-engine, rear drive

　All others ....Rear engine, rear drive
Clutch:
　356, 356A 1500 GS....................................Fichtel & Sachs
　　　　　　　　　　K12 200 single dry-plate
　356A GS GT, GS Deluxe,
　　1600 GS GT, Carrera 2B ....Haussermann
　　　　　　　　　　A-10 single dry-plate
Transmission:
　904 GTS ....Porsche five-speed, all-synchromesh
　All others ....Porsche four-speed, all synchromesh
Axle ratio: 4.428:1
Rear suspension:
　904..............................Independent, with reversed A-arms,
　　　　trailing links, coil springs, tubular shock
　　　　　　absorbers, and anti-roll bar
　All others..............Independent, with parallel trailing arms,
　　　　transverse laminated torsion bars, shock
　　　　　absorbers, and (after 1954) anti-roll bar

General

Wheelbase, mm/inches
　(356-based)..2100 /82.7
　904...2300 / 90.6
Track: front, mm/inches: 356 ....1290 /50.8
　904 GTS ....1314 / 51.7
　All others ....1306 / 51.4
rear, mm/inches: 356 ....1250 / 49.2
　904 GTS ....1312 / 51.6
　All others ....1272 / 50.1
Brakes:
　356, 356A 1500GS, GS-GT, 1600 GS-GT ....Drum
　Carrera 2s ....Porsche ring disc
　Carrera 2C, C-GT, Abarth GTL,
　　GTL I & II, 2000 GS-GT........................Porsche ring-disc
　904 GTS ....Dunlop/Ate disc
Tire size, front and rear:
　356..5.00-16
　356A 1500GS, GS-GT, GS Deluxe 5.90-16
　1600GS-GT, Abarth GTL,
　　GTL I and II, 2000 GS-GT 5.90-15
　Carrera 2B, 2C, and C-GT 165-15
　904 GTS...5.50/6.00-15
Wheels:..Stamped steel disc
Body Builder:
　Abarth GTL, GTL I and II ....Abarth
　904 GTS ....Heinkel
　All others ....Reutter

Carrera engines didn't leave much room for mechanics to work—prompting the factory joke of hiring an asbestos octopus to change spark plugs. A 1600 Carrera engine from the front, complete with flywheel, pressure plate, and clutch disc. The double-entry fan can just be seen. *Porsche A. G.*

in the car according to the manual (no more than 4500 rpm for the first 750 miles and not over 5000 rpm for the next 2,400 miles) ". . . the car seemed to lose all its pep and would not pull the skin off a rice pudding in any gear." The rings had not seated properly in Bentley's engine, and it was subsequently pulled down and rebuilt under warranty. "Now," said the factory representative, "go out and beat the hell out of it. Take it to 7000 rpm if you like—just for short bursts. But don't baby the engine. This is a Carrera GT!"

What Bentley hadn't known before, but found out then, was that Carrera engines were bench-tested at 4000 rpm for several hours and given a full-throttle test that lasted several minutes, before the engine was installed in a car.

Writing in the September 1959 issue of *Sports Cars Illustrated* Jesse Alexander wrote of the 1600 Carrera GS: "By the end of our trip [more than 1,000 miles], we had added exactly three quarts of oil, apparently a good figure judging from the experience of other Carrera owners with whom we talked." But Jesse liked the Carrera, and finished his report by saying: "As in any car, the Carrera had its failings—most troublesome was its inability to get off the mark smartly without slipping the clutch. Apart from this, we enjoyed driving the car tremendously; she'll cruise all day long at 100 mph and is equally at home in the midst of city traffic. With the Carrera's flexibility in the gears, one is able to overtake or to shoot through narrow gaps almost at will—all in all a very satisfying car to drive."

The 356 Carrera variants were fantastic cars for their time—or any other time, probably. They were fast, comfortable and reliable. Both owners and magazine road testers were impressed by the Carrera's mechanical state-of-the-art design, and spectators at road races had to be impressed with its racing performance. And as a collector car, the Carrera has to be one of the most desirable, if costly, vehicles.

Chapter 7

901/911

★★★★	**1963-1964 Type 901**
★★★	**1965-1968 Type 911**
★★★★★	**1967 Type 911R**
★★★	**1967-1968 911S (shorter wheelbase)**
★★★★	**1969-1973 911S (longer wheelbase)**
★★★	**1969-1973 911E, T**
★★★★★	**1973 Carrera RS 2.7**
★★	**1974 911**
★1/2	**1975-77 911**
★★1/2	**1976-1979 Turbo Carrera**
★★★ 1/2	**1978-1988 911 SC**
	1980-1985 Turbo (EUR only) *
★★★	**1986-1988 930 Turbo**
★★★★★	**1986 Type 959**
★★★1/2	**1987-1988 930S**

*Note: In the United States, any Turbo from 1980 through 1985 would be a "gray market" car, imported and "federalized" by a number of independent companies with lesser or greater skills in meeting federal emission and safety regulations. Be extremely wary of any Turbo offered to you from these years. Most of these companies have disappeared. In the event that compliance with previous regulations is more strictly enforced today, you as new owner may be faced with paying for enormously expensive work or sacrificing the car to a crusher. There were 80 1980 Turbo models delivered before January that were U.S. legal.

It was evident to Porsche management as early as the mid-1950s that the 356 series would someday come to an end. The body shape was becoming dated, and the four-cylinder pushrod engine was reaching the end of its potential. The four-cam Carrera engine was considered briefly as an across-the-board replacement for the pushrod and rocker arm engine, but was too costly and too complicated to be considered seriously for general use.

In 1959, Ferdinand "Butzi" Porsche (Ferry's son) started designing a body for the new car. His father had decreed that the new Porsche would be an evolutionary design, to continue in the established Porsche tradition, would have no more than a 2,200 mm wheelbase (100 mm longer than the 356), and would carry two adult passengers and two children in small rear seats with folding seatbacks to accommodate more luggage if only two persons were aboard.

Reutter and old Porsche stalwart Erwin Komenda shared the responsibility of preparing the car for production.

The new car was introduced at the Frankfurt auto show in September 1963 as the Porsche 901. The 901 met all the criteria set by Dr. Porsche: It had a family resemblance to previous models, it was more powerful, smoother, more comfortable, quieter, had more space for people and luggage and was only minimally larger than the 356. The

wheelbase had grown from 2,100 to 2,211 mm (from 82.7 to 87.04 inches), and overall length had increased 153 mm (from 158 to 163.8 inches), but width had decreased by 60 mm (from 65.8 to 63.4 inches).

The body structure was similar to that of the 356, utilizing an all-steel form welded into a single unit-body chassis. Front suspension had a MacPherson strut and lower wishbone with a longitudinal torsion bar on each side, and an anti-roll bar connecting the two sides. Torsion bars were also used at the rear, but mounted transversely, and the suspension members were triangulated trailing links. The rear axles, unlike the 356, had inner and outer U-joints. Tubular shock absorbers were used all around, and the brakes were almost identical to the last 356s: Ate-built discs with the parking brakes working inside drums in the rear brake discs.

The steering was ZF rack and pinion, with two universal joints in the column, which connected to the steering rack at its center. Two purposes were served by the design: It made left- or right-hand-drive models easier to assemble, and the double-jointed column was a safety feature in a front-end accident.

In debating the power plant and its subsequent location in the new car, Dr. Porsche felt that front-engined cars were likely to become less popular, and a mid-engined design was impractical for general customer road use. Therefore, the engine, if light enough, should remain at the rear. Remember, he was thinking of high performance sports and GT cars, not four-door sedans, and the 356 replacement was destined to be a sports car in the established Porsche tradition.

The new engine, designed by Dr. Porsche's nephew, Ferdinand Piech, and developed by Hans Tomala, was an opposed six-cylinder unit with single chain-driven overhead camshafts—one on each bank—and two inclined valves per cylinder. Intake was through two triple-choke Solex floatless carburetors, and the car had a 12-volt electrical system.

Cast aluminum was used for the crankcase, a forged steel crankshaft ran in seven bearings (with a bearing between each cylinder) and the oiling system was of the dry-sump type. Not only did it aid in engine cooling, but resulted in a bit more ground clearance because a shallower sump could be used.

The 1991 cc engine produced 148 SAE horsepower at 6100 rpm, and drove through a Fichtel & Sachs single dry-plate clutch to the Type 901 all-synchromesh, five-speed transmissions. The shift pattern of the 901 confused old Porsche hands. Second through fifth gears were in the normal "H" pattern while first was left and down and reverse was left and up, outside of the "H." It was adopted from racing gearboxes where first was used only at the start of the race.

The 901 rode on fifteen-inch steel disc wheels with 4.5-inch-wide rims carrying 15-165 radial tires. Weight was up to 2,380 pounds, 405 of which were engine, clutch, and engine accessories.

Before the new Porsche began production in the fall of 1964, its designation was changed to 911 because Peugeot had copyrighted all three-number combinations with a zero in the middle. Peugeot was an old, respected company, and France was an excellent market, so Porsche acquiesced to Peugeot's demands. Unpredictably, Peugeot did not object to Porsche's Type 904, it being a

The early 911 models, like this 1968, were devoid of the garnishment that was to give later models more pizzazz—fender flares, alloy wheels, spoilers, whale-tails, and so on—but were also some of the cleanest looking of the series. *Porsche Cars North America*

By 1969, when the 57-mm-longer-wheelbase 911 B series came out, all models had fender flares as shown on this 1969 911T. *Porsche Cars North America*

racing car not intended for production beyond FIA requirements of 100 cars. Porsche designated subsequent competition cars 906, 907, 908, and 909 in order of their development study numbers.

One body style was all one could get on the early 911 but in September 1965, the Targa was introduced at the Frankfurt show. At this time, Wilhelm Karmann GmbH joined the Reutter division of Porsche as a producer of Porsche bodies. The demand for 911s had been such that Porsche's capacity was inadequate to keep up with sales. The first right-hand-drive 911, for the U.K. market, was made.

In July 1965, transmission gears were changed to a higher ratio (lower gear) and maximum speed was attained at 6700 instead of 6500 rpm. This gearing was the same as the 912 and the four-speed transmission was the standard production unit.

Early 911 customers had complained about front-end float and handling, because even with an extremely tail-heavy weight bias, the combined suspension design and narrow wheels and tires caused understeer unless the car was really pushed, at which time violent oversteer was induced without warning. The factory cure for this, for customers who could bring the car back to the factory, was to install an eleven-kilogram (24.2 pounds) cast-iron weight at each end of the front bumper. These weights were bolted and glued (to prevent vibration) inside the front bumper contour and flush with the backside so that the majority of owners never

knew what had been done to cure the front end "float."

Owners also complained of fouled plugs after driving in traffic, and severe carburetion "flat spots" from the floatless Solex carburetors. In February 1966, Weber 40 IDA 3C carburetors replaced the Solexes. This eliminated the necessity for two mechanical fuel pumps, in addition to a Bendix electric pump, because the Webers had float bowls, and one Bendix pump was subsequently used. The Webers also had flat spots, and this problem was cured by the addition of adjustable accelerator pump rods.

Porsche replaced the old Nadella axle shafts with Lobro shafts with Rzeppa constant-velocity joints, and the shafts were canted rearward from the inner to the outer joints. This gave better weight distribution—from 41.5 front/58.5 rear to 43/57—and a much better ride. Part of the improved weight distribution also came from placing two batteries in the front of the car.

1967

When the 1967 models went into production in July 1966, a new 911, the "S" model, was introduced. With new camshafts, larger valves, larger ports, 9.8:1 compression ratio and Weber 40 IDS carburetors, the 911S produced 160 DIN and 180 SAE horsepower at 6600 rpm. An anti-roll bar was added at the rear, Koni shocks were standard as were vented brake discs, and the five-spoke Fuchs alloy wheels (which were five-pounds-per-wheel lighter than the steel wheels) made their Porsche debut.

The 1969 911S, with its Fuchs five-spoke, forged-alloy wheels that were introduced on the model in 1967. The S model and the alloy wheels were two of Porsche's most popular products. *Porsche Cars North America*

Porsche management had thought that some sort of automatic transmission—one that would allow clutchless shifting without losing the Porsche sporting feel—should be developed for the American market. In 1967, the Sportomatic was introduced. This transmission, the Type 905, developed by Fichtel & Sachs, had a three-element hydraulic torque converter and a four-speed transmission connected by a single dry-plate clutch.

Performance was altered only minimally, and it was felt that the American driver would take to this clutchless shifting (a switch in the gearshift knob was connected by a solenoid to a vacuum reservoir and the clutch was disengaged by merely touching the shift lever). In 1975, the Sportomatic became a three-speed unit when the three-liter engine was introduced, but the system was phased out in May 1979, rejected by the American buyers—the very market it was designed to conquer.

In typical Porsche fashion, models appeared from time to time that *may* have been meant for production but surely were planned for competition. One such car was the 1967 911R. These cars used plastic front fenders, doors, hood and deck lids and bumpers, and plexiglass windows. The Rs weighed less than 2,000 pounds. Aided by 10.3:1 compression and 46 mm Webers, engines produced 210 hp at 8000 rpm. Only twenty "production" Rs were built, following four prototypes.

1968

In August 1967, when the A series 911s were introduced as 1968 models, a lower-priced 911T was offered for the European market. It had cast-iron cylinders instead of Biral (cast-iron barrels with aluminum fins cast in place to improve cooling) and a crankshaft without counterweights. Cast-iron rocker arms replaced the steel ones, and compression was reduced to 8.6:1. With its milder camshaft, the engine developed 110 hp. The 911Ts had solid steel disk brake rotors, steel wheels, four-speed transmission, and a lighter front anti-roll bar. The interior was similar to the 912.

The 911S was available only in Europe in 1968 as it failed to meet the U.S. emission standards, and the other U.S. emission-equipped models were not up to Porsche's running standards; the air injection pump caused the engine to backfire. Porsche later produced a kit to correct these faults, and it is unlikely that many 1968 911S have escaped the conversion. If you find one that hasn't been corrected, it can still be done.

The poor running of these cars was due mainly to inadequate carburetor jetting, which is where the adjustable accelerator rods came into play. Many manufacturers were in the same performance predicament. U.S. specs were slow in coming and reduction of jetting, even to the point of poor performance, seemed the only solution. Only 911s and 911Ls were brought to the United States in 1968. Mechanically the same, the L had the more luxurious S trim.

1969-1971

When production started on the 1969 B-series 911 in August 1968, the wheelbase had been stretched 57 mm (2.224 inches), to 2,268 mm. The increase was obtained by lengthening the rear trailing arms, but the engine and transmission remained in their original positions in the chassis.

B models included the 911T (which was new to the U.S. market), 911E (which replaced the L), and the 911S. Brake discs on the E and S were ventilated, and were thicker, which widened the track about 0.4 inch. To accommodate the wider track, the wheel openings were flared, and this styling was carried on all 1969 versions of the 911. The S now had six-inch rims as standard equipment, and the E was equipped with Boge hydro-pneumatic, self-leveling front struts, which eliminated the torsion bars (although many have since been converted to torsion bar suspension).

On the Targa, the rear window became a wraparound glass assembly to replace the zip-out soft rear section that was never completely satisfactory—leaky and noisy.

Significant changes were made to the engines of the 1969 cars; the T now had two Weber model 40 IDT carburetors, but the E and S were equipped with Bosch high-pressure mechanical fuel injection. The E, with 9:1 compression ratio, had 140 DIN horsepower at 6500 rpm, and the S, with 9.8:1, produced 170 at 6800. The Bosch pump was driven by a toothed belt from the left camshaft. Revs, throttle opening, and fuel were monitored by a control system, which operated a cam lobe in the injection pump. A centrifugal mechanism moved the cam axially as it was rotated by the throttle linkage.

Transmission options for the T, E, and S models were four- or five-speed manual gearboxes or the Sportomatic.

An even bigger change in the 911 engine came with the C-series cars in September 1969, when the 1970 models went into production. A bore increase of four millimeters brought the displacement up to 2195 cc and along with that the horsepower increased by about the same percentage; and T, now with twin Zenith 40 TIN carburetors, went from 110 to 125 horsepower, the E from 140 to 155, and the S was up from 170 to 180—both of the latter with Bosch fuel injection. To handle the extra power, the Fichtel & Sachs clutch was enlarged from 215 to 225 mm.

911, 911E, 911L, 911R, 911S, 911T

Engine
Design: ....Air cooled, flat (opposed) six
Bore x stroke, mm/inches: 80x66/3.15x2.60
Displacement, cc/cubic inches:.........................1991/121.5
Valve operation:....................Chain driven single overhead camshaft on each bank with rocker arms and inclined valves
Compression ratio:
911T..8.6:1
911, 911L..9.0:1
911E..9.1:1
911S..9.8:1
911R...10.3:1
Carburetion:
911...Six Solex 40 PI
911E, L, T.................................Two Weber 40 IDA
911S...Two Weber 40 IDS
911R......................................Two Weber 46 IDA3C
BHP (Mfr.):
911T..125 SAE @ 5800
911, L, E.......................................148 SAE @ 6100
911S..180 SAE @ 6600
911R..210 SAE @ 9000

Chassis & Drivetrain
Transmission:
1965...Porsche five speed
1966 ....Porsche four-speed (five speed optional)
1967–1968................................Porsche 4 or 5 speed or optional Sportomatic
Axle ratio:
911, E w/Sportomatic 3.86:1
911T, E, R (4 or 5 speed)................................4.43:1
optional...4.38 or 4.83:1
Rear suspension: ....Independent, semi-trailing link on each side with transverse torsion bars and telescopic shock absorbers. (911 S and R add anti-roll bar)
Front suspension: ....MacPherson telescopic shock strut and triangulated wishbone on each side with longitudinal torsion bars. (911 S and R add anti-roll bar)

General
Wheelbase, mm/inches:.....................................2211 / 87.1
Track: front, mm/inches:...................................1367 / 53.8
rear, mm/inches:
911 L, R, S:...1339 / 52.7
911 T:..1335 / 52.5
Tire size, front & rear:
911 T..165 HR 15
911, S, R.....................................185/70 VR 15
911 E (U.S.) ....185 HR 14
Wheels, front & rear:
911, E, T:..............................5.5 inch Bolt-on steel disc
911 R, S ....Forged alloy, 6 in. front; 7 in. rear
Weight, kg/lb:
911, E, L, S, T:...2376 lbs
911 R ....1782 lbs
Body builder:....................................Porsche and Karmann

New in 1969 was the 911E, which replaced the 911L. The E model was equipped with Boge hydro-pneumatic, self-leveling front struts that eliminated the front torsion bars. *Porsche Cars North America*

The 911C series was introduced in September 1969 as 1970 models and had engines that displaced 2195 cc. These cars carried a decal of an engine silhouette with 2.2 superimposed on it in the back window of each car, as on this 1970 911T coupe. *Porsche Cars North America*

Typically, handling was not ignored, and the front strut upper attachment points were moved forward 14 mm (0.55 inch), which lightened the steering effort and reduced kickback to the wheel.

The Boge self-leveling hydropneumatic front struts were phased out in 1971 as they weren't all that popular with buyers of the 911E (where the struts were standard) and were seldom ordered by buyers of the T or S versions.

Not much else of significance was done to the B- or C-series 911. As before, the cars underwent constant minor modifications and improvements as the Porsche engineers developed new ideas. And it may be unfair to say that there were no other significant changes because the myriad minor improvements made almost monthly by Porsche taken together all added up to a significantly improved automobile.

1972-1973

A further increase in engine displacement, for the 1972 911 series, was the big news for Porsche enthusiasts in the fall of 1971. The increase was accomplished by lengthening the stroke from 66 to 70.4 mm, while the bores remained at 84 mm. The cars were called 2.4s, but the actual displacement was 2341 cc. As before, the T, E, and S versions were offered, all with slightly increased horsepower. The goal, though, in making the engine larger was not more power to achieve more performance, but was to enable an emission-legal U.S. engine to have the torque and flexibility to result in good driveability.

Compression ratios were lower: The T was down to 7.5:1 from 8.6, the E was now 8:1 instead of 9:1, and the S ratio was lowered from 9.8 to 8.5:1. Horsepower was up fifteen in the T, to 140, and ten each on the E and S, to 165 and 190 respectively. All three ran on regular gas in the United States, and "two-star" petrol in Britain.

The T now came with Bosch mechanical fuel injection like the E and S on U.S. models, while the rest of the world continued with Zenith carburetors for 1972 and 1973. With new cam timing and larger ports, the torque peaks were at lower revs, contributing to greater flexibility. A four-speed transmission was offered in all three versions, but the Sportomatic and five speed, the 915 gearbox, were options. The latter now had a "standard" shift pattern with fifth gear outside the "H". With the Sportomatic, Porsche fitted 3.85:1 rear axle ratios and used 4.428:1 for either manual gearbox. The British importer offered only the five-speed for E and S models into the U.K.

The oil tank for the dry-sump system was moved from the right rear wheel arch to a position between the right rear wheel and the door, with a filler flap similar to the one for gasoline on the left front fender. This lasted only a year (to the fall of 1972) because service station attendants too often put fuel into the oil tank with unfortunate results.

Boge shock absorbers were standard equipment in 1972, but Konis or Bilsteins were optional. The 911S was equipped with anti-roll bars of 15 mm diameter, front and rear. To further aid handling, the higher-powered S had an air spoiler under the front bumper, which came about as a result of aerodynamic work by Porsche engineers. Front-end lift was reduced from 183 to 102 pounds at 140 mph. This "chin spoiler," as it

was sometimes called, was optional on the T and E, and the demand was so great it was made standard on all three versions.

For 1973, the fuel tank became larger (eighty-liter capacity) by stamping the upper half to fit the space-saver spare tire. Unfortunately this type of spare is illegal in Britain because the law prohibits mounting a bias-ply tire on the same axle as a radial tire. Porsche provided a plastic bag into which the driver could put the road wheel with its flat tire, because the full-size tire (which would be dirty and smell bad after the car was brought to a stop with a flat tire) could not be put into the space normally occupied by the space-saver spare in the luggage compartment—it would have to be carried inside.

Chassis design and dimensions of the 1972–73 911 were almost identical to the '69, '70, and '71 but the wheelbase was once again lengthened, by a mere three millimeters, to 2,271 mm.

For 1973, the Carrera name returned to a Porsche model for the first time since 1967 (the 906 Carrera Six). The 911RS, as it was called officially, used the body shell of the 911S, but was lightened in almost every way possible. It had no sound insulation, thinner

The Targa body style, shown here on a 1970 911S, was introduced in 1967 and has always been one of the more popular models. The first cars had zip-out back windows like those of normal convertibles, but problems caused Porsche to go to a fixed, glass rear window—maybe not quite as sporty, but eminently more practical. *Porsche Cars North America*

Buyers in 1970, as before, could order their 1970 911 with either steel wheels or the Fuchs five-spoke alloys that were standard equipment on the S shown here. *Porsche Cars North America*

body sheet metal, fiberglass rear lid, thinner windshield glass, no rear seats, and the two front seats were mere shells with thin padding, and every nonessential amenity was left off. The Carrera RS was meant for competition and had no emission equipment on it, so it couldn't be sold in the United States for road use.

These lightweight RS Carreras weighed in at under 2,000 pounds, and to give them added push, the engines were enlarged to 2687 cc. The stroke remained at 70.4 mm, as in the 1972–73 911, but the bore was increased from 84 to 90 mm. Because the Biral cylinders couldn't be bored to more than 87.5 mm (which would put it too near the limit) the Biral cylinder liners were eliminated and the aluminum cylinder walls were coated with Nikasil, which is made up of nickel and silicon carbide. The result was a reduction in both friction and wear. Bosch timed injection was used on the Carrera as well as the T and E; with 8.5:1 compression ratio, the Carrera's power was 210 DIN/230 SAE at 6300 rpm.

Original plans called for 500 Carreras to be produced to qualify the RS in the Group 4 Special GT category, but approximately 1,580 of this version were built during the 1973 model year. The reason for the higher production figure was that the Carrera could be used on the road in Europe, and enthusiast drivers took advantage of the opportunity. Of the total production, 217 were stripped lightweights, and the rest were trimmed as per 911S specifications.

To get, and keep, the extra power on the road, rear wheel rims were widened to seven inches (fronts remained six, as on the 911S), and a real front air dam was augmented by a "ducktail" spoiler mounted on the rear fiberglass engine compartment lid. The ducktail spoiler reduced rear-end lift from 320 to 93 pounds at top speed, and it moved the aerodynamic center of pressure about six inches to the rear, improving high-speed stability even in cross-winds.

Peter Gregg won both the Trans-Am and IMSA championships in 1973 with a Carrera RSR, which was a further modification of the RS (the RSR had a displacement of 2806 cc, and 300-plus horsepower), and the model won outright victory in the Targa Florio, in Sicily.

1974

Throughout the years Porsche had made running changes, in addition to the annual model changes, to improve its cars. Speed, both acceleration and top, was always sought after, but flexibility and ease of driving were just as important—maybe more so. Speed for speed's sake isn't that difficult to achieve; but speed coupled with a flexible engine is the ultimate goal.

Factory engineers know, just as hot rodders do, that bigger is better (or, when in doubt get out the boring bar). Unlike hot rodders though, factory engineers have other things to consider—like manufacturing economy, and reliability of the car when driven by a large number and variety of customers.

So, after only two years of the 2.4-liter Porsches, the 1974 911 and 911S (the T and E designations were dropped) displayed at the 1973 Frankfurt auto show had larger engines. Matching the Carrera, which continued from 1973, all 911 series cars now had a bore of 90 mm and a stroke of 70.4 mm resulting in 2687 cc displacement. Further standardizing the model, Bosch CIS (Continuous Injection System) fuel injection, introduced in mid-1973 on the 2.4-liter T model, was used on all 911 models, regardless of the state of tune.

The standard transmission for all models sold in the United States was the four-speed manual-shift unit (the five-speed manual and four-speed Sportomatic optional. Rear axle ratios were 3.857:1 for Sportomatic-equipped cars, and 4.429:1 for manual-transmission cars.

Power actually decreased on the 1974 Porsches; the 911 was rated at 133 SAE and both the 911S and Carrera rated 167 SAE. Engine stroke was increased, providing greater torque and improving drivability. Unfortunately, the cars are known to run hot; it was the beginning of a four-year cycle of troubles as Porsche wrestled with smog controls and metallurgy problems in Germany that allowed cylinder studs to pull loose easily. With their higher weight and lesser horsepower, these 1974 models have poor resale value at the present time.

Porsche continued the 911 with Coupe or Targa bodies, four- or five-speed all-synchromesh or Sportomatic three-speed transmissions, and T, E, or S engines. This T, with optional sunroof, has the Mahle cast magnesium ten-spoke wheels. These were the lightest wheels Porsche ever offered for the 911. *Porsche Cars North America*

To meet ever-increasing U.S. safety regulations, heavy-duty aluminum bumpers, front and rear, were incorporated into the design. The bumpers projected several inches from the bodywork and were attached by collapsible aluminum alloy tubes that crushed under severe impact—protecting the body—but had to be replaced after each incident. A hydraulic shock-absorbing attachment that didn't have to be replaced was standard on U.K. cars and optional in other markets. Accordion-pleated rubber boots covered the gap between bumpers and body, and the overall result was one of the better adaptations of safety bumpers to an existing body (in this case, one that had been in production for more than ten years). Other car companies, particularly some of those in Europe, should have taken note.

Underneath, a 16 mm front anti-roll bar was standard on the 911 and 911S, while the Carrera carried a 20 mm front bar. Cast aluminum alloy rear trailing arms, with large wheel bearings, replaced the welded steel arms of previous models.

Inside, Porsche redesigned the steering wheel with extra padding, used new instrument panel knobs as well as higher-backed lightweight seats. The Carrera also was equipped with the electric window lifts which had been optional on all 911 models. Now they were standard on the Carrera.

Outside, visual identification in addition to the safety bumpers were the front air dam, or chin spoiler, which was now standard on all versions; a new tail-pipe/muffler arrangement because of the new bumpers; large rubber "cushions" on the rear

---

911T, 911E, 911S (1969–1971)

Engine

Design: Air-cooled, flat (opposed) six
Bore x stroke, mm/inches:
1969 ....80x66/3.15x2.60
1970–1971 ....84x66/3.31x2.60
Displacement, cc/cubic inches:
1969 ....1991/121.5
1970–1971 ....2195/133.8
Valve operation: Chain-driven single overhead camshaft on each bank with rocker arms and inclined valves
Compression ratio:
911T 8.6:1
911E 9.1:1
911S 1969 ....9.9:1
911S 1970–1971 ....9.8:1
Carburetion:
911T 1969 ....Two Weber 40 IDT
911T 1970–1971 ....Two Zenith 40 TIN
911E, 911S ....Bosch timed fuel injection
BHP (Mfr.):
911T 1969 ....110 DIN/125 SAE @ 5800
911T 1970–1971 ....125 DIN/145 SAE @ 5800
911E 1969 ....140 DIN/160 SAE @ 6500
911E 1970–1971 ....155 DIN/175 SAE @ 6200
911S 1969 ....170 DIN/190 SAE @ 6800
911S 1970–1971 ....180 DIN/200 SAE @ 6500
Chassis & Drivetrain
Transmission:
911T, 911E ....Four- or five-speed all-synchromesh, or Sportomatic
911S ....Porsche five-speed all-synchromesh

Axle ratio:
911T, 911E (Sportomatic) 3.86:1
911T, 911E (with standard four-speed
or 911S five-speed) 4.43:1
911T, 911E, 911S (optional ratios
with four- or five-speed) ....4.833 or 4.38:1
Rear suspension:
911, 911T ....Independent, semi-trailing link on each side with transverse torsion bars and telescopic shock absorbers (add anti-roll bar standard on 911S, optional on T and E)
Front suspension:
911T, 911S ....Independent, MacPherson telescopic shock strut and triangulated wishbone on each side with longitudinal torsion bars and anti-roll bar
911E ....Boge hydro-pneumatic gas/oil shock strut and triangulated wishbone on each side and anti-roll bar
General
Wheelbase, mm/inches: ....2268 / 89.3
Track: front, mm/inches: ....1374 / 54.1
rear, mm/inches: ....1355 / 53.3
Brakes: ....Ate disc
Tire size, front & rear:
911T ....165 HR 15
911S ....185 / 70 VR 15
911E (U.S. version) ....185 HR 14
Wheels:
911T, 911E ....Bolt-on steel disc
911S ....Pressure-cast alloy
Body builder ....Porsche

The interior of the 1972 911 models continued the tradition of comfortable elegance. Three transmissions (four- or five-speed manual or three-speed Sportomatic) were offered. *Porsche Cars North America*

bumpers; and rear fender flairs. On the Carrera, only a trim change from U.S. 911S models, the ducktail spoiler was still on the rear engine lid and large script lettering on the lower body sides identified the model as a Carrera in case anyone was in doubt. The 911, 911S, and Carrera were available in both coupe and Targa body styles.

While the "2.7-liter" engine for the production 911 series seemed adequate, a further step was taken for competition when Porsche built the RSR version in 1974. Designed as a customer racer, with a planned production of 100 units to satisfy FIA homologation requirements, the RSR had a full three liters displacement, obtained by combining a 95 mm bore with the existing 70.4 mm stroke; the result being 2993 cc. The crankcase was made of aluminum rather than magnesium as before.

Because the FIA requirements dictate a "road" car rather than "race" car, these RSR models could be, and were, used by customers on the road (in Europe at least, as they weren't U.S. road-legal) as well as on the track. Out of a total production of 109 vehicles, only forty-nine were stripped racers, while the other sixty carried at least some passenger amenities. This RS version was rated at 230 horsepower, and the RSR at 315 initially, but a switch from throttle butterflies to slide valve throttle opening brought power up to 330 at 8000 rpm on the RSR.

The RSR was not raced by the factory in either 1974 to 1975, but private entrants upheld the marque's honor everywhere Porsches were raced.

Another addition for 1974, appreciated mainly by those who actually drove their Porsches in the winter (skiers mostly), was the headlight washers. Because some form of on-board automatic headlight washer is required in Sweden, which is a good Porsche market, Porsche engineers experimented with wash and wipe, using water jets and miniature wipers like those on the windshield, and with straight jets of water without wipers—which they finally settled on. A nine-quart reservoir, which was filled through a "neck" beside the fuel filler in the left front fender, supplied water to the high-pressure jets mounted in front of each headlight on the front bumper.

1975

For 1975, Porsche introduced a die-cast, or pressure-cast, aluminum crankcase for the Turbo. The heating system was improved both in amount and control of hot air, with driver and passenger able to control each side individually. Up-rated alternators could handle the load of new electrical equipment either standard or optional, including electric windows, sunroof, rear-window defogger and the heater fan itself.

The 2.7-liter engine problems that began in 1974 got worse in 1975 with the arrival of

911T, 911E, 911S, Carrera 2.7 (1972–73)

Engine

Design: ....Air-cooled, flat (opposed) six
Bore x stroke, mm/inches:
  911T, E, S...84x70.4/3.31x2.77
  Carrera (1973 only)* 90x70.4/3.54x2.77
Displacement, cc/cubic inches:
  911T, E, S...2341/142.8
  Carrera...2687/163.9
Valve operation: ....Chain-driven single overhead
camshaft on each bank with
rocker arms & inclined valves
Compression ratio:
  911T (to mid-1973 model year)..............................7.5:1
  911T (from mid-1973 model year)..............................8:1
  911E...8:1
  911S, Carrera...8.5:1
Carburetion:
  911T (to mid-1973 model year).................Two Zenith 40
  911T (from mid-1973 model year) ....Bosch CIS
fuel injection
  911E, 911S, Carrera ....Bosch timed fuel injection
BHP (Mfr.):
  911T
   (to mid-1973 model year).......130 DIN/150 SAE@5600
  911T
   (from mid-1973 model year) ...140 DIN/157 SAE@5600
  911E...165 DIN/185 SAE@6200
  911S...190 DIN/210 SAE@6500
  Carrera 2.7 ....210 DIN/230 SAE@6300
*Note: The 911 Carrera 2.7 was introduced in 1973 for
track use only in the U.S. but could be used on the
road in Europe.

Chassis & Drivetrain

Transmission: ....Four-speed, all-synchromesh
(five-speed or Sportomatic optional)
Axle ratio: ....3.87 or 4.43:1
Rear suspension: ....Independent, semi-trailing link
on each side with transverse torsion bars,
telescopic shock absorbers,and anti-roll bar
Front suspension: ....Independent, MacPherson
telescopic shock strut and triangulated
wishbone on each side, with longitudinal
torsion bars and anti-roll bar

General

Wheelbase, mm/inches:....................................2271 / 89.4
Track: Front, mm/inches:
  911T ....1360 / 53.5
  911E, 911S, Carrera 2.7................................1372 / 54.0
Rear, mm/inches:
  911T ....1342 / 52.8
  911E, 911S...1354 / 53.3
  Carrera 2.7 ....1394 / 54.8
Tire size, front & rear: ....185/70 VR 15
Wheels:..Pressure-cast alloy
Body Builder:..Porsche

more smog equipment. A severe back-fire problem existed on start up. The very lean fuel mixture (to meet emissions standards) burned so slowly that it was still burning a full engine cycle later when the intake valve reopened to provide more fuel. This ignited the mixture all the way back to the thermal reactor air boxes, causing them to explode. Porsche added a vacuum controlled warm-up regulator to force the engine to run faster when it started so it would not hesitate and backfire. As if that wasn't enough, the metallurgy problems with the magnesium crankcases continued from 1974.

1976

Cold start-up problems continued to plague the 2.7-liter engined cars. Engineering was at work on a permanent fix, but it would not really arrive until 1981. The 1976 engines were equipped with an auxiliary air regulator to ensure fast idle while cold. The problems lingered in part because engineering was hard at work completing final development of both 924 and 928 projects.

On the other hand, some battles were won decisively. After fighting the rust and corrosion problem for many years, as had every other car builder in the world, Porsche adopted the use of a zinc coating (galvanizing) to each side of the car's sheet metal (both chassis and body), which allowed the company to issue a six year no-rust warranty.

The European 3.0 Carrera got a die-cast aluminum crankcase. This was the first step toward finally solving the case bolt problems. Elsewhere on the cars, Porsche further improved the heating system, adding a temperature dial for the driver to set from one to ten according to desires. Two sensors, one inside the car and one in the left heater hose maintained that temperature. With model year 1976, Porsche introduced an electronic speedometer along with the electronic tachometer in use since the 356C of 1965. Also, for the first time on a Porsche, cruise control was offered. This was aimed directly at the American market, where it would reduce driver fatigue and improve mileage on long stretches of interstate highway.

Porsche offered three cars for American buyers in 1976, the 3.0 Turbo, the 911S 2.7, and a 912E with a 2.0 liter 914 engine for the gas crunch (see Chapter 8 and Chapter 9 for 914). The S had most of the standard equipment from the 1975 Carrera including tinted glass, two-speed plus intermittent windshield wipers, two-stage rear window heating, front and rear anti-roll bars, and five-speed transmissions. Options included Koni adjustable or Bilstein gas/oil shocks, an external oil cooler mounted in the right front fender, forged alloy wheels, sport seats, electric sunroof, electric windows, and air conditioning.

There were some good 1974-through-1977 cars produced for sale outside the United States. Mechanical injection 2.7 Carreras, called "Euro Carreras," and 3.0 Carreras were not burdened with the miserable emissions control devices that caused so many problems. They were not originally imported here, but they sometimes can be found here now.

1977

In 1977, Porsche started using Dilavar head studs on the bottom row of the magnesium cast crankcases to try to prevent the situation in which these studs pulled out. Unfortunately, this was not entirely successful either. Meanwhile, engineers continued transmission ratio juggling that had begun as early as 1975, again with a goal of meeting emissions standards without compromising performance. It took a while for the engineers to accept that, in those early days, it was simply not possible.

Inside the cars, the interior door locks were changed, with shorter door lock buttons and knurled nobs set into the door lining in an accelerated attempt to thwart thieves. Porsches rank alongside Corvettes as the most stolen cars in the world. It took much more than this effort to secure one but this did deter the amateurs.

The cars received a brake servo booster for the markets that bought left-hand drive cars (a year later all Porsches were so equipped), which seemed mainly to help when the brakes were cold, and at lower speeds.

The 1977 models, then, had running detail improvements that had become a Porsche hallmark, but were devoid of any significant changes. In the fall of 1977, when the 1978

In 1972, displacement was increased to 2341 cc, and the cars carried 2.4 lettering on the rear air intake as on this 911T. The oil filler for the dry-sump tank was under the cap just below the right rear quarter window. This lasted only for 1972, as too many cars had gasoline put into the oil filler by careless gas station attendants. Decals along the rear of the engine compartment told the owner everything from tire pressures to valve clearances. *Porsche Cars North America*

models were introduced, Porsche made another big change in the 911 series cars: Only two 911 types were available—the three-liter SC and the 3.3-liter Turbo.

1978

With the introduction of the SC, Porsche alleviated one big problem that had plagued the 2.7-engined cars. Studs pulling out of the magnesium crankcase—by adopting the cast aluminum crankcase that had been introduced in 1976 as the basis of the 3.0 Carrera and the Turbo, studs remained in the crankcase.

To handle smog considerations, Porsche engineers fitted both an air pump and a breakerless capacitive discharge (CD) distributor to cars for all markets. The SC was virtually a Carrera without the name, because it had the same mechanical specifications, flared wheel openings, and wider wheels. Horsepower was down to 180 from the Carrera's 200, but a higher and flatter torque curve made the car more enjoyable to drive. A new, stronger crankshaft with larger bearings was used, as was a new clutch disc hub for the five-speed manual

The 911S for 1972 came equipped with a front "air dam" or "spoiler," which reduced front end lift from 183 to 102 pounds at 140 mph—the top speed of the S. The spoiler was optional on the T and E, and became so popular that it was made standard equipment on all three models later in 1972. This car has European Quartz Iodine lights (which can be installed on any 911/912). Below are the typical U.S.-style sealed-beam units. *Porsche Cars North America*

In 1973, some new alloy wheels became available, called "cookie cutters" by the press and Porsche enthusiasts. *Porsche Cars North America*

transmission, which eliminated gear chatter at low speeds.

1979-1982

The 1979 911SC would continue with the same specifications as the 1978 version, but the Sportomatic transmission was phased out of production.

A two-millimeter bore increase, to 97 mm, and a stroke increase of four millimeters, to 74.4, gave the 930 Turbo a displacement of 3299 cc, the largest and most powerful production Porsche engine to date. With a 7:1 compression ratio, the Turbo produced 300 DIN horsepower at 5500 rpm, and 303 pounds-feet of torque at 4000 rpm. An air-to-air intercooler was squeezed into the engine compartment, which necessitated moving the air-conditioning condenser to the right side of the air-intake grille on the spoiler.

To cope with the added performance, in 1978 the 930 Turbo received the vented and cross-drilled brake discs and four-piston calipers of the 917. Performance of the 3.3 Turbo was and is sensational, and in tests conducted by *Motor* magazine, in England, the car went from 0–60 in 5.3 seconds, 0–100 in 12.3 seconds, and 0–120 mph in 19.1 seconds. In braking tests, *Motor* staffers found that the 930 would stop in 174 feet from 70 mph, and there was no brake fade evident in twenty successive stops (at forty-five-second intervals) from 100 mph.

When the new clutch disc hub was introduced in 1978, its larger sizes caused the engine to be mounted farther toward the rear of the car by 30 mm (1.18 inches); and even though no handling difference was discernible in any but racetrack conditions, Porsche engineers called for the rear tire pressure to be increased from thirty-four to forty-three pounds per square inch.

At the Frankfurt auto show in October 1981 and then at the Geneva show in March 1982, Porsche showed its 911 SC Turbo Cabriolet, its first true convertible since the 1965 356C and SC. (Nicknamed the "Roadster" by Porsche engineers, this car was particularly provocative to careful observers because it was not only a convertible but it was also an all-wheel drive study vehicle, hinting openly

The Carrera name returned to the Porsche line in 1973 on the 911RS (for Rennsport, or race sport). It had a 2687 cc engine, no sound insulation, thinner sheet metal and glass, fiberglass rear lid with a small ducktail spoiler, and no emission equipment so it couldn't be sold for road use in the United States (it was raced in the United States, however). It was popular as a road car in Europe. *Porsche Cars North America*

The 1973 Euro 911T Targa with its top on here, showed how open-air motoring could incorporate safety: the Targa "T-handle" was also a roll-over bar. Larger rubber bumper pads were used instead of bumper guards to help U.S. cars pass the crash tests. *Porsche Cars North America*

at projects years ahead.) Several after-market sources in Germany and the United States had begun removing the tops from Coupes or Targas with varying degrees of competence and success, and the company acknowledged the interest. Porsche's open cars never appealed to all Porsche customers. To this day, there are lifelong owner/enthusiasts who would not have one as a gift and there are others who support their local lotteries in an unending desire for one of Porsche's cabriolets. To be sure, once it was in production, it returned a portion of the high-performance car market to Porsche. (Ironically, Porsche was more anxious from an engineering standpoint to introduce all-wheel drive. Initial plans were to do that for 1983 production;

the Cabrio, however, caught the public's imagination.)

1983

The 911SC Cabriolet went into production, joining the Coupe and Targa, each getting minor improvements as Porsche engineering saw fit. The wisdom of Porsche's decision to produce the car was borne out by uniformly favorable magazine reviews worldwide and by sales of the entire production run.

1984

Porsche renamed the 911SC the Carrera, a designation change for 1984 first displayed at the Frankfurt auto show in late 1983. The

Carrera name had appeared first in 1953, was dropped in 1965, resurrected again in 1972 and discontinued once more in 1977. For 1984, engine size increased to 3164 cc by using the 74.4 mm stroke crankshaft of the

---

911, 911S, Carrera, Carrera RS and RSR (1974)

Engine

Design:...................................Air-cooled, flat (opposed) six
Bore x stroke, mm/inches:
  911, 911S, Carrera.............................90x70.4/3.54x2.77
  Carrera RS, RSR...............................95x70.4/3.77x2.77
Displacement, cc/cubic inches:
  911, 911S, Carrera....................................2687 / 163.97
  Carrera RS, RSR ....2993 / 182.57
Valve operation: ....Chain-driven single overhead
                      camshaft on each bank with
                      rocker arms and inclined valves
Compression ratio:
  911..8:1
  911S, 911 Carrera, Carrera RS, RSR 8.5:1
Carburetion: ....Bosch CIS timed fuel injection
BHP (Mfr.*):
  911.....................................150 DIN/143 SAE @5700
  911S, Carrera ....175 DIN/167 SAE @ 5800
  Carrera RS...............................230 DIN/220 SAE @ 6500
  Carrera RSR ....330 DIN/320 SAE @ 8000

Chassis & Drivetrain

Axle ratio: with four- or five-speed........................4.429:1
  with Sportomatic.......................................3.857:1
Rear suspension:......................Independent, semi-trailing
                  link on each side with transverse
                torsion bars and telescopic shock
             absorbers (and anti-roll bar on Carrera)
Front suspension: ....Independent, MacPherson
             telescopic shock strut and triangulated
           wishbone on each side, with longitudinal
             torsion bars and anti-roll bar

General

Wheelbase, mm/inches:....................................2271 / 89.4
Track: Front, mm/inches:
  911 (with 5J-15 wheel)....................................1360/53.5
  911S, Carrera (with 6-15 wheel)......................1372/54.0
Rear, mm/inches:
  911 (with 5J-15 wheel)....................................1342/52.8
  911S, Carrera (with 6-15 wheel)......................1354/53.3
  Carrera (with 7J wheel)..................................1380/54.3
Tire size, front & rear:
  911..165 HR 15
  911S ....185/70 VR 15
  Carrera......................................185/70 VR15 front and
                      215/60 VR 15 rear
Body builder...Porsche

***Note**: In 1973 the SAE (Society of Automotive Engineers) changed its horsepower rating system, using net instead of gross power, so SAE ratings were lower than DIN (Deutsche Industrie Normal) ratings from 1974 on.

Turbo with the 95 mm bore of the SC. Bosch's Digital Motor Electronic (DME) injection and ignition system replaced the K-Jetronic. Horsepower rose to 207 SAE at 5900 rpm. The European versions produced 231 hp.

Porsche improved braking to cope with the increased power. Engineers enlarged the brake booster and the brake rotors were cast 3.5 mm thicker to enlarge ventilation passages for better cooling. The brake pressure regulator from the 928S was adopted to help prevent rear wheel lockup under severe braking. Inside, leather upholstery was standard in either the Coupe, Targa, or Cabriolet. Porsche offered only its five-speed transmission in the Carrera. The European-market-only Turbo was virtually unchanged, and it continued with its four-speed gearbox.

1985

By 1985, Porsche had built more than 200,000 of the 911 series in its various forms. As before, small changes that might be considered insignificant in themselves (but when added up made a considerable difference in the car over the years) continued to be made. Considering that the 911 design was twenty years old (from a marketing standpoint, but several years older considering conception and development time), the 911 series had evolved into a car that was not yet at its peak of development.

Few had thought the model would last this long, but it did—and continued to get better. Almost any option one could want, except an automatic transmission, was available on a 911 Carrera, and it is doubtful if the lack of an automatic has harmed sales.

1986

The 911 Turbo Coupe once again was offered to U.S. customers but the revolutionary all-wheel drive (AWD) Type 959, developed as a result of engineering fascination with the 1981/1982 Frankfurt/Geneva auto show all-wheel drive "Roadster," would not be. A working prototype all-wheel drive car was drivable even before the Frankfurt show. This vehicle showed the tremendous potential of AWD in racing and international rally applications. Several prototypes, designated the

Visually, the 1974 911 models could be identified by the heavier side strip below the doors, and the U.S.-required "safety" bumpers. To Porsche's credit, the adoption of the mandatory bumpers was accomplished better than on any other make, as they blended well into the existing body forms. Underneath, the engine was enlarged once more, this time to the 2687 cc of the previous year's Carrera. All three 1974 models—911, 911S, and Carrera—had the same displacement. The horsepower rating was 150 DIN/143 SAE for the 911; 175 DIN/167 SAE for the S and Carrera. *Porsche Cars North America*

959, were built to compete in the arduous Paris-Dakar rallies starting in 1984, resulting in outright victory in 1986. Ferry Porsche himself authorized initial production beginning in 1987 of a limited number of road-going models, essentially a 959 *de luxe* after the style of the 1959 and 1960 Carrera Deluxe. As such, it soon became a showpiece for every advanced technological idea that the most imaginative of Weissach's engineers could conceive. It was powered by a 2.85-liter six with air-cooled cylinders but water-cooled heads and twin turbochargers. It developed 450 hp at 6500 rpm, would reach 60 mph in 3.9 seconds and would exceed 200 mph. It was to sell for 430,000 DM, approximately $200,000 at the time. It ran afoul of U.S. Environmental Protection Agency (EPA) and Department of Transportation (DOT) regulations and, after a lengthy standoff, Porsche decided not to modify the car to meet U.S. regulations. (Of

course, unbeknownst to Porsche loyalists at the time, engineering was at work on a more affordable version that would arrive in mid-1989 as the Carrera 4.)

Only one was legally imported, by Californian Otis Chandler for permanent display in his museum. Another dozen came into the United States under sketchy terms. At this writing, special legislation has slipped through Congress that has allowed these cars U.S. legal status following expensive modification. More than a decade after their production, they will finally be allowed to run on U.S. roads. (One imagines their owners poised up at the border of Montana, the only state with an unposted speed limit on Interstates.) Porsche factory figures indicate that 283 of the 959s (including the prototypes) were produced in 1987 and 1988.

Warranty coverage was extended for 1986, with vehicle coverage for two years and

The 911 Carrera was offered to American buyers in 1974; other than the bumpers and side trim, it was visually much like the 1973 2.7 RS, one of the most sought-after Porsches. However, the American 1974 model was much less automobile. *Porsche Cars North America*

Porsche is one of the few companies that has been successful in convincing buyers that cloth upholstery is as good as, and in some cases better than, leather—particularly on either very hot or very cold days. This is a 1974 911 interior. *Porsche Cars North America*

959	
Engine	
Design:	Air-cooled cylinders, water-cooled heads flat (opposed) six cylinder
Bore x stroke, mm/inches:	95x67 / 3.74x2.64
Displacement, cc/cubic inches:	2847/171
Valve operation:	Four-per-cylinder
Compression ratio:	8.5:1 (13.5 @ maximum turbo boost)
Carburetion:	Two water-cooled turbochargers, two air-cooled intercoolers
BHP (Mfr.):	450 @ 6500
Chassis & Drivetrain	
Transmission:	Six-speed with Variable electronic transfer case and front/rear differentials
Axle ratio:	4.13:1
Rear suspension:	Unequal wishbones with two adjustable Bilstein shocks per wheel; progressive coil springs. Ride height controlled by road speed. Manually over-rideable for height and stiffness
Front suspension:	Unequal wishbones with two adjustable Bilstein shocks per wheel; progressive coil springs; ride height controlled by road speed. Manually over-rideable for height and stiffness
General	
Wheelbase, mm/inches:	2272/89.4
Track: Front, mm/inches:	1504
Rear, mm/inches:	1550
Tire size, front & rear:	235/45VR17; 275/35VR17
Wheels, front & rear:	8x17; 10x17
Weight:	2970 lbs
Body builder:	Porsche

unlimited mileage (1985 carried it for one year and unlimited mileage), five years or 50,000 miles on the power train, and ten years on rust perforation (up from seven years).

As before, the 911 Carrera and 911 Turbo were available worldwide—the Carrera in Coupe, Targa, and Cabriolet body styles; the Turbo in Coupe only.

1987

The 1987 911 Carrera and 911 Turbo saw very pleasant changes. Porsche changed to the G50 five-speed transmission, which abandoned its own servo synchro technology in favor of the Borg-Warner system. This bigger, stronger transmission shifted better. Horsepower increased from 207 to 217 for the Carrera. Top speed was quoted as 149 mph and 0–60 came in 6.1 seconds. The 911 Turbo developed 282 bhp, providing a top speed of

<table>
<tr><td colspan="2">

911, 911S, 911S/C Carrera, Turbo (1975)

</td></tr>
</table>

911, 911S, 911S/C Carrera, Turbo (1975)

Engine

Design: ....Air-cooled, flat (opposed) six
Bore x stroke, mm/inches:
  911, 911S, Carrera, 911S/C (U.S.) 90x70.4/3.54x2.77
  Turbo...................................95x70.4/3.74x2.77
Displacement, cc/cubic inches:
  911, 911S, Carrera, 911S/C ....2687 / 163.97
  Turbo ....2993 / 182.70
Valve operation: ....Chain-driven single overhead
      camshaft on each bank with
      rocker arms and inclined valves
Compression ratio:
  911...8:1
  911S, Carrera, 911S/C 8.5:1
  Turbo 6.5:1
Carburetion: ....Bosch K-Jetronic fuel injection
BHP (Mfr.):
  911..........................150 DIN/143 SAE @5700
  911S..........................175 DIN/167 SAE @ 5800
  Carrera ....210 DIN/200 SAE @ 6300
  911S/C (U.S.) ....165 DIN/157 SAE @ 5800
  Turbo..........................260 DIN/248 SAE @ 5500

Chassis & Drivetrain

Axle ratio:...3.87:1
Rear suspension:......................Independent, semi-trailing
    link on each side with transverse torsion bars ,
    telescopic shock absorbers, and anti-roll bar
Front suspension:...................Independent, MacPherson
    telescopic shock strut and triangulated
    wishbone on each side, with longitudinal
    torsion bars and anti-roll bar

General

Wheelbase, mm/inches:
  911, 911S, Carrera, 911S/C ....2271 / 89.4
  Turbo ....2272 / 89.4
Track: Front, mm/inches:
  911, 911S, Carrera, 911S/C ....1372 / 54.0
  Turbo ....1438 / 56.6
Rear, mm/inches:
  Carrera..1380/54.3
  Turbo ....1511 / 59.5
  911S/C ....1342 or 1368/52.8–53.8
    (depending on wheels)
Tire size, front and rear:
  911 Turbo....................185/70 VR 15 and 2115/60 VR15

911, Carrera 3.0, Turbo, Turbo Carrera (1976–1977)

Engine

Design: ....Air-cooled, flat (opposed) six
Bore x stroke, mm/inches:
  911 ....90x70.4/3.54x2.77
  Carrera 3.0, Turbo,
    Turbo Carrera (U.S.) 95x70.4/3.74x2.77
Displacement, cc/cubic inches:
  911 ....2687 / 163.90
  Carrera 3.0, Turbo, Turbo Carrera................2993/182.57
Valve operation: ....Chain-driven single overhead
      camshaft on each bank with
      rocker arms and inclined valves
Compression ratio:
  911, Carrera 3.0..................................8.5:1
  Turbo, Turbo Carrera 6.5:1
Carburetion:
  911, Carrera 3.0...............Bosch K-Jetronic fuel injection
  Turbo, Turbo Carrera.......................KKK Turbocharger &
      Bosch K-Jetronic fuel injection
BHP (Mfr.):
  911 ....165 DIN/157 SAE@5800
  Carrera 3.0 ....200 DIN/191 SAE@6000
  Turbo ....260 DIN/248 SAE@5500
  Turbo (U.S. and Japan) ....245 DIN/234 SAE@5500

General

Wheelbase, mm/inches:........................2272/89.4
Track: Front, mm/inches:
  911, Carrera 3.0.....................................1369/53.9
  Turbo, Turbo Carrera 1438/56.6
Rear, mm/inches:
  911 ....1354/53.3
  Carrera 3.0...1380/54.3
  Turbo, Turbo Carrera 1511/59.5
Body builder...Porsche

---

157 mph and reaching 60 mph in 5.5 seconds.

New colors were added, as well as additional leather trim options, and new electrically adjustable seats had additional lumbar support. All of which added up to better cars, with a higher price; the 911 Carrera Coupe at $38,500, the Targa at $40,500, the Cabriolet at $44,500, and the Turbo Coupe at $58,750.

In March 1987, a slant-nose "935 look," called the 930S, became an option for the 911 turbo—for $23,244 extra. The sloping nose included retractable headlights, functional air outlet vents behind the lights, and air scoops in front of the rear wheels for additional engine and brake cooling. The 930S package was available on Coupe, Targa, and Cabriolet models.

1988

The 911 Carrera name continued for 1988, in Coupe, Cabriolet, and Targa body styles; still with 3164 cc displacement and 217 hp. The 911 Turbo and 930S, also in all three body configurations, were also to continue, and they retained the 3299 cc and 282 hp flat-six engine.

There were few mechanical or body changes, none of them major, for the 1988 911 series cars although Porsche, as usual, continued to add safety and comfort convenience features to all its cars.

In honor of the twenty-fifth anniversary of the 911, a Silver Anniversary model, with diamond blue metallic paint and body-colored wheels, and silver blue leather interior with "F. Porsche" signature on the head restraint was built in a run of 300 cars. Production was divided between the three body styles and the manufacturer's suggested retail price was $45,200 for the Coupe, $47,485 for the Targa, and $52,050 for the Cabriolet.

In 1975, the Carrera got what is now referred to as the "whale-tail" rear spoiler. This device was designed by Porsche for the 930 Turbo and 935 race cars so it had plenty of development before application to the Carrera. *Porsche Cars North America*

The 1975 911 silver anniversary edition had silver cloth in seats and doors to complement the black vinyl trim and black carpeting. *Porsche Cars North America*

While the basic body shell of the 911 didn't change much after 1965, the engine compartment kept getting more added to it. This is a 1976 911S engine. *Porsche Cars North America*

The detachable Targa (this is a 1975 911S) top section could be stowed in the front luggage compartment. A soft top could also be ordered as an option, which stowed in a smaller area leaving more space for luggage. The Carrera was also available as a Targa. *Porsche Cars North America*

U.S. customers could buy Turbo Carreras beginning in 1976 (they were available in Europe as the Turbo in 1975). The cars had a large rear spoiler with two intake vents, one for the engine and the other for the air-conditioning condenser. The CIS-injected U.S. engine developed 234 horsepower. This was not a car for inexperienced drivers; it was quick to spin under trailing throttle deceleration and it required extremely smooth cornering technique. *Porsche Cars North America*

The Turbo Carrera was continued in 1977, with no discernible visual difference from 1976. The standard Turbo Carrera was fully equipped, including air conditioning, stereo, leather interior, and power windows. *Porsche Cars North America*

911SC, 930 Turbo (1978–)

Engine
Design: ....Air-cooled, flat (opposed) six
Bore x stroke, mm/inches:
  911SC.....................................95x70.4/3.74x2.77
  930 Turbo 97x74.4/3.82x2.93
Displacement, cc/cubic inches:
  911SC 2993/182.57
  930 Turbo.....................................3299/201.24
Valve operation: ....Chain-driven single overhead
                                camshaft on each bank with
                                rocker arms and inclined valves
Compression ratio:
  911SC ....8:5:1, 9.8 (from 1981)
  930 Turbo...7:1
Carburetion:
  911SC ....Bosch K-Jetronic fuel injection
  930 Turbo......................................KKK Turbocharger and
                                Bosch K-Jetronic fuel injection
BHP (Mfr.): 911SC........................180 DIN/172 SAE @5500,
                                204 DIN/196 SAE @
                                5500 (from 1981)

Chassis & Drivetrain
Transmission:
  911SC ....Porsche five-speed, all-synchromesh
  930 Turbo ....Porsche four-speed, all-synchromesh
Axle ratio:
  911SC..3.875:1
  930 Turbo..4.22:1
General
Wheelbase, mm/inches: 2271/89.4
Track: Front, mm/inches:
  911SC ....1369 / 53.9
  930 Turbo...1433 / 56.4
Rear, mm/inches:
  911SC ....1379 / 54.3
  930 Turbo...1501 / 59.1
Tire size, front & rear:
  911SC ....185/70 VR 15 & 215/60 VR 15
  930 Turbo ....205/55 VR 16 & 225/50 VR16
Wheels, front & rear:
  911SC ....Cast alloy 6J 115 & 7J 15
  930 Turbo ....Forged alloy 7J 16 & 8J 16
Body builder: ....Porsche

By 1976, all 911 series cars were beginning to look alike, with few and very minor visual differences from year to year. The outside rearview mirror is the only visual difference from 1975. This is a 1976 911S. *Porsche Cars North America*

The 1978 911SC, with more flare to the rear wheel openings but otherwise looking like Porsches of the previous few years, boasted more creature comforts and conveniences. The outside rearview mirrors were electrically adjusted and heated, and the door locks supposedly made the car theft-proof. Unfortunately, it has been proven, that if a thief wants the Porsche badly enough, there isn't much to stop him short of an armed guard. *Porsche Cars North America*

Porsche replaced the 1976 two-air-intake whale-tail with this version in 1978 to accommodate an enlarged intercooler. This tea tray-style also provided better air management than the whale-tail.

911, 930 Turbo (1985–1989)

Engine
Design: ....Air-cooled, flat (opposed) six
Bore x stroke, mm/inches: 97x74.4/3.82x2.93
Displacement, cc/cubic inches: ....3299 / 201
Valve operation: ....Chain-driven single overhead camshaft on each bank with rocker arms and inclined valves
Compression ratio...7.0:1
Carburetion: ....Bosch K-Jetronic fuel injection
BHP (Mfr.): ....282 @ 5500

Chassis & Drivetrain
Frame:...Unit body
Component layout: ....Rear engine, rear drive
Clutch:.............................Fichtel & Sachs single dry-plate
Transmission: ....Porsche four-speed
Axle ratio:..4.22:1
Transmission ratios: 2.25, 1.30, 0.89, 0.63:1
Rear suspension: ....Independent, semi-trailing link on each side with transverse torsion bars, telescopic shock absorbers, anti-roll bar

General
Wheelbase, mm/inches:...................................2271 / 89.4
Track: Front, mm/inches: ....1369 / 53.9
        Rear, mm/inches:...............................1379 / 54.3
Brakes: ....Hydraulic, dual-circuit system, four ventilated discs, brake servo
Tire size, front & rear:.......205/55 VR 16 and 245/45 VR16
Wheels, front & rear: ....J7-16/J9-16, cast aluminum
Body builder:...Porsche

The interior of the 930 Turbo looked much like the 911SC in its most deluxe forms. Turbos were available only with four-speed transmissions (SCs have five-speeds) and the tachometer read to 7000 rpm, redlined at 6800, with a boost gauge across the bottom.

The 930 engine compartment got more crowded as it had to accommodate the air-conditioning condenser and compressor.

The 1980 911SC "Weissach Special" was a limited edition model that resembled the 1975 Carrera. It was offered in metallic silver and metallic black with light platinum-center wheels. *Porsche Cars North America*

Nineteen years after the 901 was first shown to the public, the basic body shell was unchanged; the wheel openings were flared, the bumpers protruded farther out from the body, and several styles of alloy wheels were available with fatter tires, but the total look was not unlike 1963—which is just fine with me. *Dean Batchelor*

By careful attention to top detailing, including padding and insulation, the 911 Cabriolet is one of the quietest convertibles—except for the intrusion of the air-cooled rear engine noises. Well, at least wind noises are low. *Porsche A. G.*

A good comparison of the three 911 boy types is shown here—Coupe, Targa, and Cabriolet. All three models are the same mechanically, and in most other respects except for the top itself. *Porsche A. G.*

Unfortunately, the third, high-mounted, taillight now required in the United States poses a problem that designers can't always solve—particularly in a retrofit situation. The light for the Coupe can be concealed in the rear window, but it won't work for the Targa and Cabriolet, so the light sticks out of the body above the engine grille. *Porsche A. G.*

The slant-nose "935 look," called the 930S, became an option in 1987 for the 911 Turbo—for $23,244 extra. The sloping nose included re- tractable headlights, functional air vents behind the lights, and air scoops in front of the rear wheels for additional engine and brake cooling. *Porsche A. G.*

Chapter 8

★★	**1965–1967**
★	**1968**
★★	**1969**
★	**1975–1976**

912

When the Porsche 911 was introduced for sale in the fall of 1964 as a 1965 model, it was met with enthusiastic response from all quarters, but its high price eliminated many potential buyers. Porsche management felt that this was not in the best interests of the company. It appeared that Porsche could sell all the 911s it could produce, but the market "base" was too narrow for Porsche's goals.

In 1965, the lowest-priced 911 was the equivalent of $5,496 in West Germany, which was an increase of about $1,500 more than the 356 1600SC. While the 911 price wasn't out of line, considering quality, handling, and performance, it was quite a bit more than old Porsche customers (other than the few who had bought Carreras) were used to paying.

Typically, Porsche management had considered this possibility so the problem was solved quickly and directly for the home market in April 1965: Install the old four-cylinder pushrod Porsche engine in the new body to create a lower-priced Porsche. Americans didn't get the new car, the 912, however, until September 1965 when 356 production came to an end.

The 912 engine was the 1582 cc flat-four with pushrods and rocker arms, taken directly from the 356SC. It was slightly detuned from the SC's 95 hp to 90, due to larger air filters and 911 look-alike exhausts. Because of the 911/912 body's slightly better aerodynamics, 90 horsepower was sufficient to propel the 912 to 115 miles per hour, marginally faster than the 356SC even without the SC's five additional horsepower. At 2,190 pounds, the 912 weighed 220 less than the 911 and weight distribution was 44/56 for the 912 compared to 41/59 for the 911 at the time.

A 12-volt electrical system was standard on both the 911 and 912, which was a vast improvement over the six volts of the 356 series. Both four- and five-speed transmissions were available. The five-speed, which had second, third, fourth, and fifth in the usual H-pattern with first and reverse to the left of the H, was basically the same gearbox as used in the 904, but turned around in the chassis.

If the lesser performance of the 912 was considered a disadvantage compared to the 911 (which had forty more horsepower), the lower price of the 912 was a resounding advantage.

A *Car and Driver* report in the October 1965 issue priced a five-speed 912 at $4,696, while a month earlier *The Autocar* (London) listed a 912 at £426 purchase tax, or £2,466 (about $6,500 at the then-current $2.80-per-British-Pound exchange rate). The 911, at that time, was selling for about $6,300 in the United States. As usual, American buyers fared better than their English counterparts.

Some observers complained about the Spartan interior of the 912, but this was obvious only if you'd just stepped from a 911. The instrument panel on the first early cars with its three dials—speedometer, tachometer, and combined fuel and temperature

The 912 (this is a 1969) was so much like the 911 in appearance that only very knowledgeable observers could spot the difference without looking inside to see the less-fancy interior or into the engine compartment. The rear lid had "912" just below the air intake grille. *Porsche Cars North America*

gauges—were similar to the 356C, which the 912 was meant to replace.

The 912 was mainly austere in its performance (again, if compared to the 911) and, to some extent, visually. It had many of the comfort, and all of the safety, features of the 911, including three-speed wipers, windshield washer, rear window defroster, back-up light, and reclining seats. During the 1965 model run, both the 911 and 912 were available with the Webasto gasoline heater and, in September, the Targa body style.

Improvements to the 912 came steadily, as they did (and do) on other Porsche models, and in 1966 the track was widened. In 1967 the five-dial dash became standard in the 912, and safety door locks were added. Interior carpeting was upgraded, and new engine mounts were fitted.

Generally speaking, all running changes made to the 911 (with the exception of the engine) were made to the 912 at the same time. This was a production economy, but one that was beneficial to the buyer at the same time. When the 1969 models were introduced, the wheelbase had been lengthened on both the 911 and 912 by installing longer rear trailing links. These 2 1/4 inches of extra wheelbase improved weight distribution by a small amount, but improved handling even more. The engines in both cars remained in the same location, but the half-shafts were canted backward in plan view from the transmission toward the outer hubs.

The least expensive 912 cost more than $5,000 by 1969, and could top $6,000 if all the available options were ordered. This seems like a tremendous bargain today; and it was a

The 912 was revived in 1976 after the 914 was dropped and it looked even more like the 911. This new 912E used the four-cylinder fuel-injected engine from the 914 2-liter, and it was rated at 32 highway miles per gallon on the EPA test. *Porsche Cars North America*

912 Coupe, Targa (1965–1969), 912E (1976)

Engine
Design: ....Air-cooled flat (opposed four)
Bore x stroke, mm/inches:
1965–1969 ....82.5x74 / 3.25x2.91
1976 ....94x71/3 / 70x2.80
Displacement, cc/cubic inches:
1965–1969 ....1582 / 96.5
1976 ....1971 / 120.2
Valve operation: ....Single camshaft with pushrods and rockerarms
Compression ratio:
1905–1969 ....9.3:1
1976 ....7.6:1
Carburetion:
1965–1969 ....Two Solex 40 PII-4
1976 ....Bosch fuel injection
BHP (Mfr.):
1965–1969 ....90 DIN/102 SAE @ 5800
1976 ....90 DIN/86 SAE @ 4900

Chassis & Drivetrain
Frame: ....Unit body
Component layout: ....Rear engine, rear drive
Clutch: ....Fichtel & Sachs single dry-plate
Transmission:
1965 ....Porsche four-speed, all-synchromesh
1966–1969 ....Porsche four- or five-speed, all-synchromesh
1976 ....Porsche five-speed, all-synchromesh
Axle ratio 4.43:1

Rear suspension: ....Independent, semi-trailing link on each side with transverse torsion bars and telescopic shock absorbers
Front suspension: ....Independent, MacPherson telescopic shock strut and triangulated wishbone on each side with longitudinal torsion bars and anti-roll bar

General
Wheelbase, mm/inches:
1965–1968 ....2211/87 1
1969 ....2268/89.3
1976 ....2272/89.4
Track: Front mm/inches:
1965 ....1337/52.6
1966-68 ....1351/53.2
1969 & 1976 ....1361/53.6
Rear, mm/inches:
1965 ....1317/51.9
1966–1968 ....1321/52.0
1969 and 1976 ....1346/53.0
Brakes: ....Ate-Dunlop disc
Tire size, front & rear:
1965–1969 ....165-15 SP
1976 ....165-15 HR
Wheels:
1965–1969 ....Bolt-on steel disc
1976 ....Pressure-cast alloy
Body builder: ....Porsche

be in the same ratio as purchase price. Chassis maintenance for the two should be comparable. Engine maintenance for the 912 will be less, but not as much less as you might hope. On top of that, certain years have unique problems. Emissions parts for some are impossible to find. The "smog pumpers" as 1968 912s are known, are particularly undesirable. Keeping them running may become extremely difficult.

Some mechanics recommend replacing the 912 engine with a 911 if major repairs are needed. This would probably be wise in the case of a 1968, but otherwise it is not necessarily the best solution. The 912 crankshaft (which is from the 356C) is the weak link in the engine. A new 912 crank will cost $2,041 (mid-1997) while a 356C crank goes for $1,188. A rebuild with a C crank should end most of a 912's engine problems but it will lower the rev limit from 6000 to 5000. A

good, nonfactory German forged 912 crank from the original dies is now available for about $1,600 (mid-1997 prices).

In either a 911 or 912, look for the worst rust at the bottom of the front fenders just ahead of the doors, at the top of the rear fenders just behind the doors, and around the turn signal/taillight housing. Check the front trunk carefully, especially around the battery or batteries and at the front mount for the A-arms. Poke around the rear torsion bar tube. Rust repair here can be very costly.

In all, Porsche produced 27,738 912 Coupes and 25,632 Targas. If you're looking for Porsche design, quality, handling, safety, and looks, and you don't need 911 acceleration or top speed, the 912 may suit your needs. It takes a certain individual to be content with a car of this type when it's underpowered compared to its look-alike 911.

★★	914/4
★★★★	914/6

914/4 and 914/6

In Karl Ludvigsen's book, *Porsche: Excellence Was Expected,* the philosophy, development, and production of the 914, 914/6 and 916 occupy fifty-two pages. It is a fascinating exercise worked out with the cooperation of three of Germany's automotive industrial giants: Porsche, Volkswagen and Karmann. For our purposes, the explanation can be more brief. I recommend Ludvigsen's book to anyone who wants to go into more depth than is possible here.

Dr. Ferdinand Porsche had designed the Auto Union racing cars in 1933 to carry their engines in what was then called the "rear" and is now called "mid" position. When he designed the Volkswagen, and later the Porsche road cars, he put the lightweight air-cooled engine behind the rear axle in what was truly the "rear" location. However, when Porsche resumed competition in 1953, those cars carried their engines behind the driver but ahead of the rear axle once more.

Porsche management believed that the trend of the future might well be toward the mid-engined road car, and it could have been their own racing successes that gave them the impetus to proceed. Porsche's all-out racing machines had all been designed with the engine in front of the rear axle: 550 Spyder, 550A/1500RS, RSK, RS60 and 61, Formula 1 and 2, 904 GTS, 906, 908 and 917.

Mid-engine-placement advantages for a racing car are too numerous to repeat them all, but the major ones are: compactness, with resulting light weight, which aids acceleration and reduces braking effort; low polar moment of inertia (from a central grouping of major heavy components), which makes the responsiveness better, although it takes a better driver to recover from an incipient spin in this type of car; and good weight distribution.

The disadvantages, which would have to be overcome for a customer road car (luggage space, sound deadening for the engine location is just behind the passenger compartment, and chassis construction which would allow easy access to both passenger and engine compartments) are simply ignored for the racing cars.

Porsche management's desire to produce a relatively inexpensive car came coincidentally with Volkswagen's (under the direction Heinz Nordhoff) plan to produce a sportier car to help broaden the VW image away from a producer of strictly utilitarian transportation. It also came at a time when Volkswagen wanted to drop the Type 2 Karmann-Ghia, which was not selling well.

After meetings between Ferry Porsche and Heinz Nordhoff, an agreement was reached whereby Porsche would design a new car for Volkswagen (to use the new 411 engine), which would be a VW-Porsche. But Porsche retained the right to buy back body shells in which Porsche could install its own engine.

The 914/4, 1970 model shown, was an agile and responsive car due to its mid-engined placement and resultant low polar moment of inertia. Engine access and luggage space suffered, although there were luggage compartments in front and at the rear. *Porsche Cars North America*

The 914/6 could be identified by five-lug wheels. Shown here are optional Mahle die-cast magnesium wheels. *Porsche Cars North America*

Standard 914 for the U.S. markethad side-marker lights just behind front turn indicator lights, and this early European version had driving lights set into the bumper face-bar. Later U.S. versions had optional driving/fog lights. *Porsche Cars North America*

European 914s carried the Wolfsburg crest in the steering wheel center because the car was sold in Volkswagen showrooms, while the U.S. 914 carried the Porsche crest in its steering wheel because of the Porsche+Audi distributorship, and was sold through Porsche dealers. *Porsche Cars North America*

The new project would be a two-way benefit to Volkswagen because the 914, as it was to be called, would replace the 1500 Karmann-Ghia and, at the same time, the new car would be assembled at Karmann's factory in Osnabruck. Thus, VW would get its sportier car, Karmann would use it to replace the production of the Ghia, and at the same time keep its trained workforce employed, and Porsche would be able to get bodies directly from Karmann to use as it saw fit.

The body shape was based on a design by Gugelot GmbH which was originally intended to be a front-engined car made from layers of fiberglass bonded together with a foam layer inside the "sandwich." BMW, Daimler-Benz, Volkswagen, Karmann, and Porsche were all interested, and conducted tests of the materials. The conclusion was that it wouldn't work for mass production.

A Porsche team, directed by Butzi Porsche, changed the Gugelot design to accommodate the mid-engine placement, and made other styling changes to suit Porsche's needs or desires. Before the 914 got into production, however, Nordhoff died in April 1968, and the new director of Volkswagen, Kurt Lotz, denied Porsche some of the agreement terms that had been verbal between Porsche and Nordhoff.

As a result, Porsche and Volkswagen entered into a joint marketing venture, creating the VG (Vertriebsgesellschaft), whereby each company owned exactly fifty percent of the sales organization which would now handle Volkswagen, Porsche, and Audi; and Porsche could buy bodies from Karmann, but at a much higher price than Porsche had expected.

The final outcome of all this negotiation and agreement, was that Karmann built the 914 as an out-the-door-ready-to-go car bearing the VW-Porsche name for Europe, and just Porsche for America. The 914/6 bodies ware assembled, trimmed and painted in Karmann's Osnabruck facility but were shipped to Porsche for final assembly where they went down the same production line with the 911.

Public introduction of the 914 was at the Frankfurt auto show in September 1969, and the first cars reached German showrooms

February 1970, with the American versions arriving in U.S. showrooms in March 1970.

Porsche's first advertising for the 914 played up the benefits of the mid-engine car's handling by saying, "If there's one thing we've learned from racing, it's where to put the engine . . . We think it's time you shared those advantages. So we've built a couple of mid-engined cars for the street." After listing several reasons why this configuration is better, including low center of gravity, handling, braking, tire life, and safety, Porsche concluded with: "So if you're thinking about a true, two-seat sports car, think about this: When you don't get a back seat, you should at least get an engine in its place."

At the Frankfurt show introduction in 1969, the 914 was priced at DM 11,955 and the 914/6 at DM 18, 992 which, when translated in U.S. dollars, worked out to $3,495 and $4,775. By the time the cars arrived in the United States in March, advertisements gave the prices (East Coast) at $3,495 and 914/6 at $5, 595 (with a note at the bottom of the page: "Prices subject to change without notice"). A $200 Appearance Group was available for the 914, which included chrome bumpers and chrome-trimmed vinyl covering for the roof pillars. Car prices were $100 higher on the West Coast.

While the appearance of the 914 was a departure for Porsche, the mechanical pieces were familiar. The MacPherson telescopic shock strut front suspension with its longitudinal torsion bars was taken almost intact from the 911; but while the rear trailing link independent suspension had similar geometry to the 911, the links themselves and the coil springs were new.

Both 914s had disc brakes at all four wheels with solid rotors on the rear. Front rotors on the 914/4 were also solid but the fronts on the 914/6 were ventilated. Both models used dual master cylinders activating separate front and rear brake systems through a rear brake pressure limiter. Both used an odd rear caliper that had the hand brake built into it. These were different in size but identical in design and operation. The 914's 4.5x15 wheels mounted on VW411 four-lug hubs, while the 914/6's were delivered on 5.5x15

The 914 interior harks back to the 356 Speedster for austere simplicity. *Porsche Cars North America*

steel wheels or optional Mahle alloy 5.5x15 wheels attached to Porsche five-lug hubs. The Mahles were referred to as "gas burner" or "bottle cap" wheels.

Boge shocks were standard with the gas-pressure Bilsteins available as an option, and neither 914/4 nor 914/6 had anti-roll bars standard, as Porsche engineers thought they weren't needed. With the factory-recommended tire pressures, 26 psi front and 29 rear, to compensate for the 46/54 front/rear weight bias, both the four and six had near to neutral handling. Engineer Helmuth Bott said the 914 was about six-to-eight-percent better (cornering) than a comparable 911. If the 914 was driven into a corner it would display oversteer.

Power for the 914 came from the new Volkswagen 411, and the "traditional" four-cylinder flat (opposed), air-cooled over-head-valve design. In this application the Bosch fuel-injected 1967 cc unit produced 80 DIN horsepower with a net SAE rating of 76. The fuel injection, developed by Bosch under Bendix patents, allowed the early 914 and VW 411 to meet the U.S. emission standards without using an air pump. The 1975 and 1976 914s had air pumps.

The 914/6 shared the six-cylinder, single overhead cam engine with the 1968-69 911T

The 914/6 engine was from the 911T, but mounted ahead of the rear axle in the 914. *Porsche Cars North America*

By utilizing both front and rear compartments, quite a bit of luggage could be carried—assuming careful planning and packing. The 1973 had big rubber bumper guards at the front, the '74 had them front and back, and '75 and '76 had the "crash bumpers" shown above. *Porsche Cars North America*

All 914s had the removable roof section and fixed Targa-type roll-over bar. The only Porsche identifying feature on the outside was the lettering on the engine air intake behind the roll bar. This is a 1971 model. *Porsche Cars North America*

(the 1970-71 911T had a 2.2-liter engine). This engine had capacitive discharge ignition system, dry-sump lubrication system as on the 911—the oil reservoir tank was on the left side of the engine compartment—and two triple-choke Weber carburetors. In this form it produced 110 DIN and 105 SAE net horsepower. The six-cylinder engine ran usually ten degrees hotter than the four, which was notorious for overheating. One 914 owner says that some oil-temperature gauges were inconsistent, and because the 914/4 gauge was not marked with actual numbers, it was difficult to know what the temperature really was. He calibrated his, after getting tired of driving slowly because it got into the red so often, and found the *start* of the red section was 195 degrees.

The fuel pump on the 914/4 was located immediately adjacent to the right heat exchanger, causing vapor lock. Oil temperature gauges were unmarked, but the cars got hot when driven for long distances at high speeds. Like all other air-cooled Porsches, 914s are subject to starter solenoid/electrical system overheating. When driven long distances in high temperatures, the cars wouldn't restart. The culprit is unclear: starter, solenoid, bad ground, ignition switch, etc. Vapor lock was the car's worst problem. The demise of the car could partly have been Porsche's lack of a cure for vapor lock from 1970 to 1975, when the fuel pump was relocated to a cooler position up front.

Sportomatic transmissions were advertised an as option for the 914/6 and a few were produced. Otherwise, both cars used the five-speed gearbox from the 911. Because of the engine location, the transmission was turned around and the ring gear was installed on the opposite side of the pinion gear. The axle ratio was the standard 4.428:1 on both 914 versions.

The unitized steel body was strictly for two passengers, and had no provision for additional seating. It did have more luggage space than would be expected from a car of this size, or from a mid-engined car, by having two luggage compartments. One was behind the engine, over the transmission; the other was at the front, with the spare tire.

In addition to the bigger, more powerful engine, the 914/6 was fancier and better

The 1972 four-cylinder 914 carried only that number on the rear panel; the six would carry 914-6 in the same spot. *Porsche Cars North America*

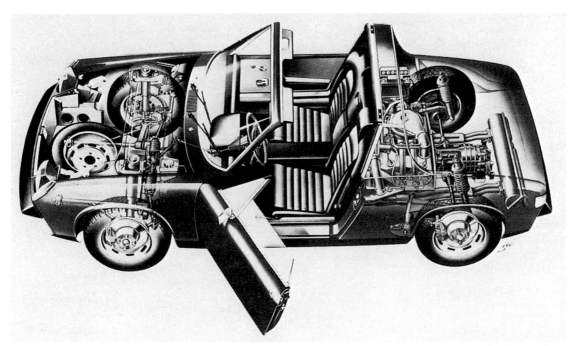

Phantom view of the 914/4 shows the basic mechanical layout of both four- and six-cylinder versions. *Porsche Cars North America*

equipped. It had three-speed windshield wipers, electric windshield washers, and chrome-plated bumpers. The 914 had painted bumpers, and the driver had to activate the pneumatic windshield washers by hand. The six also had headlight flasher, hand throttle, dual-tone horns, external trim strips, wider ten-spoke wheels, and vinyl trim on the "roll bar."

The instrument panel contained three dials, the center one being a tachometer that went to 7000 on the 914 and 8000 on the 914/6. At the right was a speedometer (120 mph for the four and 150 for the six). The left dial on each model carried a fuel-level indicator at the bottom, but the top of the dial on the bigger-engined model displayed oil temperature,

The U.S. version of the 914 received the European-style bumper-mounted driving lights in 1972. Also new were improved ventilation and an adjustable passenger seat as standard, but no other visual changes. *Porsche Cars North America*

Introduced in April 1974 was a limited-edition 2.0-liter 914, which had a front spoiler, Mahle cast-alloy wheels, a special interior, and only black or white body colors with contrasting yellow or orange, respectively, accent trim. *Porsche Cars North America*

while the top part of the 914's left dial had warning lights for fuel level, hand brake, and low brake fluid.

The one-piece fiberglass roof (only the part between the windshield and the Targa-type roll bar) was easily removed and stowed in the rear luggage compartment.

No right-hand-drive models were made for those countries that drive on the left side of the road but conversions were made by Crayford Auto Developments, Ltd., in Kent, England.

During the six years of production for the 914—1970 through the 1976 model year—and three years for the 914/6 ending in 1972, the cars remained basically the same. Porsche has always made running changes except in major components, so minor details were improved over the model run. This led indirectly to the demise of the 914. It was never as well developed as other Porsches.

For the 1972 models, introduced at the Frankfurt show in September 1971, the passenger's seat was made adjustable—fore and aft movement as well as tilt being the same as in the 914/6. Windshield wiper and washer controls were mounted on the steering column, as on the 914/6, instead of on the panel, and the glovebox doorknob was enlarged. Adjustable air outlets were mounted at each end of the dash. Insulation and sound deadening were improved. Wider wheels, part of the Appearance Group for America, were added to the European option list. For 1973, the driver's seat was adjustable and the shift linkage improved. These improvements were significant enough to make it wise to buy a 1973 or later 914/4.

The EA-series four-cylinder engine, which would run on regular fuel, replaced the W-series engine of the original 914, but changes to the fuel-injection system mandated no performance loss.

For 1975, the 1914 received new energy-absorbing impact safety bumpers with 2.5 inches of "give" via hydro-pneumatic dampers and new wheels; but the basic body remained as before. *Porsche Cars North America*

The center console on the 914 was an option, containing gauges instead of the usual warning lights. This car also has an aftermarket air conditioning, which takes up much of the front trunk compartment space. *Porsche Cars North America*

A 2.0-liter engine was optional from 1973 on, but in 1974 the 914's standard engine displacement was increased to 1795 cc (109.5 cubic inches) by increasing the bore from 90 to 93 mm, and displacement was increased again in 1975 by enlarging the bore to 94 mm and lengthening the stroke from 66 to 71 mm with a resulting displacement of 1971 cc, or 120.3 CID. These latter 914s can be spotted by the 2.0 numbers on the rear lid. The 914/6 remained at 1991 cc (121.5 CID) during its nearly three-year tenure. Built primarily as 1970 and 1971 models, probably less than fifty sixes were built for the 1972 model year.

The 914/6 was shown in the factory driver's manual with the Porsche crest on the hood. However, it seems the car illustrated was a preproduction prototype, and in regular production the crest was deleted. The Porsche name, however, was carried on the rear deck inlet and the crest was placed in the center of the steering wheel on U.S. models, while the VW crest adorned the steering wheel of European models. European 914 hubcaps came straight off the VW411; in the United States, the 914/4 used the same caps without the VW logo. The 914/6 had a Porsche crest on the hubcaps if it was equipped with steel wheels.

The reason for not openly identifying the 914 series as Porsches stems not from company indifference, or lack of pride in the cars, but rather from a marketing decision by Porsche and VW management.

The 914 was to be sold in America as a Porsche, but in the rest of the world it would be a VW-Porsche. Management of the newly created Porsche+Audi (which in America was division of VW of America) marketing decreed that dealers would have to set up separate facilities, away from the VW showrooms, for their Porsche and Audi cars. The dealer could sell all three cars, but not on the same premises. Because Porsche+Audi wanted to separate VW from Porsche in the minds of the buyers, the 914 didn't carry the VW-Porsche name as it did elsewhere.

The reception of the 914 was not overwhelming and, in some cases, was not even gracious. Appearance was the first stumbling block. Most viewers didn't like it at all, and most of the rest were lukewarm. Reports on the 914 damned it with faint praise. They liked the handling but hated the shift mechanism (although the side-shifter transaxle introduced in 1973 was a great improvement), and performance was not considered to be up to Porsche standards or tradition. It was noisy by comparison to almost any other car, including Porsches. *Car and Driver* said it was half the cost of 911, and half as good. And even without the VW name on the car, many still considered it more VW than Porsche, overlooking the fact that the first Porsches had almost all VW mechanical parts.

So what did the 914 offer? Besides a reliability and economy it had competition potential. Its inherent balance and subsequent handling brought out the competitive spirit in many Porsche fans who hadn't thought in those terms in recent years. We eventually saw 914s in races, rallies, auto crosses, and slaloms on both club and national levels. Many were raced in international events with success.

But more than that, it was and is the affordable Porsche, at least in 914 form. The 914/6 is now considered one of the sought-after Porsches and prices are getting higher at a rapid rate. Converting a 914 to "six" status isn't advisable, for any number of reasons, not the least important of which is cost, and the fact that any Porsche enthusiast will recognize it as nongenuine. Serial numbers, which will tell buyers what they are getting, are very easy to decipher.

The 914/4 engine is basically very stout, but the fuel injection system can give trouble. Even the newest 914 is more than 20 years old. Early electronic injection systems were not very reliable. Many cars have been converted to carburetors, which is not a difficult task.

When you inspect a 914 for rust, check carefully under the exhaust system and the inside rear seam of the rear trunk. It is essential that you remove the rocker covers and check around the jacking points as well. Check carefully that the right rear wheel alignment is correct. Look under the battery tray in the engine compartment; leaking battery acid can weaken the chassis, causing the right trailing arm to pull away from the chassis.

914, 914/6 (1970–1975)

Engine

Design:
914 ....Air-cooled flat (opposed) four
914/6 ....Air-cooled flat (opposed) six
Bore x stroke, mm/inches:
  1970–1973 four ....90x66 / 3.54x2.60
  1974–1976 four ....93x66 / 3.66x2.60
  1973–1976 four ....94x71 / 3.70x2.80
  all 914/6...80x66 / 3.15x2.60
Displacement, cc/cubic inches:
  1970–1973...1679/102.3
  1974–1976 four 1795/109.5
  1973–1976 four 1971/120.3
  all 914/6 ....1991/121.5
Valve operation:
  914 ....Single camshaft with pushrods , rocker arms, and inclined exhaust valves
  914/6 ....Chain-driven single overhead camshaft on each bank with rocker arms and inclined valves
Compression ratio:
  1.7-liter four 8.2:1
  1.8-liter four 7.3:1
  2.0-liter four 7.6:1
  914/6 ....8.6:1
Carburetion:
  all U.S. fours.............................Bosch fuel injection (European models had Solex carbs)
  914/6 ....Two Weber 40 IDT 3V carburetors

BHP (Mfr.):
  1.7-liter four ....80 DIN/76 SAE @ 4900
  1.8-liter four ....76 DIN/72 SAE @ 4800
  2.0-liter four ....95 DIN/91 SAE @ 4900
  914/6 ....110 DIN/105 SAE @ 5800

Chassis & Drivetrain

Frame: ....Unit body
Component layout: ....Mid-engine, rear drive
Clutch: ....Fichtel & Sachs single dry-plate
Transmission: ....Porsche five-speed, all synchromesh
Axle ratio: 4.428:1
Rear suspension: ....Independent, semi-trailing link on each side, coil springs and telescopic shock absorbers
Front suspension:...........MacPherson telescopic shock strut and wishbone on each side with longitudinal torsion bars

General

Wheelbase, mm/inches: ....2450 / 96.5
Track: Front, mm/inches:
  (with 4 1/2Jx15 wheels) 1331/52.4
  (with 5 1/2Jx15 wheels) 1343/52.9
Rear, mm/inches:
  (with 4 1/2Jx15 wheels) 1371/54.0
Brakes:...Ate disc
Tire size, front & rear: ....155 HR 15, 165 HR 15, or 185 HR14, depending on wheels
Wheels:...................Bolt-on steel disc or pressure-cast alloy
Body builder: ....Karmann

Chapter 10

924 and
924 Turbo

★	924
★★	924 Turbo
★	924S
★★★	1980 924 Carrera GT
★★★★	1980 924 Carrera GTS

The Porsche 924 was the most "different" Porsche the company had built in twenty-five years, yet it continued a philosophy of the first cars from this company—using Volkswagen parts as the basis for the vehicle.

The first 356 in 1950 had VW suspension, brakes, steering, and a Porsche-modified air-cooled VW engine mounted at the back. The 924 had VW suspension, brakes, steering, and a water-cooled VW engine mounted at the front. One major difference, aside from the air/water cooling, was that while the 356 used many VW components, it was designed to be a Porsche and sold as such. The 924, on the other hand, was designed by Porsche to be a VW or Audi and ended up becoming a Porsche.

As far back as 1970, the VW-Porsche VG (Vertriebsgesellschaft—the joint organization formed to market the 914) saw that there was a probability that the 914 was not going to become the lasting favorite that the 356 had been. VG management therefore began planning a new car; one to be designed *by* Porsche *for* VG to sell as a VW/Audi—no more "VW-Porsche" in Europe and "Porsche" elsewhere, as the 914 had been conceived.

Requirements for the new car were formally outlined:

1. interior space comparable to the 911
2. useful trunk volume
3. higher comfort level than the 914
4. maximum use of high-volume VW parts

5. technical similarity and family resemblance to 928 (this car was in the design stage actually before the 924)
6. not to be rear-engined or mid-engined
7. independent suspension all around
8. 2+2 seating

Once the parameters had been agreed to, the components that would form the basis for the new car were selected by a process of logical application as would be expected. It was believed that air-cooled engines were nearing the end of their production at both Porsche and Volkswagen so one of the new water-cooled units under development would be used. The one selected was a Volkswagen design, built by Audi, used in carbureted form in the VW LT van, the American Motors Pacer and Spirit, and in fuel-injected form in the new-to-be Porsche.

A mid-engine location was deemed unsatisfactory because of the 2+2 seating requirement, and a rear location à la 911 was ruled out because of the required family resemblance to the 928, which would have a heavier V-8 and couldn't be rear-engined.

Once the front location was picked, Porsche engineers decided to mount the transmission at the rear to create as equal as possible front/rear weight distribution (it came out 48 front, 52 rear). The rear transmission location also resulted in a high polar moment if inertia which is a near-ideal safety factor because, although a car of this type isn't quite as agile as a mid-engined car with its inherent low polar moment, it is easier for the average-to good driver to handle in all circumstances. A car with low polar moment is difficult to "catch" once it starts to spin, for example, whereas a car with high polar moment is more forgiving; a factor that would be appreciated by old Porsche hands.

The new design had already been guaranteed an independent rear suspension, so mounting the transmission at the back in unit with the differential became only a matter of mechanical problem-solving. Besides, Porsche management liked the transaxle idea because it was "technically interesting" and that was considered important for a Porsche.

The 1984 cc single-overhead-camshaft cast-iron-block engine was just over-square with a bore of 86.5 mm and a stroke of 84.4 mm. The aluminum crossflow cylinder head had 9.3:1 compression ration (8:1 U.S.) and Heron-type chambers, which meant that the piston crowns were dished and the head surface was flat.

A Bosch K-Jetronic CIS fuel injection system fed into 40 mm inlet valves (38 mm U.S.) with 12 mm lift, and exited through 33 mm exhaust valves with 11.8 mm lift. Double valve springs were used on all valves and the exhaust valves rotated during lift for better cooling and wear characteristics. The toothed belt-driven camshaft turned in five plain bearings and operated the valves through cup-type tappets.

The first 924 came off the assembly line in November 1975 as a 1976 European model. Cars did not reach the United States until April 1976, and these were called 1977s. This was a U.S. car, fitted with large round side marker lights front and rear and bumpers that protruded further to meet safety regulations. The side molding appeared only on U.S. cars. An electric motor drove a shaft to raise or lower the headlights. The 924 Turbo body with its modest front chin spoilers and rear lip had the best drag coefficient of any European production car at the time, 0.34 Cd. *Porsche Cars North America*

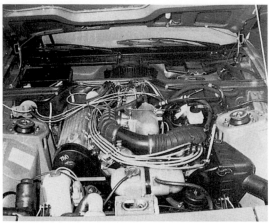

The VW/Audi engine in the 924 used Bosch CIS fuel injection. Single overhead camshaft was driven by toothed belt.

As on all Porsches after the 356 series, the electrical system was 12-volt. The European 924 had a conventional ignition system, but the U.S. version used transistor-type breakerless ignition. The engine was installed at an angle of forty degrees from vertical, to the right. The alternator, exhaust, and spark plugs were on the right side with the intake on the left. This would normally be immaterial, but in as much as the engine was tilted to the right, this was also the low side and made spark plug changing an adventure.

The engine, with its cast-iron block, although considered a VW design, was fully developed and tested at Audi Research in Ingolstadt. All 924 engines for the United States had exhaust-gas recirculation, and the forty-nine-state cars had air injection while the California cars had catalytic converters. After development at Audi, the engine was built at the VW Salzgitter plant. As delivered to Porsche it weighed 300 pounds.

Power rating for the European version was 125 DIN/119 SAE net 5800 rpm, with a compression ratio for 9.3:1. In the form in which it would go to the Unites States it produced 100 DIN/95.4 SAE at 5500 rpm with 8.0:1 compression ratio. When the automatic transmission was introduced, the U.S. version was rated at 115 DIN/110 SAE net at 5750, with a compression ratio of 8.5:1.

Drive went through a single-plate, diaphragm-spring clutch, mounted at the back of the engine. The driveshaft, 20 mm in diameter, revolved inside an 85-mm-diameter steel torque tube, which tied the engine rigidly to the transaxle assembly at the rear. The transmission, when the car was first introduced, was a four-speed unit with a cone-type synchromesh—the first Porsche since the early nonsynchro 356 that didn't use Porsche's patented synchromesh system. Because of the high rotating inertia of the driveshaft, the synchromesh cones were sprayed with molybdenum to prevent excessive wear.

The transaxle was from the 1972 and later Audis, installed in a Porsche-designed aluminum die-cast housing. The half-shafts were from the Volkswagen Type 181 "Thing" and ran at an angle of ten degrees rearward to the hubs.

Front suspension was a combination of Volkswagen parts—coil spring MacPherson shock strut from the Beetle, and lower A-arms from the Rabbit/Golf/Scirocco. These lower arms were the same, left and right. The front end suspension geometry was designed with negative roll radius (the center line of the wheel's pivot axis intersected the ground slightly outside the center of the front tire's contact patch). Steering was the rack and pinion from the Rabbit, but with 19.4:1 ratio instead of the 17.4:1 of the Rabbit.

At the rear, transverse torsion bars 22 mm in diameter were connected to flat steel trailing links, and suspension arms pivoted off the tubular torsion bar housing. Front shocks were from the VW Beetle, and either Boge or Fichtel & Sachs units were used at the rear. Anti-roll bars, 20 mm front and 18 mm rear, were options at the beginning. Brakes, too, were VW-Beetle solid disc at the front, K-70 drums at the rear, with a dual diagonal system vacuum-boosted.

The suspension was attached to a unit-body that was unique to the 924 which, once more, followed Porsche's established tradition with all its previous cars.

Body design was dictated to some degree by the previously mentioned parameters of the basic concept, but details were debated strongly among Porsche management. Some thought the car should have a grille at the front, others preferred to follow Porsche's grilleless tradition even though the new car would be water-cooled. The latter won out, and air was taken in under the front bumper—conceding the necessity to have a family resemblance to the 356 and 911.

The 924 body was designed by Dutchman Harm Lagaay, the protégé of Porsche styling chief Tony Lapine. Lagaay's body in final form had a frontal area of 18.95 square feet (slightly more than the 911) and a coefficient of aerodynamic drag (Cd) of 0.36. The 924 Turbo, with its modest chin spoiler and rear deck lip, had a Cd of 0.34, which was the best in Europe for more than a decade.

An electric motor raised and lowered the headlights. U.S. cars had aluminum bumpers—castings in front, extrusions at the back—attached to hydraulic energy absorbers. The U.S. cars also had round side-marker lights to conform to American regulations.

The instrument panel contained three dials: center, speedometer; right, 8000 rpm tachometer; and left, fuel, water temperature, and warning lights. All three were covered with conical glass as an antiglare measure. The driver sat in 911 seats, covered in cloth, vinyl, or optional leather, and looked at the instruments through a steering wheel that was offset about one inch above center to give added leg clearance.

Such was the 924 as it was first conceived. Before production began, however, problems within almost kept it from production. In 1973, the VG was disbanded, and the design became VW property in as much as it had been by VW. Then-VW director Rudolph Leiding wanted it for VW or Audi because he saw the advantage of marketing it through the 2,000 VW dealers in West Germany instead of the 200 VW-Porsche dealers that had been established to market the 914.

Then a seemingly unrelated matter added fuel to Porsche's fire—the OPEC oil embargo of 1973–74 caused Leiding to have second thoughts about an upgraded car for VW. Late in 1974 Leiding was asked to leave

Aerodynamic efficiency and cargo space dictated the shape of the rear, but it was one of the least appealing views of the 924. The rear window wiper was part of the Touring Package II for the U.S. market in 1977. The rear window/hatchback lifted for luggage stowage and access. *Porsche Cars North America*

A Championship Edition 924 was offered in February 1977, to commemorate Porsche's winning the 1976 World Championship of Makes. This special edition of 2,000 cars came in one trim: all-white body with red, white and blue side stripes; white alloy wheels; red corduroy seats with blue piping; red carpeting in both passenger and luggage areas; leather-covered steering wheel; and anti-roll bars front and rear. *Porsche Cars North America*

Steering wheel rim of the 924 was not concentric with hub (offset toward the top), for better instrument visibility and more leg room. It was still a tight fit, and got worse as the wheel turned.

Volkswagen and Toni Schmucker came into top position at VW in February 1975.

Schmucker, a former Ford executive, wanted to close one of VW's eight plants, and chose the old NSU facility at Neckarsulm as the one to go. Things were beginning to go Porsche's way now, and as a result of these and other factors Porsche and VW agreed to build the new 924 at the Neckarsulm plant, using the same workforce that had been there under NSU and, later, VW management.

Production was planned for 100 cars per day when the first 924s came off the assembly line in November 1975. By April 1976, it had reached sixty cars per day and the first production models reached U.S. dealers in April as 1977 models.

In 1976, West German models were sold for DM 23,240 ($8,900), and the base price of the 1977 model in the United States was $9,395. The optional removable roof panel was $330; air conditioning, $548; front and rear anti-roll bars, $105; metallic paint, $295; and three radio speakers and antenna, $105. The American models were designed to meet all U.S. air pollution standards.

Touring Package I, consisting of triple speakers, leather-covered steering wheel, and six-inch-wide alloy road wheels for 185/70 HR-14 radials, was $345. Touring Package II, with headlight washers, rear window wiper, and right-hand outside mirror, was another $240.

In February 1977, the engine was improved for the U.S. market; the compression ratio was raised to 8.5:1, a new camshaft with the timing advanced seven degrees, and 40 mm intake valves increased the horsepower to 110 SAE net at 5,750 rpm. At the same time the rear axle ration was changed from 3.44 to 3.88:1. They were "fifty-state" cars and all had catalytic converters for emissions control.

A three-speed automatic transmission, the first in Porsche's history, became an option on European 924s in late 1976, and on U.S. cars in March 1977. The rear axle ratio was 3.455:1 in Europe and 3.727 for the United States.

At the Frankfurt show in 1977, Porsche introduced the long-awaited five-speed transmission as an option for the 924. Unfortunately, it was the "Getrag" shift pattern with second, third, fourth and fifth in the normal H pattern, with first off to the left and below reverse. The five-speed was accompanied by a rear axle ratio change from 3.444 to 4.714:1. The difference is not quite as much as it seems because of simultaneous changes in the transmission gears. Remember, all gears are indirect in the 924 transmission, and both

With the rear seatback folded flat, a surprising amount of gear can be carried, but it's still no station wagon. *Greg Brown/Argus*

In February 1977, horsepower of the 924 was increased from 95 to 110 on U.S. models—all of which were "50 state" cars with catalytic converters for emission control. At this time the first fully automatic transmission ever offered in Porsche became an option. The model was designated a 1977 1/2 in the United States. *Porsche Cars North America*

fourth and fifth are "overdrive" in relation the ring and pinion ratio.

Performance of the 1978 model 924 was little changed from before, but the flexibility of the five-speed made it a much more enjoyable car to drive, and economy was increased measurably. Coupled with improvements in suspension attachment that decreased road noise, the 924 was finally becoming the car Porsche had wanted it to be.

The 924 interior was state-of-the-art design in 1977, but for some reason the overall package appealed more to new Porsche buyers than it did to previous owners. And in 1979 the 924 accounted for 60 percent of Porsche's production (including 911 and 928). In March 1979, Porsche sold more cars in Germany than it did in the United States for the first time. *Porsche Cars North America*

Porsche of Great Britain worked out a deluxe package for its market that included alloy wheels, headlamp washers and rear window wiper, and tinted glass, all included in the base price.

For 1979, the five-speed was made standard, with the three-speed automatic still an option. The abominable space-saver spare was utilized (except in England where it was illegal) to give slightly more luggage space, and pressure-cast alloy wheels, tinted glass, vanity mirror on the sun visor, and stereo speakers were included as standard equipment.

The big news for 1979, however, was the addition of a turbocharged version that could be identified by the four air intakes just above the front bumper, the NACA intake duct on the right side of the hood, its own unique alloy wheels, rear gravel guards, and spoilers—a "chin" spoiler at the lower front of the car, and a "ducktail" at the rear of the deck lid.

Inside, a three-spoke, leather-covered steering wheel (like the 911 Turbo) and leather boot for the shift linkage were the quick identifying features. There was no boost gauge, because Porsche engineers thought it unnecessary. European 924 Turbos had four-wheel disc brakes, while U.S. Turbos still had the disc-front, drum-rear of the standard 924. A sport package option for any 1979 924 included the four-wheel disc brakes of the European Turbo.

Visual changes through 1981 were so minor as to be almost unnoticeable. In 1980, the 914 had received a new transmission with the five-speed shift pattern in the more "normal" H (the first four speeds and fifth up to the right beside third), although the Turbo retained the Getrag pattern (with the four top gears in the H and first down and to the left). The lower body shell was covered by a limited rust-perforation warranty of six years. Four-wheel disc brakes became standard for all 914 models in 1981. *Porsche Cars North America*

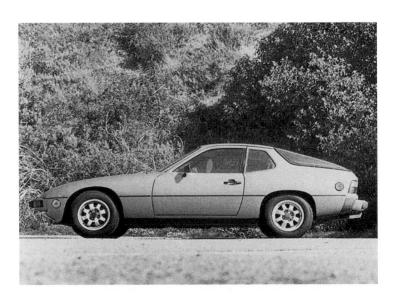

Rear ducktail spoiler, modest rear-wheel mud flaps were standard on the 924 Turbo. Button in left rear corner of backlight covered hole where optional rear window wiper would be attached. *Dean Batchelor*

The 924 engine, with its KKK (Kuhnle, Kopp, & Kausch) turbo charger produced the sort of performance the 924 should have had in the first place for the U.S. market. *Dean Batchelor*

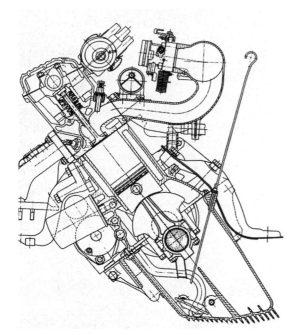

Front view to the 924 engine—which is slanted 40 degrees to the right from vertical—in cross section shows the overhead camshaft operating on cups over the valvestems, and the flat cylinder head surface (the chamber is in the tip of the piston), deep oil pan for the wet-sump lubrication system. *Porsche Cars North America*

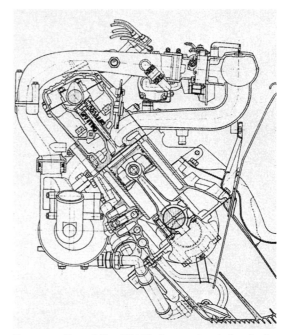

Cross section of the 924 Turbo engine is basically that of the 924 but with the turbo unit on the lower side to pick up the exhaust close to the ports. The intake goes from there up and over the valve cover to a plenum chamber on the intake side of the engine and through individual pipes to each intake port. *Porsche Cars North America*

The major changes brought about in creating the 924 Turbo were mechanical, even though the cosmetic changes were the most obvious. The "short-blocks" (cylinder block, crankshaft, connecting rods, and pistons) were the same on both 924 and Turbo, and these were assembled at Neckarsulm on the same assembly line. But before final assembly, the Turbo short-blocks were trucked to Porsche's Zuffenhausen works where final assembly was to take place adding other components unique to the Turbo.

After checking what had been assembled, a new cylinder head with recessed combustion chambers was installed. Using a "flattened hemisphere" chamber coupled with the dished pistons gave a "flattened spherical" chamber and a compression ratio of 7.5:1. Spark plugs (platinum tipped) were moved to the intake side to the head, and water seal between block and head was accomplished by a copper gasket and silicone rings.

CIS fuel injection was standard on the Turbo just as it was on the normally aspirated 924, but two fuel pumps were utilized to ensure full pressure maintenance under all driving conditions. The new pump was submerged in the fuel tank, and subsequently became the standard pump for both models, as a production economy.

The KKK (Kuhnle, Kopp & Kausch) Turbocharger was fitted to the exhaust manifold, and the system contained a wastegate downstream from the exhaust manifold. Including a wastegate provided pressure regulation, and also protected the catalytic converter from an overload of extremely high exhaust temperatures. Mounting the turbocharger on the right side required relocation of the starter to the left side of the engine.

The driveshaft was enlarged from a 20 to 25 mm diameter to handle the extra horsepower, and only a five-speed transmission could be obtained with the turbocharged engine.

In turbocharged form, the European-market engine produced 170 DIN horsepower at 5500 rpm, with 180 foot-pounds of torque at 3500 rpm. The rear axle ratio was 4.125 for European specification cars. The U.S. version was rated at 143 SAE horsepower at 5500 with 147 foot-pounds of torque at 3000 rpm, and the axle ratio was 4.71:1.

Because the Turbo engine was sixty-four pounds heavier than the standard 924 unit, some suspension changes were in order—recalibrated front springs, heavier anti-roll bar in front (and a slightly smaller one at the rear), and stiffer shocks. The rear track was widened by 0.8 inch. Weight distribution changed from 48/52 of the standard 924, to 49/51 for the Turbo (empty) or 44/56 with passengers and fuel.

For 1980, the 924 received a new transmission—a five-speed with a normal shift pattern, which was arranged by a adding a fifth gear to the old four-speed assembly. The

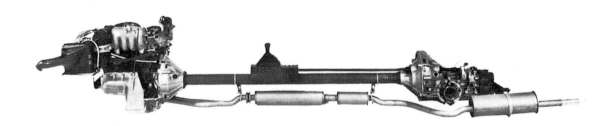

Front engine, rear transmission in unit with the axle, connected by a torque-tube driveshaft. A four-speed all-synchromesh transmission was used exclusively until a three-speed fully automatic transmission became optional on European 924s in late 1976, and for the U.S. market in March. The five-speed transmission became an option after the Frankfurt auto show in 1977. *Porsche Cars North America*

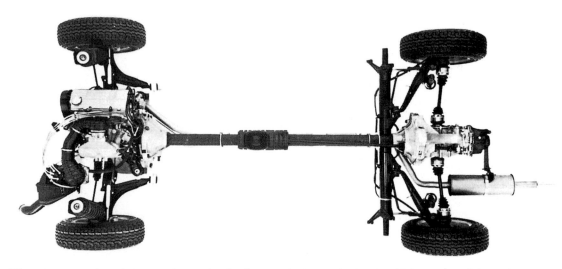

The 1977 924 chassis layout shows the Audi transmission at the back, which was used through 1978, was replaced for 1979 by the Porsche-designed gearbox, and then came back into use in 1980 and was used on the 924, 924 Turbo, and 944. The half-shafts trail toward the rear at a 10-degree angle. *Porsche Cars North America*

The 1980 924 Turbo chassis design, with the Porsche transmission which was used in the 924 in 1979, and the Turbo in 1980 only. The 924 and 924 Turbo (for Europe) and the 944 used the Audi unit exclusively. The half-shafts, for this layout, lead toward the front by a 10-degree angle. The rear suspension and mounting shown here was adopted in 1978 for both the 924 and 924 Turbo, and was carried into the 944 design. *Porsche Cars North America*

For 1981, the 924 Turbo got the standard shift pattern of the 924 and 911SC, four-wheel disc brakes as standard equipment and a modified turbocharger to give better response. The Turbo can be identified by the four air intakes above the bumper and the NACA duct on the right side of the hood. *Porsche Cars North America*

Turbo retained the five-speed with the Getrag shift pattern, since the 924's modified four-speed couldn't handle the torque of the turbo engine.

The lower body shell of both 924 and 924 Turbo was now covered by a limited rust perforation warranty for six years.

The basic car, both normal and Turbo, remained unchanged for 1981, but four-wheel disc brakes became standard for all versions—largely because of customer complaints. All models received halogen lights and rear seat belts. Other minor changes continued to be made when Porsche management thought them to be necessary. Nothing is ever static at Porsche.

Since the introduction of the first 924, customer complaints revolved around engine roughness, too much interior noise for a car of this price class, poor ventilation (U.S. owners were more insistent on air conditioning than European or British customers), rather plain interior (again, for price class), choppy ride, vibrations that shook screws out of the dash, electric options that caused more than ordinary trouble and, in American models, poor performance.

On the other side of the coin, customers and magazine road testers praised handling, brakes (except for the disc/drums on early U.S. Turbos), space, looks, and general assembly quality. Given these pros and cons, it's unfortunate that the 924 will automatically be compared to other Porsches. On its own, and standing by itself, it's not a bad car. The pluses outweigh the minuses and, if built by another manufacturer, would probably be rated higher in the automotive enthusiast's mind than it is being a Porsche.

Production of the 924 and 924 Turbo ended for the export market at the end of 1981 but continued for the home market, where engine size determined taxes to be paid on the car each year.

The 924 Turbo was a bit of a disappointment: Porsche didn't like the sales figures, and the customers didn't like the performance, which was coupled with expensive maintenance costs. The 924 Turbo is already a rare car. Another fairly rare 924 is the Sebring Special Edition, which was primarily a striped and trimmed version, but a few were made with suspension and brake changes for would-be racers. Those too, are not particularly good investments for speculators.

One limited-production series of turbo-charged, race-bred 924s will prove a good investment. These were known as the 924 Carrera GT of which some 400 were produced, and the rarer-still Carrera GTS of about 59 in number. The Carrera GT retained the two-liter Audi-based in line, four-cylinder engine revised to produce 210 horsepower. The Carreras were built to meet homologation requirements for FIA Group 4 racing events. First shown at the 1979 Frankfurt Auto Show, these were no-nonsense machines with spartan interiors in black-painted metal with cloth-covered racing seats. Weighing some 330 pounds less than the stock 924 Turbo, the GT sold for 50,000 Deutsche Marks. The 924 Carrera GTS achieved its extra 35-horsepower engine output primarily by using a higher-output highly modified 928 fuel distributor. With this, the GTS engine produced 245 horsepower at 1.0 bar (14.1 psi) turbo boost. Brakes came from the 917s. These sold for

The 924 Turbo op-art interior, standard on the first 600 sent to the Unites States, is more comfortable physically than it is visually; and fortunately, the driver can see little of the black and white checkered flag look while seated in the car. *Bill Appleton/Argus*

924, 924 Turbo

Engine

Design...Water-cooled inline four
Bore x stroke, mm/inches: ....86.5x84.4 / 3.41x3.32
Displacement, cc/cubic inches:......................1984/121.06
Valve operation: 924 ....Toothed belt-driven single overhead camshaft
Compression ratio: Europe and Great Britain 9.3:1
  U.S., Canada, California, Japan
    (manual transmission) 8.0:1
  U.S., Canada, California, Japan
    (automatic transmission) 8.5:1
  Turbo (from 1979) 7.5:1
Carburetion:
  924 ....Bosch K-Jetronic fuel injection
  924 Turbo ....Exhaust-driven turbocharger and Bosch K-Jetronic fuel injection
BHP (Mfr.):
  Europe & Great Britain ....125 DIN/119 SAE @ 5800
  U.S., Canada, California, Japan
    (manual transmission)..........100 DIN/95.4 SAE @ 5500
  U.S., Canada, California, Japan
    (automatic transmission)......115 DIN/110 SAE @ 5750
  Turbo (from 1979) ....150 DIN/143 SAE @ 5500

Chassis & Drivetrain

Frame:..Unit body
Component Layout: ....Front engine, rear drive
Clutch:...............................Fichtel & Sachs single dry-plate
Transmission: ....Porsche five-speed, all synchromesh, in unit with differential optional three-speed automatic, in unit with differential
Axle ratio:
  California, Canada, Japan
    with four-speed manual transmission 3.89:1
  Europe and rest of world
    with four-speed manual transmission 3.44:1
  U.S., California, Canada, Japan
    with three-speed automatic transmission............3.73:1
  Europe and rest of world
    with three-speed automatic transmission............3.45:1
Rear suspension:............Independent, semi-trailing arms, transverse torsion bars, and tubular shock absorbers (anti-roll bar optional)
Front suspension: ....Independent, MacPherson telescopic shock strut & lower A-arm on each side with coil springs (anti-roll bar optional)

General

Wheelbase, mm/inches:...................................2400 / 94/5
Track, Front, mm/inches: ....1481 / 55.8
  Rear, mm/inches: ....1372 / 54.0
Brakes: ....Disc front, drum rear (all-disc optional)
Tire size, front & rear: ....165 HR 14
  (185/70 HR 14 with optional wheels)
Wheels: ....5 1/2Jx14 Steel (6Jx14 alloy optional)
Body builder: ....Porsche or Karmann

The engine and drivetrain, brakes and electrical system of the 924S are taken directly from the 944 with minimal modifications to suit the chassis. The 147-horsepower engine gives the 924S a top speed of 134 mph and 0–60 in 8.3 seconds with the manual five-speed transmission.

924S

Engine
Design:...Water-cooled inline four
Bore x stroke, mm/inches: ....100x78.9 / 3.94x3.11
Displacement, cc/cubic inches:...........................2479/151
Valve operation: ....Toothed belt-driven single
overhead camshaft
Compression ratio:...9.7:1
Carburetion:................................Bosch DME fuel injection
BHP (Mfr.): ....147 @ 5800

Chassis & Drivetrain
Frame: ....Unit Body
Component layout: ....Front engine, rear drive
Clutch:...............................Fichtel & Sachs single dry-plate
Transmission:
standard.................Porsche five-speed, all synchromesh
optional ....Porsche three-speed automatic in
unit with differential

Axle ratio:
manual 3.89:1
automatic 3.46:1
Rear suspension: ....Independent, semi-trailing arms,
transverse torsion bars, & tubular shock absorbers
Front suspension: ....Independent, MacPherson
telescopic shock strut & lower A-arm on each side with
coil springs

General
Wheelbase, mm/inches:....................................2400 / 94.5
Track: Front, mm/inches: ....1419 / 55.9
Rear, mm/inches...1393 / 54.8
Brakes: ....Hydraulic, dual-circuit system, 4
ventilated disc, brake servo
Tire size, front & rear: ....195/65 HR 15
Wheels: ....6J-15 cast alloy
Body builder:...Porsche

110, 000 DM. Bodies of both Carrera versions, made of steel, fiberglass, and GFK plastic, offered observers undisguised hints of the styling of the 944.

In June 1986 the 924 reappeared on the U.S. market as the 924S. The body was the same as before, but the engine, drive train, brakes, suspension, and electrical system were from the 944. Standard equipment included air conditioning, tinted glass, electrically adjustable and heated outside mirrors (left and right), power steering, power windows, antenna, four speakers, convenience package including anti-theft wheels, and coin and cassette holders. Optional equipment included AM/FM stereo radio and cassette tape player, electric sunroof, automatic transmission, limited-slip differential, and a rear window wiper.

The 924S would hit 134 miles per hour and 0-60 in 8.3 seconds with the five-speed manual gearbox. This model was brought back to the United States as the "entry-level" Porsche, at $19,900, increasing to $21,900 in November 1986. Production stopped at the end of 1988.

Buyers thinking of a 924 should be aware that from 1977 to early 1979 (before turbos), the cars had a galvanized body but not hood, doors or front fenders. Those fenders often rust out. Dashes cracking on cars with 10,000 miles or more is common. Check carefully the upper door hinges; they are known to crack. The door will fall off.

1980 924 Carrera GT (400 built)

Engine
Design: ....Water-cooled, in-line four cylinder
Bore x stroke, mm/inches: 86x84/3.39x3.31
Displacement, cc/cubic inches: 1984/119.2
Valve operation: ....single-overhead camshaft, two valves per cylinder
Compression ratio: 8.5:1
Carburetion: ....Bosch K-Jetronic fuel injection, KKK turbocharger, intercooler
BHP (Mfr.): ....210 @ 6000

Chassis & Drivetrain
Transmission: ....five-speed manual
Axle ratio: 4.125:1
Rear suspension: ....Independent, semi-trailing arms, transverse torsion bars, coil springs, telescopic shock absorbers, anti-roll bar
Front suspension: ....Independent, single wishbones. MacPherson struts, coil springs, telescopic shock absorbers, anti-roll bar

General
Wheelbase, mm/inches: 2400/94.5
Track: Front, mm/inches:
Rear, mm/inches:
Tire size, front & rear:.......................................215/60VR15
Wheels, front & rear: 7x15
Weight: ....2,602 lbs
Body builder: ....Porsche

Chapter 11

928

★★	1977–82 928
★★	1983–84 928S
★★1/2	1985–86 928S
★★★	1987–89 928S 4
★★★	1990–92 928
★★★	1991–92 928GT
★★★★	1991–92 928GT4
★★★★★	1993–95 928GTS

There is a game still played by Porsche enthusiasts, automotive writers, and Porsche management. It goes like this. One side asks: "How long can Porsche continue to build the 911?"

The other side answers, "As long as there is a demand for the model." In recent years, the real game has been to determine who is asking and who is answering the question.

Beginning in the early 1970s, Porsche management—in the person of Ernst Fuhrmann and his engineering staff—began to worry, and not only about demand for the then-10-year-old 911. They also worried about U.S. government safety regulations that might literally outlaw an automobile with an engine not in the front. General Motors' experience with Chevrolet's Corvair and outside consumer advocate Ralph Nader convinced Fuhrmann that it was important to produce an automobile that could be sold in America, no matter what rules the U.S. government passed.

Porsche's director of research and sport, engineer Helmut Flegl, was assigned in early 1974 to complete development of the front-engine car project, designated the Type 928. He worked closely with design chief Tony Lapine, doing, as Lapine put it, "the 928 the way any intelligent development team should do. We did engineering and design simultaneously." This was remarkable because at the time, Porsche counted nearly 2,000 engineers and just 43 designers. Yet it became not a clash of egos but a marriage of compromises.

Design parameters called for performance to match—or exceed—the current 911. Yet noise pollution was becoming an issue in some countries. So engineering specified a water-cooled engine. A V-8 was a necessity to provide the power, not only to propel the vehicle but also to run the accessories that Porsche buyers were coming to expect. Large displacement also guaranteed them enough power to overcome the threatened emission controls and their strangling effects.

Fuhrmann and Flegl first considered a 60-degree V-8 but it made the hood too tall. A 90-degree engine lowered the hood, the cowl (windshield base), and the center of gravity, enhancing ride and handling. Joining the transmission to the rear differential as a transaxle further improved balance and opened up interior cabin space by allowing wider footwells and a narrower center tunnel.

The heritage of Porsche Design, from Ernst Kommenda's first 356 through Butzi Porsche's 911, required that whatever the 928 would look like, it must look like a Porsche. Compromises developed from this. Engineering needed an adequate radiator to cool a big, powerful V-8; Tony Lapine imagined laying it on an angle and setting it back from the front bumper. The first idea aided in lowering the hood, the second, after suitable engineering testing, revealed a kind of formula. Given enough room, air intake ducts placed below the bumper need not be any larger than one-third the area of the radiator. In a kind of venturi effect, air was sucked into the radiator. This also allowed increased room for front impact crushability in crash tests.

Because through the years the United States had absorbed nearly half of Porsche's entire production, Porsche had to consider the American market when designing its new cars. Then, and now, it is impossible to anticipate how far and in which direction American bureaucratic ingenuity might take automotive regulations. Porsche's management also recognized that safety and emission controls in effect in the United States may be adopted sooner or later by other countries.

After preliminary work was completed, the final go/no-go decision came in 1973. The timing couldn't have been more nerve-wracking. It coincided with OPEC's first oil embargo and it raised questions about the need for high performance sports cars at all. This same situation drove the 924 from VW/Audi back into Porsche's family (see the previous chapter). This car was already developed and paid for by Volkswagen. Its intrusion into the Porsche lineup, as an economical Sports/GT, might stop or postpone Porsche's own new V-8 luxury sports car. And it did.

The 924 was introduced in 1975 to mixed reviews. Being introduced by Porsche led to customer expectations that weren't met. The 924, decried as the Volks-Porsche, was the right car for the time. It just was not yet right. However for Porsche, it was essentially free. Thus it brought income into Porsche and it bought time. By March 1977, when Porsche introduced the powerful, luxurious 928 to a waiting world at the Geneva show, OPEC had been satisfied and oil prices had stabilized. The world, and Porsche, returned to business as usual.

It was a dazzling introduction. There had been an unacknowledged "agreement" in Germany that Volkswagen produced its economy cars, Opel and Ford made family automobiles, Mercedes-Benz (and BMW) provided its luxury cars, and Porsche created the sports cars. Yet here was Porsche with an unmistakable luxury intruder. Grand touring took on new meaning.

Porsche's engine developers produced their 90-degree V-8 with 95 mm bore and 78.9 mm stroke, for total displacement of 4474 cc (273 cubic inches). The cylinder block and heads were cast of Reynolds 390 aluminum alloy requiring no liners for the cylinder bores. A toothed Gilmer-type belt drove a single overhead camshaft on each bank.

The U.S. version produced 219 horsepower at 5250 rpm (European and English

When introduced at the Geneva auto show in March 1977, the Porsche 928 was viewed as a daring departure from Porsche philosophy. The water-cooled 4.5-liter V-8 was mounted in the front, driving the rear wheels through a five-speed transaxle (three-speed automatic optional). In true Porsche tradition, however, all four wheels were independently sprung, and great attention was paid to aerodynamics. This was later to prove an embarrassment as the Cd was no better than many family sedans and not as good as that of the 924Turbo, which was the best in Europe at the time. *Porsche Cars North America*

From the rear the American 928 differed from its European counterpart with the addition of running lights and rubber bumper inserts around the license molding. *Porsche Cars North America and Porsche A. G.*

buyers got 229 hp at 5500), using Bosch's K-Jetronic injection system (CIS). The cars were fitted with 22.7 U.S. gallon plastic tanks (86 liters in Europe), located at the extreme rear of the car, with an electric fuel pump submerged in the tank.

Porsche specified a Fichtel & Sachs 7.875 inch-diameter (200 mm) double disc clutch and used a one-inch (25 mm) diameter solid steel driveshaft running inside a nearly four-inch (100 mm) torque tube to the transaxle. Engineers revised Mercedes-Benz's three-speed automatic transmission from the monstrous 6.9 sedan (with torque converter) and offered it as an option for the 928. With this option, there was a starter ring gear at the engine but no flywheel. A 2.75:1 set of differential gears transferred the power to short half-shafts, each with inner and outer constant-velocity U-joints.

Unlike the transaxle of the 924, the transmission of the 928 was mounted ahead of the differential and was more like a transmission found in a "normal" front-engined, rear-drive car. All Porsches prior to the 928 had indirect gears on all speeds, with the driveshaft lining up to a secondary shaft in the transmission. The 928 driveshaft, in line with the upper main shaft, was linked directly to the pinion gear in the differential. One advantage to this layout was quieter operation, which had been one of the original goals for the 928s. The shift pattern resurrected the earlier "H" pattern with first and reverse outside the H.

Engineers created a front suspension consisting of parallel but unequal-length A-arms on each side, with a concentric tubular shock absorber and coil spring attached to the lower A-arm and passing through the upper arm to its chassis attachment point at the top. A power-assisted ZF rack-and-pinion steering assembly was mounted behind the front wheel center line. This entirely new passenger car suspension was based on Porsche's earlier Type 804 (1962 Grand Prix single seater) and the 904 race cars.

At the rear, engineers mounted a single upper arm on each side laterally—from frame to hub—while each lower arm pivoted at an angle from its mounting points on the chassis forward of the axle, in effect making a semi-trailing arm. This new suspension,

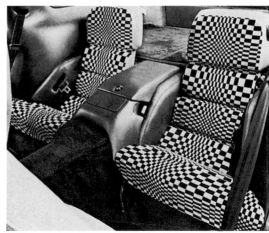

The op-art interiors of the first 928s didn't impress the viewers and elicited more sarcasm than praise. It was not one of Porsche's better designs. *Porsche Cars North America*

Power for the 928 was furnished by a V-8 engine with cylinder block and heads made of Reynolds 390 aluminum alloy. Displacement was 273 cubic inches (4,474 cc), and fuel was metered to the engine by Bosch electronically controlled AFC fuel injection. A toothed, belt-driven single camshaft on each bank operated the in-line valves. Horsepower rating was 231 DIN in the U.S. and 240 DIN in Europe and England. *Porsche A. G.*

An electric motor operated a shaft common to both headlights to raise them. High and low beam filaments worked in these pop-up lights, while the front bumper housed driving lights (inboard) and fog lights (outboard). The black button below each headlight was the nozzle for headlight washers, operated by the windshield washer switch. *Porsche A. G.*

called the "Weissach axle," caused the outward rear wheel to toe inward instead of outward during cornering when power was reduced or during braking. It helped prevent oversteer in which the rear of the car slid further outward. Rear springs were concentric with tubular shock absorbers as at the front, and a 21 mm anti-roll bar was used. The 928 placed ventilated disc brakes all around, operated by dual diagonal brake circuits.

All this running gear was attached to a unit body of welded sheet steel construction, which had been galvanized to prevent rust, and was guaranteed for seven years. The doors, front fenders and engine hood were made from a special aluminum alloy. Energy-absorbing bumpers, front and rear, were covered with polyurethane caps that were faired into the body.

Driver convenience and comfort were a high priority, so a number of innovations resulted. The adjustable steering wheel moved the instrument cluster with it when it was raised or lowered. Porsche incorporated power windows, air conditioning, cruise control, a four-speaker stereo system, rear window wiper and two-stage electric defogger, retractable headlights with washers, electrically heated and adjusted outside rearview mirrors, and even sun visors for the rear-seat passengers.

The two back seats were not something one would want to ride in across country, but for short distances they were serviceable. The 928 was Porsche's largest model ever, yet its

2+2 seating fit into a body whose wheelbase was barely 0.4 inches longer than the current Corvette. It weighed 340 pounds less than the Corvette and it was ten inches shorter in overall length.

Porsche anticipated most 928 buyers would come out of other car makes. As it turned out, during the first year of sales, 60 percent went to first-time Porsche buyers and 40 percent of the cars went to previous Porsche owners. New owners loved the cars, the repeat customers did not. They expected the 928 to be just like their last Porsche, but more so. In fact it was an entirely different automobile.

The quality was there, as was the handling and performance. But the Old Porsche Feel was not. This was for good reason. Porsche did not intend for it to be like any other Porsche. It was to be a car for the 1980s and 1990s. If the 356s could survive for 15 years and the 911 for 12 at the time of the 928 introduction, then it seemed possible the 928 could take Porsche very close to the twenty-first century.

It began to appear that Porsche management no longer saw this as a 911 replacement. Instead, they had become a full-range sports car maker with a "low-priced" 924, a "mid-priced" 911, and the "high priced" 928. Porsche had four-, six- and eight-cylinder engines in water-cooled and air-cooled front- and rear-engined cars.

General specifications of the 928 remained unchanged through the first five years of production, but as with all

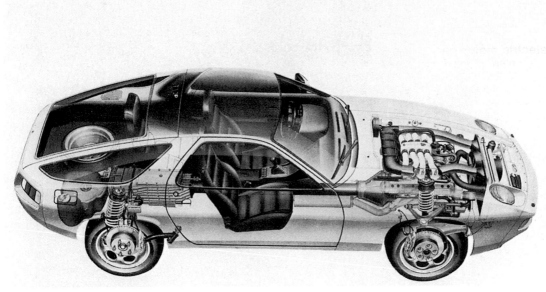

General component layout of the 928. *Porsche A. G.*

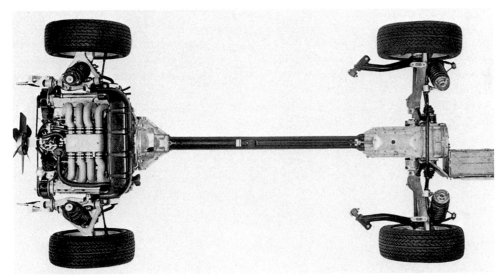

The 928 engine and clutch are connected to the rear transaxle by a torque tube. Unlike the 924, the 928 transmission is ahead of the rear axle, allowing the input to be in line with the transmission main shaft rather than on the lower, secondary shaft. Thus, it is like a normal transmission attached to the engine but moved rearward. The 60 ampere-hour battery is mounted at the rear for better vehicle weight distribution and is attached to the transaxle as a partial vibration dampener. Suspension is fully independent with coil springs and anti-roll bars front and rear. *Porsche Cars North America*

Porsches, running changes appeared that improved the car.

In 1980, several items that had been standard on 1979 U.S. cars were moved to the option list: 7x16-inch rims, radio, and partial-leather upholstery. Climate control, an open door warning light, and an electric sunroof were offered for the first time. A Sports Group, including 16-inch wheels, firmer shock absorbers, spoilers, and a limited slip differential, became a later option.

Porsche cut 220 pounds of weight by using tubular steel for the pinion shaft, transmission main shaft, and the front anti-roll bar, and aluminum for the torque tube. Electric door locks replaced the vacuum locking system, and Porsche improved the air conditioning.

Engineers increased the engine compression ratio to 9.0:1 for U.S. cars (10.0:1 for European and England), and they replaced the Bosch K-Jetronic with the newer L-Jetronic system for American models. They reduced valve overlap and lift and moved the spark plug 4 mm closer to the center of the combustion chamber. All of these increased engine output by *one* horsepower, but they increased engine flexibility and economy, which was the objective.

Despite being named the best sports car or best Grand Touring car by most automotive magazines, or best car, period, by some publications, the 928 still was not yet accepted as the best Porsche by Porsche enthusiasts. It had the potential for more power and more speed and, even if the die-hard Porsche enthusiasts couldn't use it, they wanted every bit of it.

Soon after Porsche introduced the 924 Turbo, the company gave European customers what they wanted, a 928S. It was distinguished by fashionable spoilers, new wheels, and twin exhausts. The spoilers cleaned up the aerodynamics enough that the Cd was reduced to 0.38. The aerodynamics of the 928 had embarrassed Porsche because, despite Tony Lapine's striking body design, the drag coefficient had been no better than many sedans of the same period.

American buyers wouldn't get the S until 1983; to keep them excited, Porsche offered a Competition Group, including the European S spoilers, Recaro seats, stiffer shocks, a padded steering wheel, limited slip differential, and 7x16-inch wheels. However, U.S. emissions rules prohibited any of the S engine upgrades.

Then in 1983, U.S. customers got their own S. Porsche increased engine size from 4474 to 4644 cc and raised the compression ratio to 9.3:1, producing 234 bhp at 5500 rpm, and offering a top speed of 146 mph. A new four-speed automatic transmission—with

The European 928S was more potent than versions allowed into the United States.

In 1981, a Competition Package 928 became available for the American market. With front and rear spoilers, leather interior, special shock absorbers, and forged alloy wheels, the car had the look of the 928S (without the side trim strip, however) but not the performance. The American version would go nearly 140 mph even without the S-engine tune, a respectable top speed. *Porsche Cars North America*

Daimler-Benz moving parts inside a Porsche case—was standard, while the five-speed manual became optional.

The 928S, virtually unchanged for 1984, came of age in 1985. Porsche introduced twin-cam cylinder heads with four valves per cylinder. Bore was slightly increased (from 97.0 to 100 mm), raising displacement to 4957 cc (302 cubic inches). With the new 10.0:1 compression ratio, output increased by 54 horsepower to 288 at 5750 rpm. Porsche used the Bosch LH-Jetronic fuel injection system with an air-mass flow meter and the split four-cylinder ignitions were operated by a single unit for better control.

The 928, introduced at $28,500 in 1979, had jumped up to $37,930 in 1980, then $38,850 in 1982. The 928S came in at $43,000 in 1983, then $44,000 in 1984, and $44,600 for 1985. The 1986 928 S4, (the first in the United States with twin-cam heads) sold for $51,900. For 1986, Porsche made the anti-lock braking system (ABS) standard. Power train warranties were extended to 50,000 miles, Porsche-built parts

were covered for 12 months with unlimited mileage, and the rust perforation coverage increased from seven to ten years.

Before the year was out, the late racing driver Al Holbert set a new production car speed record at the Bonneville salt flats. Holbert covered the flying mile in a completely stock S4 in 171.11 mph, fastest ever for a catalytic converter-equipped automobile.

Porsche introduced the 928 S4 (fourth development version) in 1987, with improved engine induction, which increased power output to 316 hp at 6000 rpm. A larger-diameter single disc clutch replaced the twin-plate unit.

Outside, Tony Lapine's body received a new nose and front spoiler, incorporating fog and driving lights as well as openings for engine and front brake cooling. New wraparound, flush taillights and a detached wing at the rear improved both looks and aerodynamics, dropping the Cd to 0.34 with virtually no lift at its claimed top speed of 165 mph with the optional

The steering wheel of the 928 didn't adjust in and out but moved up and down with the instrument cluster to keep it in view of the driver at all times. The glovebox was air conditioned along with the interior. *Porsche Cars North America*

928, 928S (1978--1982)

Engine
Design: ....Water-cooled V-8
Bore x stroke, mm/inches: 95x78.9/3.74x3.11;
97.0x78.9/3.82x3.11
Displacement, cc/cubic inches:...........4474/273.0; 4644/285
Valve operation: ....Toothed belt-driven single
overhead camshaft on each bank
Compression ratio:
1978–1979 ....8.5:1
1980–1982 (U.S. and Japan)......................................9.0:1
1980–1982 (Europe and England) 10.0:1
928S...9.3:1
Carburetion:
1978–1982 (Europe)..........Bosch K-Jetronic fuel injection
1978–1979 (U.S.) ....Bosch K-Jetronic fuel injection
1980–1982 (U.S.) ....Bosch L-Jetronic fuel injection
BHP (Mfr.):
U.S. and Japan, 1978–1979.......230 DIN/219 SAE @ 5250
Europe and England ....240 DIN/229 SAE @5500
U.S. and Japan, 1980–1982.......231 DIN/220 SAE @ 5500
928S...234 @ 5500

Chassis & Drivetrain
Frame: ....Unitized galvanized steel
Component layout: ....Front engine, rear drive
Clutch: ....Fichtel & Sachs double dry-plate
Transmission: ....Porsche five-speed all-synchromesh
(three-speed automatic optional); four-speed
automatic (five-speed manual optional)
Rear suspension:..........Independent, upper transverse links,
lower trailing arms, coil springs,
tubular shock absorbers, and anti-roll bar
Front suspension: ....Independent, upper A-arms,
lower trailing arms, coil springs, tubular
shocks absorbers, and anti-roll bar

General
Wheelbase, mm/inches:............................2500 / 98.4
Track: Front, mm/inches:...................................1552 / 61.1
Rear, mm/inches: ....1530 / 60.2
Brakes:...Ventilated disc
Tire size, front & rear: ....225/50 VR 16 (215/60 VR 15
with automatic transmission)
Wheels: ....Cast alloy 7Jx16 (7x15
with automatic transmission)
Body builder:...Porsche

five-speed manual or 162 mph with the standard automatic transmission.

Porsche made only a few minor changes for 1988 and 1989. For 1990, it dropped the S4 designation, calling the car simply the 928. Automatic cars continued at 316 horsepower while cars with the manual gearbox increased to 326 horsepower at 6200 rpm. The 1990 models incorporated a variable-ratio limited-slip differential adopted from the Type 959, which automatically transferred torque between rear wheels as needed to control wheel speed, slip, and lateral acceleration. Porsche fitted the tire pressure monitor system introduced on the Type 959, which alerted a driver by light and digital readout on the instrument panel when a tire was losing pressure and which one it was.

In the 1990 model year, Porsche became the world's first car maker to make driver and passenger-side airbags standard equipment on every car sold in the United States.

For 1991, Porsche announced its 928 GT with standard five-speed manual transmission while the S4 continued on with the four-speed automatic. The variable-ratio limited slip was carried over.

In the spring of 1992, Porsche introduced its 1993 928 GTS. The all-aluminum, 32-valve engine was enlarged to 5.4 liters (329 cubic inches) of displacement, producing 345 horsepower and providing 0-60 mph times of 5.5 seconds with the five-speed manual, 5.6 seconds with the four-speed automatic. Top speed was quoted as 171 mph. Weight distribution reached 50/50 because of the all-aluminum engine. The engineers fitted new

245/40 ZR 17 tires on the rear 9-inch wheels, having widened the rear track by 2.7 inches, while the fronts used 225/45 ZR 17s on 7.5-inch wheels. Inside these large front wheels, Porsche adopted the front brakes with 12.68-inch rotors from the Porsche 911 Turbo.

The new sound system provided an AM/FM cassette stereo with 10 speakers and a 160-watt six-channel amplifier/equalizer. Besides the 10-year rust warranty, Porsche offered a two-year new-vehicle unlimited mileage limited warranty with Porsche's AS-SIST, the roadside assistance program.

For 1994, Porsche discontinued the 928 S4 model and produced only one 928, the GTS, with 345 horsepower, with either a manual or automatic transmission. It continued to use the Weissach rear suspension, anti-lock brakes, and the variable-ratio electronically controlled limited slip differential first offered for 1990 cars.

Horsepower output increased incrementally for 1995 from 345 to 350 horsepower at 5700 rpm for the GTS. Porsche introduced its Pocket Commander cellular telephone, the only unit certified by Weissach to be free of interference from the 928's electronic systems. With either four-speed automatic or five-speed manual, the 928 GTS sold for $82,260 in its last year in production.

In its eighteen years, through its entire production run of 61,000 cars, the 928 never

Sports car or Grand Touring car? The 928S 4 was both, combining sports car performance with grand touring luxury and refinement. The cost was as dazzling as the car's attributes, but for those who could afford it, the 928S 4 was possibly the best GT car extant, fast, quiet, comfortable, and safe, with ABS braking on four-wheel ventilated disc brakes. *Porsche A. G.*

lost its stigma with many long-time, steadfast Porsche customers and enthusiasts. It was derided early on as Ernst Fuhrmann's "shopping car," as the kind of car Porsche would build if it produced the Mercedes-Benz 450 SL.

However, from 1985 through the end in 1995, the 928 simply matured into a better car, having fewer vices and more virtues. Its handling was neutral; experienced drivers claimed to feel exactly what the car was doing on the road right through their seat. This made it feel extremely sure-footed and confidence-inducing. It was powerful

For 1987 the 928S was given new front and rear end treatment (which improved the looks) and a

new designation, 928S 4, for the fourth series of development. *Porsche A. G.*

(although for a while, Ernst Fuhrmann's personal 928 was a turbocharged prototype with an undisclosed number of horses pounding beneath the hood) and, especially in its last subtle body variations, it was deceptively proportioned. From the outside it always seemed larger than it was. From the inside, it always felt more intimate.

The 928 was an exceptionally civilized, very high performance automobile. It was a taken-for-granted sports car, capable of performance much greater than what seemed possible.

Improving first and second gear ratios in the optional four-speed automatic, as well as revising full-throttle shift points and providing a slightly higher final drive ratio, reduced 0–60 mph times from 6.3 seconds to 6.0. The manual took 5.7 seconds. Top speed was quoted as 165 for the automatic, 168 for the five-speed.

Porsche introduced its electronically controlled automatic variable-ratio limited slip differential to the 928 for 1990. Locking varies from zero to 100 percent, based on input from each rear wheel. In addition, the tire pressure control system first developed for Porsche's Group C race cars was now standard equipment on the 928. *Porsche Cars North America*

Porsche used the S4 designation to identify its automatic and the GT for its five-speed manual transmission model. Both were listed at $77,500 suggested retail. The manual boasted 10 more horsepower, rating 326; acceleration from 0–60 mph took 5.6 seconds and the manual models were reportedly capable of 171 mph. *Porsche Cars North America*

The 1993 model actually arrived in the spring of 1992, called the GTS, with 345 horsepower, in either four-speed automatic or five-speed manual trim. Suggested retail price for either car was $82,260. Top speed was 171. The only real visual distinction is the lack of a bump strip along the body side. *Porsche Cars North America*

From the first year, Porsche design chief Tony Lapine labored to bring a family resemblance to the front-engined, water-cooled 928s. His successor Harm Lagaay continued the heritage, repeating the "bottom breather" dual horizontal air-intake slots from the Carreras and the 968 that first appeared on the 959. *Porsche Cars North America*

The car's dimensions have always been deceptive. Its overall length, 178.1 inches, is only 10 inches longer than the Carrera 4, only 4.5 inches wider, and it is full inch lower. Yet, seeing it without any basis for comparison has consistently brought complaints about its size. No one, however, complains about its handling and performance. *Porsche Cars North America*

---

928 S (1983–1986),
928 S 4 (1987–1989), 928 (1990)

Engine

Design: ....Water-cooled V-8
Bore x stroke, mm/inches:
  1983–1984 ....95x78.9 / 3.74x3.11
  1985–1986 ....97x78.9 / 3.82x3.11
  1987–1990 ....100x78.9 / 3.94x3.11
Displacement, cc/cubic inches:
  1983–1984 ....4474/273.0
  1985–1986 ....4644/283.2
  1987–1990 ....4957/302.0
Valve operation:
  1983–1984 ....Toothed belt-driven single overhead
    camshaft on each bank., two valves per cylinder
  1985–1990..........Toothed belt/chain-driven dual overhead
    camshafts, four valves per cylinder
Compression ratio:
  1983–1984 ....9.3:1
  1985–1990 ....10.0:1
Carburetion: ....Bosch LH-Jetronic fuel injection
BHP (Mfr.):
  1983–1984 ....234 SAE @ 5500
  1985–1986 ....288 SAE @ 5750
  1987–1989 ....316 SAE @ 6000
  1990 ....326 SAE @ 6200

Chassis & Drivetrain

Frame:..Galvanized, unitized steel

Component Layout: ....Front engine, rear drive
Transmission: ....Porsche five-speed manual all
  synchromesh or four-speed automatic (1983–1990)
Clutch:
  1983–1986 ....Fichtel & Sachs double dry-plate
  1987–1990 ....Fichtel & Sachs single dry-plate
Rear suspension: ....Independent, upper-A-arms,
  lower trailing arms, coil springs, tubular
  shock absorbers, and anti-rollbar (1983–1989).
  Independent Weissach suspension system
  with upper links, lower A-arms, self-stabilizing
  toe characteristics, hollow anti-roll bar.
Front suspension:..................Independent, upper transverse
  links, lower trailing arms, coil springs,
  tubular shock absorbers, and anti-roll bar.

General

Wheelbase, mm/inches: ....2500 / 98.4
Track: Front, mm/inches: ....1549 / 61.0
  Rear, mm/inches:.....................................1521 / 59.9
Brakes: ....Power-assisted, dual-circuit,
  anti-lock system, four-piston aluminum calipers
Tire size, front & rear: 225/50ZR16; 245/45ZR16
Wheels, front & rear:.............................7.5Jx16; 9Jx16
Weight: ....3,505 lbs

This was the last year of a great automobile. Over the 18 years of the car's life, it had grown from 219 horsepower up to 350 in this, its final appearance. The 928 introduced anti-lock brakes to Porsche as well as the "Weissach" rear suspension, which cants the rear wheels into the turn, similar to what a downhill slalom skier does on skis. *Porsche Cars North America*

**928 S 4 (1991), 928 GT (1991),
928 GTS (1993–1995)**

Engine

Design: ....Water-cooled V-8

Bore x stroke, mm/inches:

    1991 ....100x78.9 / 3.94x3.11

    1993–1995 ....100x85.9 / 3.94x3.43

Displacement, cc/cubic inches:

    1991 ....4957/302.5

    1993–1995 ....5400/329

Valve operation: (1991–1995) ....Dual overhead cams,
four valves per cylinder,
belt-chain driven, hydraulic lifters

Compression ratio:

    1991 ....10.0:1

    1993–1995 ....10.4:1

Carburetion: ....Bosch LH-Jetronic fuel injection

BHP (Mfr.):

    1991 ....326 @ 6200

    1993–1995 ....345 @ 5700

Chassis & Drivetrain

Frame:....................................Unitized, fully-galvanized steel

Component Layout: ....Front engine, rear drive

Transmission:.........................Porsche five-speed manual or
four-speed automatic

Axle ratio: ....2.73:1 manual; 2.54:1 automatic

Rear suspension:.....................Independent Weissach design

aluminum alloy suspension system with
upper links, lower A-arms; self-stabilizing
toe characteristics, hollow stabilizer bar

Front suspension: ....Independent, aluminum alloy
unequal length A-arms, double action shock
absorbers and coil springs with height
adjustment, hollow stabilizer bar, negative
steering roll radius

General

Wheelbase, mm/inches: 2500/ 98.4

Track: Front, mm/inches: 1551/61.1

    Rear, mm/inches:...1546/60.9

Brakes:.............................Power-assisted, dual circuit, four-
piston aluminum alloy fixed calipers,
anti-lock braking system

Tire size, front & rear:

    1991 ....225/50ZR16 / 245/45ZR16

    1993–1995 ....225/45ZR17 / 255/40 ZR17

Wheels, front & rear:

    1991 ....7.5Jx16; 9Jx16

    1993–1995 ....7.5Jx17; 9Jx17

Weight:

    1991 3505

    1993–1995 ....3593 manual; 3638 automatic

Chapter 12

944

In September 1981, Porsche introduced its long-awaited 944 at the Frankfurt auto show. The engine had been through thorough testing and development for at least four years and many people knew about it, anxiously anticipating something better than the 924 engine.

The 924's engine had been a VW/Audi power plant, not even assembled by Porsche, and its performance, even turbocharged, was not really inspiring. In 1977, Weissach began design and development work on their own successor.

The 944 engine has been called "half a 928" but this is only half true. The research, experience, and technology gained from the ongoing development of the 928 V-8 was applied to the new in-line four. However, no major part of the 944 engine was interchangeable with a 928. Yet the store of knowledge and information gathered during the creation and improvement of the 928 enabled engineers to get the 944 engine into production much quicker than previous engines.

There were certain similarities to the 928, however. Both the cylinder head and block were cast of Reynolds 390 aluminum alloy, like the V-8, with identical bore and stroke of 100 mm by 78.9. for total displacement of 2479 cc, (half the V-8, this being the real reason for the analogy). The crankshaft ran in five main bearings and a single overhead camshaft operated two valves per cylinder through hydraulic tappets. The Digital Motor

Electronic (DME) "Motronic" fuel injection system also monitored ignition timing. U.S. models operated with a compression ratio of 9.5:1, producing 143 SAE horsepower at 5500 rpm while European models claimed 10 more at 5800 rpm.

Porsche solved the problem of rough-running four-cylinder engines that plagued the 924 by using two counter-weighted shafts. This was an idea developed by Frederick W. Lanchester in 1911 and whose patents were held by Mitsubishi at the time. The Lanchester shafts turned at twice the crankshaft speed and in opposite directions to each other. This successfully dampens the vibrations inherent in a large displacement four-cylinder engine.

Porsche drove these counter-balance shafts from a toothed Gilmer-type belt. However this belt had teeth on both sides, for right and left shafts. After experiments to develop its own counter-shaft technology, Porsche engineers concluded it was quicker, easier, and more cost effective to pay the estimated eight dollars per engine license fee to Mitsubishi and use their patents.

Engineers also addressed complaints of engine and drivetrain noise that invaded the passenger compartment of the 924. For the 944, they isolated the engine from the frame using one antifreeze liquid-filled rubber mount on each side between the cast-aluminum engine mount and the cast-aluminum

Above and at right
The basic body shell and chassis of the 944 were taken directly from the 924 and 924 Turbo, but the flared fenders, to accommodate wider wheels and tires, front air dam, and rear-deck spoiler were unique to the 944. Even though introduced to America in May 1982, the 944 was a *1983* model according to Porsche+Audi -no matter when it was built and sold. *Porsche Cars North America*

frame cross member. In the middle of this hollow rubber mount was a divider with a small hole permitting the fluid to flow back and forth as the engine moved, acting much like a hydraulic shock absorber. At the rear of the car, two more normal rubber mounts attached the transaxle to the unit-body. The steering rack also was attached to the chassis by rubber bushings.

Porsche unveiled the new engine three months before the car introduction at Frankfurt, using it to power its 924 GTP (Grand Touring Prototype) at Le Mans in June 1981. At the end of the 24-hour race, the car finished third in class, seventh overall. A few weeks later, the car raced in Germany.

Dry weight of the production 944 engine was 340 pounds while curb weight, with all fluids, of the car was 2,778. All inner body and suspension pieces were those of the 924, although the 944 used the ventilated four-wheel disc brakes of the 924 Turbo. Outwardly, the car resembled the 1980 924 Carrera

Other than the heater control, the 944 interior looks almost identical to the 924 and 924 Turbo. *Greg Brown/Argus*

GT. Outer body panels were like those of the Carrera, but the 944's were made of galvanized steel instead of polyurethane plastic.

Drivers familiar with the 924 were right at home in the 944 with the same seats, instrument panel, and interior accouterments carried over. The 944 came standard with air conditioning, electrically adjustable outside mirrors (each side for U.S. cars, driver's side only for European cars), sunroof, power windows, and tinted glass, 7Jx15 cast alloy wheels and 215/60VR15 steel-belted radials. There was an optional sports suspension package offering stiffer shocks, limited-slip differential, and 205/55VR16 tires on 7x16 alloy wheels.

The 944 did everything well that earlier buyers hoped the 924 would do at all. The

Standard equipment on the 944S included air conditioning, electric windows, outside mirrors, fog lights, and sunroof. *Porsche Cars North America*

Its unique front-end treatment distinguished the 944 Turbo from other 944s. The "telephone dial" wheels were similar to the ones used on the 928s. The Turbo would exceed 150 mph in fifth gear and would reach 60 mph in six seconds. *Porsche A. G.*

924 Carrera-bred front and rear spoilers and flared fenders greatly enhanced the appearance. The 944 suspension, essentially picked up intact from the 924, was nonetheless tuned and tweaked to improve handling. While its top speed fell short of the 924 Turbo by just four miles per hour (130 versus 134), the 944 reached 60 miles per hour in 8.3 seconds compared to 9.1 for the turbo 924. And the introductory price, in early 1982 but labeled a 1983 model, was affordable for a Porsche: $18,450.

Porsche engineers continued to make running changes in the first years of the 944. They replaced the DME fuel injection with Bosch's newer LE-Jetronic, and they substituted alloy cast front suspension A-arms for the original welded, stamped steel pieces from the 924 Turbo.

Most of the interior was redone in mid-1985. Instruments were regrouped and a smaller steering wheel was raised a bit higher, the better to clear driver's legs and view the instruments. At the end of that year, Porsche introduced the 944 Turbo. Compression was, naturally, reduced to 8.0:1; horsepower, however, surged from 143 to 217 at 5800 rpm and torque swelled from 144 lb-ft at 3000 to 243 at 3500. Top speed also increased greatly to 155 mph.

Continuing its practice of mid-year releases, Porsche brought out its twin-cam, four-valve-per-cylinder 944S in mid-1986. With compression increased from the introductory 9.7:1 up to 10.9:1 and both intake and exhaust ports and manifold runners enlarged to improve engine breathing, horsepower increased to 188 at 6000 rpm with torque up to 170 lb-ft at 4300. The factory quoted top speed at 142 mph. To haul the cars down from these loftier speeds, Porsche introduced optional four-channel ABS for 1987 models. This reduced braking distances from 62 mph (100 km/h) by between 15 and 20 percent. If that still was not short enough, driver and passenger airbags were included on S and Turbo models.

For 1988, Porsche produced a limited run 944 Turbo S. Only 700 were produced, only in 1988. This was a turbocharged version of the four-valve head engine. Horsepower was

The twin-cam, four-valve-per-cylinder-head 944S was introduced in mid-1986. It produced 190 DIN or 188 SAE horsepower at 6,000 rpm. In 1989, displacement was raised from 2.5 to 3.0 liters, and horsepower was increased to 208 SAE at 5,800 rpm, and the designation changed to 944 S2. *Porsche A. G.*

rated at 247, 30 more than the two-valve head turbo, and 0-60 mph time was only 5.5 seconds, while top speed was up to 162 mph. Clearly, these were performance figures approaching 911s at the time, while offering water-cooled, front-engine handling in a more lithe package than the luxurious 928s.

Standard equipment for all four 1988 model 944s (944, S, Turbo, and Turbo S) included air conditioning, power windows and steering, central locking, electric height adjustment for the driver's seat, and brake pad wear indicators. Turbos and the Turbo S also came with partial leather seats, four-piston fixed-caliper ventilated discs and pressure-cast alloy wheels. (The 944 Turbo S got forged alloy wheels, seven inches wide in front, nine inches at the rear, fitted with 225/50VR16 front and 245/45VR16 rear tires, instead.)

A Cabriolet 944 S2 was first offered in 1989 (top). The Cabrio body was not available on the 944 or 944 Turbo and for 1990 the S2 Coupe and S2 Cabriolet (bottom) were the only 944 models available. *Porsche A. G.*

The 944 interior (944S shown) is unique to the model, but the instrument layout is similar to the 911 series. Driver and passenger comfort are much better than the 924 series cars, primarily because of steering wheel placement. The 944 could reasonably claim to be the best new Porsche for the dollar. *Porsche A. G.*

For 1989, the one-year-wonder 944 Turbo S was discontinued but the lineup still counted four cars: 944, 944 Turbo, 944 S2, and the new S2 Cabriolet. Engine bore was increased to 104 mm, enlarging overall displacement to 2682 cc. The compression ratio of this now-standard 944 engine was raised from 10.6 to 10.9:1, matching the S. Horsepower was quoted at 162 at 5800 rpm. Anti-lock brakes were made standard on all 944s. An electric tilt/removable sun roof, cruise control, and a one-key/central locking/theft alarm system with an LED in the door were added to all the 944 standard equipment lists.

For 1990, the 944 model carried on only with the S2 and S2 Cabriolet with a new 3.0-liter, 208 horsepower engine. The 2.7-liter, 162 horsepower 944 and the 2.5-liter 247 horsepower Turbo were discontinued. Driver and passenger-side airbag restraints were introduced as standard equipment. The Cabriolet, while 111 pounds heavier, matched the coupe in performance (6.9 seconds to 60 mph) and top speed (149 mph). The Coupe and Cabriolet remained unchanged through the 1991 model year, after which they were replaced by the new 968.

Earlier assessments of Porsche's involvement with and dedication to "entry level" cars had questioned how much longer the company would produce such vehicles. As Porsche continues to demonstrate, with its 968 and, as of this writing in mid-1997, with the Boxster, there is an audience that Porsche does much more than merely acknowledge. If you are seeking great driving enjoyment, even excitement, and you are wary of your driving skills with a rear-engined 911, look just *above* entry level to find a 914/6 or a 944 S2 or Turbo S and you'll see clearly Porsche's ongoing commitment to "entry level."

Output increased by 30 horsepower over the 1988 model, up to 247 horsepower out of 2.5 liters. Acceleration from 0 to 60 mph was 5.7 seconds, comparable to the 928 manual and only four-tenths slower than the 911 Turbo. Four-piston fixed caliper brakes and anti-lock braking were new for 1989. *Porsche Cars North America*

Introduced for the first time for 1990, the Cabriolet was a very civilized package with standard equipment electric convertible top, air conditioning with climate control, power steering and windows, and driver and passenger side air bags. Anti-lock brakes were also included. *Porsche Cars North America*

The S2 engine featured a belt/chain driven dual overhead camshaft with four valves per cylinder. This helped the 3.0-liter inline four produce 208 horsepower at 4,100 rpm. The 3,109 pound cabriolet would reach a top speed of 149 mph. As the "entry level" Porsche, however it was pricey at $50,350. *Porsche Cars North America*

For its introductory year, Porsche set suggested retail prices at $48,600 for the Cabriolet and $41,900 for the Coupes. Model year 1990 was a big launch for open Porsche cars, as both Carrera 4 and Carrera 2S also were introduced in Cabriolets. *Porsche Cars North America*

---

944 (1982–1989) & 944T (1986–1989)

Engine
Design: ....Water-cooled inline four
Bore x stroke, mm/inches
1982–1988 ....100x78.9 / 3.94x3.11
1989 ....103.8x78.9 / 4.09x3.11
Displacement, cc/cubic inches
    1982–1988 ....2479 / 151
    1989 ....2688 / 164
    Valve operation: ....Toothed belt-driven twin
                                                             overhead camshaft
Compression ratio:
Europe & Great Britain
    1982–1988 ....10.6:1
U.S., Canada, Japan
    1982–1988 ....9.5:1
    1989 ....10.9:1
    944T (1986–1989) 8.0:1
Carburetion
    944: ....Electronic fuel injection with oxygen
                                                        sensor DME controlled
    944T: ....Same, with KKK turbocharger
BHP (Mfr.)
    944 (1982–1985): ....150 DIN/143 SAE @ 5800
    1986–1989 ....147 SAE @ 5800
    944T (1986–1988): ....217 SAE @ 5800
    1988 and 1989 Turbo S* ....247 SAE @ 6000

Chassis & Drivetrain
Frame: ....Unit body
Component layout: ....Front engine, rear drive
Clutch: ....Fichtel & Sachs single dry-plate
Transmission: ....Porsche five-speed all-synchromesh,
                                        in unit with differential; optional three-
                                        speed automatic, in unit with differential
Axle ratio: with five-speed 3.89:1
    with three-speed automatic 3.45:1
Rear suspension: ....Independent, semi-trailing
                                        arms, transverse torsion bars & tubular
                                        shock absorbers (rear anti-roll bar optional)
Front suspension: ....Independent, MacPherson
                                        telescopic shock strut & lower A-arm
                                        on each side with coil springs & anti-roll bar

General
Wheelbase, mm/inches: 2400/94.5
Track: Front, mm/inches: 1478/58.2
    Rear, mm/inches: 1450/57.1
Brakes: ....Disc
Tire size, front & rear: 215/60VR 15
                                        (205/55VR 16 with optional wheels)
Wheels: ....7Jx15 cast alloy
                                        (7Jx16 forged alloy optional)
Body builder: ....Porsche
Note: 470 944S Turbos were built in 1988 as a special edition.

The four-valve S2 Coupe weighed 111 pounds less than the Cabriolet and sold for $7,000 less, at $43,350. The integrated rear spoiler was introduced for model year 1991, and it was inspired by the form and function of the 959's rear wing. *Porsche Cars North America*

944S (1986–1988), 944 S2 (1989–1991)

Engine

Design: ....Water-cooled inline four
Bore x stroke, mm/inches
  1986–1988 ....100x78.9 / 3.94x3.11
  S2 1989– ....103.8x87.9 / 4.09x3.46
Displacement, cc/cubic inches
  1986–1988 ....2479 / 151
  S2 1989– ....2990 / 183
Valve operation: ....Toothed belt-driven twin overhead
                  camshafts, four valves per cylinder
Compression ratio: 10.9:1
Carburetion: ....Bosch Motronic M2.1 fuel injection
BHP (Mfr.)
  944S ....188 @ 6000
  944 S2 ....208 @ 5800

Chassis & Drivetrain

Frame: ....Unit body
Component layout: ....Front engine, rear drive
Clutch: ....Fichtel & Sachs single dry-plate
                 with diaphragm spring, hydraulic operation
Transmission: ....Porsche five-speed all-synchromesh,
                   in unit with differential
Axle ratio: 3.889:1

Rear suspension: ....Independent, semi-trailing arms,
                  transverse torsion bars, tubular
                  shock absorbers, and anti-roll bar
Front suspension: ....Independent, MacPherson
                  telescopic shock strut and lower
                  A-arm on each side with coil
                  springs and anti-roll bar

General

Wheelbase, mm/inches: 2400/94.5
Track: Front, mm/inches: ....1477 / 58.1
  Rear, mm/inches: ....1451 / 57.1
Brakes: ....Hydraulic, dual-circuit system,
                  four ventilated discs, brake servo,
                  optional ABS (ABS standard 1989 on)
Tire size, front & rear:
  standard ....195/65 VR 15
  optional ....205/55 VR 16, 225/50 VR 16
Wheels, front and rear:
  standard ....7J-16 cast aluminum
  optional ....7J 16-8J-16 forged aluminum
Body builder: ....Porsche

Chapter 13

959

When Ferry Porsche hired Peter Schutz, Ferry largely had been marginalized by Ernst Fuhrmann, whose efforts to replace the rear-engine, air-cooled 911 with the front-engine, water-cooled 924 and 928 models had not succeeded. Porsche had moved his office out of Zuffenhausen and worked in a satellite facility a short distance north of the factory. Ferry told Schutz that the company was not making any money and that this seemed to be because the workers were not working together. He hired Schutz to "get this whole organization unified and working together."

In a series of masterful moves, Schutz did exactly that. He overturned recent history and trends, extending the 911's straight-line bar graph in Helmuth Bott's office that charted the life expectancies of various models and going after top honors at Le Mans in 1981. He also remodeled the largest office in Werke I and invited Ferry to move back in. Then, every morning, the two men had coffee together. Over their morning coffee some weeks after the Le Mans victory with the 936, Schutz posed the question to Ferry that had been nagging at him for nearly a year. "Whatever got into you," he asked, "to take a Volkswagen Beetle, remove the body, replace it with a streamlined two-seater, and charge five times as much money for it?"

"Without hesitation, he looked me in the eye and said, 'Herr Schutz, I didn't listen to anybody. I simply built my dream car and thought that others would share my dream.'"

Before Schutz arrived, that dream had been under assault.

"Often people think you go in a wrong direction," Helmuth Bott explained years later, "because you have an air-cooled engine, because you have the engine in the rear. . . . . But Porsche always had an outstanding concept, different from others. And that's the key for Porsche, even in the future.

"If you have a water-cooled engine in the front, that's a system everybody can do . . . cheaper than we can do it. But the exciting things are sometimes more difficult for the engineers, and in the end you have advantages others do not. And with the advantages you can motivate customers. That is the secret of Porsche. We do things other people cannot."

Fuhrmann, who planned 911 production to end at the end of the 1981 model year, had withdrawn Turbo sales from the U.S. market starting in January 1980. Tighter exhaust emissions limits required catalytic converters to meet the regulations. Weissach engineers reviewed catalyst technologies available up to that time. Combined with the quality of unleaded gasoline available in the United States, they estimated a constrained Turbo would develop only 240 brake horsepower, which offered little appeal. Schutz's arrival in 1981 put the Turbo back on Bott's wall chart, but it was not until the 1986 model year that Porsche sold the Turbo in America. Better catalytic converters and higher-octane unleaded fuels made it possible. The 1986

Porsche delivered the first production 959s to customers in 1986. Cars sold for nearly 500,000 Deutschmarks at the factory, which set a price of around $270,000 for U.S. customers.

models offered 282 horsepower, closer to European versions with 300 horsepower.

Throughout this time, however, Bott and his colleagues worked on the *ultimate* 911. The concept had begun life as an all-wheel-drive model for competition in 1984, known as the Typ 953.

Bott had a willing collaborator in Peter Schutz. The new chairman was born in Germany in 1930. His family emigrated to the United States in 1939 ahead of the war. Schutz graduated with a mechanical engineering degree from Illinois Institute of Technology. He understood and spoke German, and he quickly became fluent with Porsche. To him, all-wheel-drive technology belonged beneath a Porsche 911.

The F.I.A.'s 1982 Gruppe B was an umbrella classification in which manufacturers could create a racer in advance of series production. It incorporated the earlier Groups 4 through 7 and called for closed two-seaters with production of at least 200 examples within 12 months. Ferdinand Piëch's all-wheel-drive Audi Quattros often had won European rallies, and they demonstrated the value of this new drive system.

Bott's racing engineers wanted to do a mid-engined car for Gruppe B, building something based on the 914. Jürgen Barth knew that 80 percent of Porsche's customers participated in some kind of paved-road competition but just 20 percent rallied. Bott argued against both groups. Porsche already did so many mid-engined race cars he felt the engineers would not learn anything new. Their 956 had succeeded from the start. He worried if Porsche built a mid-engined Gruppe B car and no one else entered the category, would there even be a class?

"If you have to do a car which you must build two hundred times," he said, "you can also build one a thousand times. If we do build a Gruppe B car, let's have a look at the future of the Nine-Eleven." In early January, he formalized his concept on paper, envisioning a pure competition version at first, with series production later that utilized technologies they developed for the competition car.

Bott completed his first prototype all-wheel-drive 911 in late 1981, and he and his staff constantly upgraded it. In 1983, Porsche racer Jacky Ickx had entered and won the Paris–Dakar Rally driving a Mercedes-Benz

The 959 was the most exotic, powerful, and expensive 911-derivative Porsche ever produced, limiting assembly to 200 "production" cars and around 30 development prototypes through 1988. Its appearance hinted at production models to come.

The six-speed transmission fitted a creeper gear in first position, meant to help extricate the car from deep snow or sand. Instrumentation told drivers how much torque—under acceleration or braking—was divided between front and rear wheels.

factory-prepared 280GE Gelandewagen. Through this experience, Ickx brought practical knowledge to Bott's program. In advance of the 1984 run, they took Bott's personal four-wheel-drive 911 prototype to Africa. On the third day, one of the front axles broke. Bott's mechanics disconnected the axle on the other side to make the car drivable. It was a revelation to them. Ickx had negotiated passages between dunes with six inches on either side of the car because he could place the car precisely. With only rear drive, Ickx needed more than six feet of clearance to feel comfortable racing through dunes.

"We thought," Bott said, "if a car is so much better under bad conditions, then you must feel it on the dry road. . . . Our concept with the Nine-Eleven always has been that it's an all-around car. With very few changes you can drive a desert rally and then to the racetrack at Le Mans, to show the people that, without changing the concept, this Nine-Eleven is capable of completely different things.

"So we thought, let's see if there is anything against our building this car for the next ten years, fifteen years. It was a goal, a task much greater than to build a race car." Bott's concept went long range: There would be a desert rally car, the Typ 953, developed by Manfred Bantle, followed by 20 copies as a road-racing Typ 960 and then the next-generation series Turbo as the Typ 961.

Bantle's Typ 953 went straight to victory in 1984, finishing first at the end of the 7,500-mile event. The race was more frustrating in 1985, and none of the three cars finished. But 1986 made up for that. Jacky Ickx captained three 959s to finish first, fourth, and sixth.

Stylist Wolfgang Möbius, who had designed the 928 and made 911 safety bumpers look attractive for U.S. customers, asked Dick Soderberg to create the look of this ultimate 911. Soderberg had worked with Norbert Singer on the radical racer 935/78, nicknamed "Moby Dick," and he understood how Singer interpreted rules. The Gruppe B show car greatly advanced Moby's appearance. He retained the existing roof and doors of a 911, as he had had to do

The "Komfort" models used multicolored leather on seats and console trim and plush carpeting on the floors. The interior looked familiar to any driver with 911 experience.

with Moby. Unable to design a more aerodynamic roof, Soderberg and Möbius, Bott and Bantle accepted that a large rear wing was necessary. Soderberg developed a design icon with an elegantly integrated wing morphed into the widened rear fenders. This elevated structure effectively lengthened and flattened the roofline. It treated detached airflow as if it were still laminar

and attached to the car body. Two years after Bott's all-wheel-drive cabriolet startled Frankfurt show visitors, the September 1983 offering—a pearlescent-white-painted coupe—again stunned the audience.

Paul Hensler's production engine group devised a 2,849 cc engine using 95 mm bore and 65 mm stroke. Two sequential turbochargers helped to develop 450 brake horsepower. But development costs and delays were affordable in the early 1980s when U.S. dollars bought 2 1/2 or 3 DM. Porsche's profits for 1984 finished 33 percent higher than 1983. Schutz's projections suggested another 30 percent profit growth for 1985. Cars produced with costs in German Marks seemed cheap to purchasers in the United States. American sales consumed two-thirds of Porsche's total output. Model year 1985 saw factory production reach a record of 54,458 cars.

At the Frankfurt show in 1985, Porsche announced two versions of the 959, a Sport with cloth interior and roll cage (of which it produced only 37 examples), and a *Komfort* model with elaborate leather trim and heated leather seats. Stylist Steve Murkett had taken Dick Soderberg's startling show

The car's widened bodywork allowed for better stability. The integrated rear wing became the 959's iconic design feature as well as one having tremendous aerodynamic benefit.

The importation saga for hopeful American buyers was stormy at best. Soon after assembly began, Porsche decided not to bother federalizing 959s for U.S. customers. Only a few cars filtered into the country until laws changed in the early 2000s, allowing their use in the States.

This U.S. Sport version came with a full padded roll cage, since, in 1988, importing the 959 either as a race car or a museum show piece was the only way to bring one in. The speedometer read to 220 mph.

The "Sport" version of the car fitted cloth-covered seats with five-point seat harnesses. Porsche finished the fully triangulated roll cage with typical attention to function and finish.

The modest 2.86-liter flat six utilized dual turbochargers and intercoolers to develop 450 horsepower. Acceleration from 0–62 mph took just less than 5 seconds. Most 959s topped 200 mph.

Porsche set 959 production at 200 cars, a number that the Federation International de l'Automobile required for classification as a Group B racer. But Group B seldom raced on pavement, and international rallying had much smaller production requirements. However, the number satisfied customer demand.

car and translated it to limited production, making the necessary adjustments to take a dream onto the road. Porsche priced these at 420,000DM, about $142,850 at the time of the show, but these passed $200,000 as deliveries began. After struggling to meet U.S. DOT and EPA safety and emissions standards, Schutz and Bott concluded that they could not make the costs work for U.S. markets. They were required to crash test four production cars, vehicles that cost Weissach more to develop and manufacture than the money the company made from selling them, even as the numbers climbed. Porsche sold the entire production throughout the rest of the world without absorbing additional charges and delays to meet U.S. regulations, despite having accepted 50 U.S. deposits. Production totaled 337 cars, including 16 prototypes and 21 *Vorseries* (or preproduction models) in 1985, as well as those *Komfort* and Sport versions manufactured in 1987 (106 and 7) and 1988 (149 and 1 plus a series of 29 U.S. Sport versions). This also included a small run of 8 fabricated for special customers from extra parts in 1992.

The 959 was not really legal in the United States until 1999 when a number of existing American owners led by Microsoft founder and Porsche enthusiast Bill Gates "lobbied" members of Congress to pass a "Show and Display" law. This allowed limited use to and from shows for those with an existing, recognized collection.

The passage of time, however, has been both friend and foe to the 959. In 2003, entrepreneur Bruce Canepa launched a program to "federalize" the 959. By modifying the turbos, exhaust, and computerized engine management systems, he got the engines to meet U.S. emissions requirements at the time. Verdicts were mixed on Canepa's work, and it was widely known his conversion was extremely expensive and took many months and thousands of test miles to accomplish. Canepa sold converted cars complete for just about $600,000, roughly the price of four new Turbos with comparable performance and new car warranties.

The good news for those still lusting after a 959 is that, after 21 years—as of the end of 2008—the 959 no longer needs to be converted to EPA standards to make it U.S. road legal. Detailed information is available at the U.S. EPA website: www.epa.gov/otaq/imports/quiktest.htm#21years. The other important site for anyone considering importing and enjoying a 959 is operated by the National Highway and Traffic Safety Administration. See its rules at www.nhtsa.dot.gov/cars/rules/import/Show/Display?sdist06202005.

More than 20 years after introduction, the 959 still looks startling. Extreme attention to aerodynamic lift produced a car that developed *no* lift, a situation in which air forces pushing down on the car equaled those attempting to elevate it off the pavement.

While this EPA regulation change represented a significant savings for an importer/owner, remember that the 959 was an exceptionally complex automobile with incredibly expensive parts, only some of which were shared with regular production models. Body panels were aluminum or carbon-fiber/Kevlar composites. At this writing in mid-2009, the four-wheel-drive pump could be found for $4,000; wheels were $1,000 each, though tires were readily available at TireRack. The ABS controller was $5,000, and brake rotors were $1,300 each. The integral "air" suspension system on the *Komfort* models actually used nitrogen. The canisters that raised or lowered the car at speed or at the flick of a switch do wear out. New ones were $5,000 each in 2009, and the car requires four of them. The shock absorbers were $1,000 each. Some *Komfort* owners have converted their suspensions to Sport configuration, but others have worried about the resale value of such converted cars. PelicanParts owner

Wayne R. Dempsey, a 959 *Komfort* owner, has detailed his experiences and expenses and has shared this information willingly on a website: www.959registry.com. This site is an excellent source of information—and inspiration—for anyone considering a 959 purchase.

While a pre-purchase inspection is a good idea for any Porsche, it is crucial for a 959. You first must find a service facility that has the code reader for this model. Without this device, the shop would not have the accompanying knowledge, skills, or information to repair or service the car. Any inspector must read the codes to determine performance history and characteristics of the car and engine, inspect the transmission for leaks, inspect the shock absorbers for fluid leaks, inspect the A/C computer, check turbo boost and inspect the electronic bypass valves, inspect tire pressure sensors, inspect active-suspension nitrogen canisters, and be certain the toolkit is complete and in the car. In southern California, Tony Callas, at Callas Rennsport in Torrance, has cared for several of these vehicles, with the proper tools, technical manuals, and documentation at hand. Some of these cars arrived by air from owners around the United States, Asia, and elsewhere.

Many 959s have been kept for long periods in collections. According to Dempsey's

Even with a $271,000 price on each 959, Porsche lost money on the car. On the other hand, the model earned the company and its engineers tremendous publicity and an unmatched reputation for its technological innovations.

959 (1986–1988)

Engine

Design............................Water-cooled flat (opposed)
6-cylinder twin turbochargers,
twin intercoolers
Bore & Stroke, mm/inches.......95.0x66.0 / 3.74x2.60
Displacement, cc/cid............................ 2,849 / 173.9
Valve operation ....dual-overhead camshafts, duplex
chain driven four-valves per cylinder
Compression ratio..8.3:1
Fuel feed ...... DME sequential multi-port fuel injection
HP (SAE net) (mfr)................................450 at 6,500

Chassis & Drivetrain

Frame.........Unitized, fully galvanized steel, aluminum
Component layout .... rear engine, all-wheel drive
Transmission.......... six-speed transaxle with 1st gear
as creeper active traction control
Axle ratio (manual/Tiptronic)...........................4.125:1
Front suspension .....Independent, double wishbones,
twin coil springs with variable and
lift-regulating shock absorbers anti-roll
bar, active suspension control

Rear suspension ......Independent, double wishbones,
twin coil springswith variable and
lift-regulating shock absorbers anti-roll
bar, active suspension control

General

Wheelbase, mm/inches...........................2,300 / 90.5
Track:
    front, mm/inches.................................1,504 / 59.2
    rear, mm/inches..................................1,550 / 61.0
Brakes.............................power-assisted, ventilated,
and drilled discs, four-piston
fixed aluminum calipers.
Tire size:
    front, rear .... 235/45ZR17 / 255/40ZR17
Wheels:
    front, rear ....8Jx17 / 9Jx17
Weight...........................3,190 Sport / 3,344 *Komfort*

---

experience, prolonged periods of inactivity may cause some of the performance-oriented systems to fail but not necessarily those affecting drivability. In other words, it could still be safe to drive the car to a show but not to use it on a race-track. Dempsey recommends that owners exercise their cars regularly and that all high-performance systems be inspected and serviced by experienced mechanics.

Prices for these cars in Europe varied from $200,000 to $500,000. Those at the higher end in Europe more likely would have been adequately used (enough to keep seals moist and systems working), factory maintained, and factory correct. For a car of this rarity and value, seeing the service history is essential, and flying in a capable mechanic to inspect it would be sensible

968

To hardcore purists, cynics, and terminal skeptics, no matter how great the 944 became in its S2 and Turbo S variants, it still bore the aftertaste of its Audi legacy. As such, it was not ever *really* a Porsche. So the company, content to continue experimenting with the breed (front-mounted four-cylinder engine driving rear wheels), did so and, in all likelihood, aimed to put to rest the snobbish sniping.

What its new engineering project number, 968, wrought was not so much a new car as what writer David Vivian called, "another well-timed evolutionary spasm." This project resulted in an 80-percent new car, with, as Porsche's chief designer Harm Lagaay protested to *Road & Track* writer Joe Rusz, only the doors that carried over from the 944. Well, Vivian's analysis is more apparent than Lagaay's plaints. The 968 was nothing if not subtle. Its appearance was decidedly evolutionary, its shape evolving from Lagaay's mentor, Tony Lapine and the zaftig 928s. If imitation is the highest flattery, then the 968 echoed the luxury V-8 from its fold-down headlights and integrated driving lights and turn signals to its rear taillights, plastic fascia, and basket-handle rear spoiler. It was, in short, a highly effective, understated design that belied its very impressive performance. Its appearance never screamed that it was a 150+ mph Porsche, never broadcast that its buyer had spent $44,500. And that may have been its problem, at least in the United States.

The car arrived in late 1991 as a 1992 model, near the peak of America's public display of affluence. And while the 968 went like the hammers of hell, it still resembled too much the Volks-Porsche.

Porsche's engineers continued to develop the 3.0-liter Audi-derived in-line four, retaining its counter-rotating vibration dampening shafts while managing to squeeze another 33 horsepower, a total of 236 SAE net at 6200 rpm, from an engine that was still normally aspirated. Torque also increased, from 207 to 225 lb-ft at 4100 rpm. Compression ratio was increased to 11:1. This was mainly accomplished through Porsche's new VarioCam, a variable valve-timing system of devilish complexity that, controlled by the Bosch Motronic injection and ignition brain, acted on the camshaft chain tensioner to delay drive to the inlet camshaft by as much as 15 degrees. This provided progressive spark advance as engine speed increased, thereby improving power outputs. Top speed was quoted at 156 mph and 0-60 mph times were in the 6.1 second range with Porsche's newly introduced Getrag six-speed manual gearbox. With the four-speed Tiptronic automatic, the run took 7.5 seconds while top speed was 153 mph.

In earlier times, Porsche took advantage of the great torque offered by its 930 Turbo engines and retained the four-speed gearbox, partly because only this box could handle the power. Yet with the 968, this revised, torquey

The cutaway shows every delicious detail of the inaugural 1992 model 968 coupe. Its in-line, water-cooled four-cylinder 182-cubic-inch engine produced 236 horsepower at 6200 rpm. Available with either a six-speed manual or the Tiptronic four-speed dual-function transmission, the car weighed 3,086 pounds with the manual. *Porsche Cars North America*

The family resemblance between Porsche's "entry level" 968 and its mid-model-year reintroduction 928 is apparent in this view of the 1992 coupe. However, dimensionally, the 968 was the smaller sibling. It was 7.2 inches shorter overall, 6.1 inches narrower and 0.3 inches lower. It also sold for just less than half the cost of a 1992 928. *Porsche Cars North America*

The 968 was introduced from the start in both Coupe and Cabriolet versions, the open car, however, selling for $11,150 more than the Coupe, at $51,000. Both cars were offered with either the six-speed manual or the four-speed Tiptronic. *Porsche Cars North America*

engine ran through six speeds. When David Vivian asked Porsche powertrain chief engineer Paul Hensler about it, he answered quickly, "It's simple. Porsche drivers like changing gears."

The 968 carried over the 944's MacPherson strut front suspensions with its aluminum alloy control arms and wheel hubs. Spring and shocks were revised to provide the tighter ride and handling of the 944 Turbos. Porsche engineers achieved the ideal weight

distribution of 50/50 front versus rear (as they had done with the 928 GTS). At the rear, the S2's semi-trailing arms and transverse torsion bars were used as well. Standard 16-inch wheels, sevens at front, eights at rear, carried the same tire combinations as the previous 944 S2. However, an optional M-030 sport suspension package included pressure-cast light alloy 17-inch five-spoke Turbo-design wheels and tires with a "run-flat" feature, as well as adjustable rebound-rate gas shocks

Prices for the 1993 968 Cabriolet rose very slightly to $51,900. Specifications, however, remained unaltered. Performance from 0 to 60 mph was 6.3 seconds and the top speed was quoted as 156 mph. The 968 Cabriolet and Coupe had the feel of Porsche quality, and they were fine cars for the track or a favorite mountain road. *Porsche Cars North America*

The lines of the 968, in this instance, the 1994 model, were clear and simple, and their derivation, from the 944 and even the 924 before it, was clear. Still, Harm Lagaay's stylists pared the appearance down to its uncluttered minimum. *Porsche Cars North America*

and larger ventilated and cross-drilled front brakes (11.97 inch diameter by 1.26 thick versus the entirely adequate 11.73 x 1.10 inch rotors, on Coupes only). Antilock braking was standard on all Porsches.

The Tiptronic transmission is a remarkable dual-function automatic-and-clutchless manual gearbox controlled through side-by-side operating slots. The change from fully automatic to clutchless manual can be done while moving and its computer brain interprets road speed, how fast the driver depresses the accelerator, and how much braking or cornering force is being generated and adjusts the shift program through five distinct ranges, from no-compromise performance to frugal economy. This transmission was originally developed in the mid-1980s as the PDK (Porsche Double Clutch) and was used experimentally on several factory-entered Type 962 Group C endurance racing cars.

Inside the car, features from the 944 S2 were carried over. The Coupe provided fold-down individual rear seat backs to provide additional storage capacity while the Cabriolet, with its electrically operated (and fully insulated) top, was a pure two-seater, offering additional lockable storage compartments underneath the exposed rear parcel shelf.

The biggest news for the 1993 model year was a substantial price reduction to $39,950

for the "base" coupe. The Tiptronic added another $3,150 to the price of either Coupe or Cabriolet (at $51,900 with the standard Getrag six-speed.) In an effort to meet global consciousness and responsibility, Porsche began labeling all recyclable plastic containers on its cars. At the point when any Porsche reaches the end of its useful life, this new practice ensured that even plastics might find a useful purpose.

Model year 1994 saw only subtle changes. Seats and wheels were restyled and several new exterior colors were added to the list of those available. Mid-year, Porsche introduced an optional Torsen differential to replace the conventional clutch-pack limited slip differential that was available as an option on six-speed-equipped cars. Traditional "reactive" traction control differentials reduced power to the spinning wheel only after it had begun to spin. This differential, because it was TORque SENsing, rather than speed-sensing, reacted instantly to transfer engine power to the wheel with the most traction. Under normal driving conditions where rear-wheel traction is equal on both sides, the Torsen behaves as a conventional (nonlimited-slip) differential. Prices for both the Coupe and Cabriolet remained identical to those from 1993.

Porsche changed the designation of its optional sport suspension package for the

1995 968 from M-030 to P31. Elements of the package included the adjustable-height MacPherson struts up front, additional barrel-type springs fitted over the shocks at rear, front and rear shocks adjustable for rebound, a 10 percent thicker front anti-roll bar and 15 percent thicker bar at the rear, and larger, thicker cross-drilled front brake rotors and larger brake caliper pistons. In addition, front wheels and tires were 7.5x17s with 225/45 ZR17s and rears were 9x17s with 255/40/ZR17s.

Then, just when Porsche seemingly had it right, it discontinued the 968 Coupe and Cabriolet at the end of 1995. Even in the 968's last year, prices remained unchanged from 1993. With the end of 1995 production, Porsche's manufacture of front-engined, water-cooled cars, an engineering love affair that had continued for twenty years came to an end.

Rear-engine Porsche purists lament the existence of these cars, often commenting disdainfully that large percentages of Porsche enthusiast clubs are made up of car owners who have never even driven a 911 and wouldn't recognize a Gmünd coupe if it parked next to them at the golf or tennis club.

Porsche, thankfully, was more catholic in its view. Its front-engined cars introduced thousands of buyers to the company, individuals without the interest or desire to perfect the skills necessary to get the most out of a 911.

Porsche's history of nearly five decades suggests it would be foolish for any writer—or prognosticator—to presume that Porsche is finished with front-engined cars. Politics and public tastes change, as do vehicle regulations. At this writing, Porsche has introduced its Boxster. History repeats.

The Boxster is liquid cooled, like the 924, 928, 944, and 968. It is mid-engined, like the 914 and like Professor Porsche's very first 356.

History repeats.

For 1995, its final year, the 968 was once again unchanged in any measurable manner. Prices held steady after the only increase in 1993. The new torque-sensing differential was introduced in mid-year 1994, to replace the conventional clutch-pack differential as an option for six-speed cars *Porsche Cars North America*

---

968 Coupe, Cabriolet (1992–1995)

Engine
Design:.........................Water-cooled, in-line four-cylinder
Bore x stroke, mm/inches: ....104x88 / 4.09x3.46
Displacement, cc/cubic inches:.........................2990/182.5
Valve operation: ....Dual overhead camshafts, belt-chain driven with VarioCam variable valve timing, hydraulic lifters
Compression ratio:...11.0:1
Carburetion:.......................Sequential fuel injection Digital Motor Electronics ME Version 2.10.1 fuel injection and ignition system
BHP (Mfr.): ....236 @ 6200

Chassis & Drivetrain
Frame:....................Unitized, fully galvanized steel
Component Layout: ....Front engine, rear drive
Transmission: ....Porsche six-speed manual or Tiptronic four-speed dual function
Axle ratio: ....3.78:1 manual; 3.25:1 Tiptronic
Rear suspension:............Independent with aluminum alloy semi-trailing arms, transverse torsion bars, stabilizer bar
Front suspension:.............Independent MacPherson struts with aluminum alloy lower control arms, coil springs, stabilizer bar, negative steering roll radius

General
Wheelbase, mm/inches:...................................2400 / 94.5
Track: Front, mm/inches:...............................1472 / 58.2
        Rear, mm/inches:..............................1450 / 57.1
Brakes:..........................Power-assisted, dual circuit, four piston aluminum alloy fixed caliper, anti-lock braking system
Tire size, front & rear:..............205/55ZR16 - 225/50ZR16
Wheels, front & rear: 7Jx16; 8Jx16
Weight:
    coupe, manual 3086
    tiptronic: 3152
    cabriolet manual: 3240
    tiptronic: 3306

Chapter 15

Carrera 2, 4, 911 Turbo 3.6

★★★1/2	**1989 Carrera Coupe, Cabriolet, Targa**
★★★★	**1989 911 Club Sport, Speedster, 930S Turbo**
★★★1/2	**1990–1996 Carrera 4**
★★★★	**1991–1993 911 Turbo 3.3**
★★★	**1990–1994 Carrera 2 Coupe, Cabriolet, Targa**
★★★1/2	**1990–1992 Carrera 4 Cabriolet, Targa**
★★★★	**1992–1993 911 America Roadster**
★★★★	**1993–1994 911 Speedster, RS America**
★★★★	**1994 911 Turbo 3.6**
★★★1/2	**1994 911 Targa**
★★★★	**1995–1996 Carrera Coupe**
★★★★★	**1996–1997 911 Carrera 4S**
★★★★	**1996–1997 911 Carrera 4 Cabriolet, Carrera Targa**
★★★★1/2	**1997 911**
★★★★	**1997 Carrera S**
★★★★★	**1997 911 Turbo, Turbo S**

1989

Three new models—actually two variations on the 911 theme, the 911 Club Sport and 911 Speedster, as well as the all-new 911 Carrera 4—arrived during the 1989 model year.

The Club Sport was simply a lightened cafe racer. Porsche eliminated air conditioning, power windows and door locks, the radio, sound insulation, fog lights, front hood lock, door arm rests, and the rear seat, reducing the Club Sport's weight by 155 pounds from the stock Carrera Coupe. The 3.2-liter engine, still rated at 217 horsepower, had the DME control system and hollow intake valves, allowing a maximum engine speed of 6840 rpm instead of 6520 for the stock Carrera.

The minimal engine changes and weight savings improved performance so the Club Sport could do 0-60 mph in 5.6 seconds and it had a top speed of 149 mph. Cars sold for $45,895.

The 911 Carrera Speedster became available in January 1989, based on the Carrera Cabriolet. The aluminum-frame windshield was raked back five degrees more than the Cabriolet and the top, like the original 356 models, was unlined. The 930S slant nose body style was available as an option; known as the "Turbo Look," it was a popular option. Porsche produced 2,104 Speedsters worldwide; 1,939 of them sported the swollen bodies and fat tires.

Porsche's technical highlight of 1989 was the introduction of its Carrera 4 (as a coupe only). It was powered by the 3.6-liter single overhead-cam flat-six air-cooled engine but with twin-spark plug ignition that pulled out 247 horsepower at 6100 rpm. The "C4" would accelerate from 0-60 mph in 5.7 seconds and would reach 162 mph.

The Carrera 4 utilized a four-wheel drive system that was full-time and the center differential normally split the torque 31 percent to the front wheels and 59 percent to the rear. Two computer-controlled multiple disc clutches in the center transfer case and rear differentials apportioned power to each wheel in the maximum amount it would accept without spinning. One clutch controlled front-to-rear torque split while the second acted as a limited slip differential between the rear wheels. Actuation of these clutches was accomplished by hydraulic pressure and fast-acting solenoid valves. This was the most sophisticated road-going Porsche since the

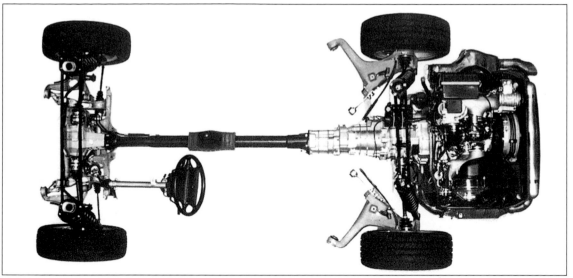

The ultimate in chassis sophistication: four-wheel drive with computer-managed traction distribution via multiple-disc clutches in center and rear differentials, and ABS make the Carrera 4 the supreme high-performance machine. *Porsche A. G.*

Typ 959 was introduced in 1986, and of course, it had been teased to the Frankfurt and Geneva auto show visitors in late 1981 and early 1982 in the Cabriolet design study. However, since this Carrera 4 was road legal in the United States from the start and cost $69,500 instead of more than $200,000, it was a more realistic dream.

The Carrera 4 chassis (floor pan and suspension) was completely new. Referred to internally as the Type 964, it came about as a result of seeking production solutions to the problem of locating the front drive shaft: early prototypes ran the transaxle tube on top of the center tunnel under a plastic cover. Once Porsche engineers decided to mount the driveline below, they realized it would require a complete new layout of the floor pan and front of the car. Once that was accepted, redesigning the front and rear

The Carrera 4 spoiler lifts automatically at about 40 mph, and retracts flush with the body at about 6

mph; all in the interest of downforce when needed for maximum traction and anti-lift. *Porsche A. G.*

For 1990, the Carrera 2 was added. Based on the chassis of the Carrera 4, it also has coil-spring suspension, anti-lock brakes, a speed-actuated rear spoiler (which raises at 40 mph and retracts flush with the rear body at 6 mph). Like other 911 models, the Carrera 2 has only rear-wheel drive. *Porsche A. G.*

An option available for the Carrera 2 is the "Tip-tronic" shift; a system that allows full automatic transmission shifting when the lever is in the left slot. When the lever is in the right side of the gate, shifting is fully manual—with a push forward to up-shift, a pull back to downshift, but with no clutch pedal to push. *Porsche A. G.*

suspension became possible as well. The Carrera 4 used coil springs instead of torsion bars all around, and the front suspension consisted of MacPherson struts with lower control arms while the rear suspension utilized semi-trailing arms.

The body carried on the stove-pipe fenders that are near and dear to 911 enthusiasts as well as the traditional low sloping hood. However, the entire car was redesigned to accommodate the new chassis and running gear, as well as various brake and engine oil cooling obligations. Coefficient of drag was slightly reduced, to 0.32 for the Coupe, owing in part to a full undertray that helped manage air flow beneath the car.

A real spoiler lay flush with the rear deck lid while the car was at rest or traveling below 40 mph. Once elevated, it lowered again automatically at just above a crawl, about 6 mph. Even though the Carrera 4 strongly resembled previous 911 models, there were virtually no mechanical and few body parts that were interchangeable. Engineers and designers heard long-time customers very clearly: do not change the 911 shape.

1990

Further consolidation of the Porsche product line for 1990 eliminated the 3.3-liter 282 horsepower 911 Turbo from U.S. markets and the 3.2 liter Carrera (in Coupe, Cabriolet and Targa body styles) was replaced by the 3.6-liter, 247 horsepower Carrera 2, a designation harking back 30 years to the two-liter four-cylinder four-cam 356 Carreras)

The Carrera 2, with rear, two-wheel drive only, shared body and chassis with the Carrera 4, introduced a season earlier. For 1990, both models were offered in Coupe, Cabriolet, and Targa bodies, and the 911 Speedster was dropped after its brief 1989 production run. Of the 2,104 cars worldwide, 800 were imported to the United States.

Porsche introduced its PDK Porsche Double Clutch "Tiptronic" transmission first for the Carrera 2, expanding the offering two years later to include the new 1993 Type 968 (see Chapter 13 for a complete description).

Anti-lock brakes and driver- and passenger-side airbags were standard on all 1990

The Carrera 4, introduced in 1989, was the first of the 911 series to have a completely new chassis/floor pan, and had coil springs instead of torsion bars. Utilizing technology gained from development of the 959, the "C4" was the most sophisticated and complex Porsche ever made available to the general public as a production model. It has full-time four-wheel drive and anti-lock brakes. *Porsche A. G.*

Porsche models, and the Carrera 2 and 4 had force-sensitive power steering.

1991

Porsche introduced no changes to either its Carrera 2 or 4 for the 1991 model year but the company did resurrect a long-time sentimental—and performance enthusiast—favorite, the 911 Turbo. Discontinued from the end of 1989, the new model, turbocharged and intercooled, incorporated enough changes to the previous 3.3-liter engine that

Reminiscent of the 935 racing car, the 930 S "slant nose" body work was an option available for 1989 on production 911 Turbo Coupes and Cabriolets. This represented a $29,555 additional cost on top of the Turbo Coupe at $70,975 or the Cabriolet at $85,060. *Porsche Cars North America*

The 911 Carrera was offered in Coupe, Cabriolet and Targa body styles, with 214 horsepower on tap. With five-speed manual transmission, the cars were capable of 149 mph top speed, 0–60-mph in 6.1 seconds, and highway fuel economy of 24 mpg at the Federal 55 mph speed limit. *Porsche Cars North America*

Porsche introduced the rear-wheel-drive-only Carrera 2 in the fall of 1989 for model year 1990. Modifications and improvements to valve train, engine breathing and fuel injection, and ignition management brought power output up to 247 horsepower. The body designation was referred to in-house as the Type 964. *Porsche Cars North America.*

After a brief interruption, the Turbo returned in the 964 body style for 1991 with an additional 33 horsepower, bringing the total to 315. Engineers retained the intercooler to increase the density of the fuel mixture, partially accounting for the additional power. *Porsche Cars North America*

engineers coaxed 33 more horsepower out of the engine. Total horsepower was 315 with an equally impressive 332 lb-ft of torque. The turbocharger itself used a larger but lower mass turbine wheel to achieve higher peak boost and better response. Following boosting, the fuel mix passed through an air-to-air intercooler with much greater airflow efficiency than previously achieved. Then, in an intricate resculpting of intake passages and corners, engineers further refined and maximized intake air flow. After combustion, exhaust passed through a metal honeycomb catalytic converter, offering 30 percent reduction in back pressure.

Turbo brakes have always inspired enough confidence to allow their drivers to go fast. The new 911 Turbo was no exception. But the revised chassis and suspension, new to the Turbo and reminiscent of the innovations on the 964 Carrera 2 and 4 models, further helped keep the tires planted on the ground whether accelerating, cornering, or braking. Coil springs over tubular shocks were fitted on all four corners. A curious, variably limited-slip differential offered a simple mechanical control for slippage, varying between 20 percent on acceleration to 100 percent lock-up under severe braking. The variability allowed precise driver control under widely different vehicle dynamics. The 1991 911 Turbo sold for $95,000.

European Porsche buyers got an unusual Carrera, derived from the Porsche Carrera 2 Cup cars and named in honor of the legendary 1973 Carrera RS 2.7. This new car, called the 911 Carrera RS, developed 260 horsepower and was designed to be raced with a minimum of modification. Yet it was road legal—in Europe—as delivered. Porsche needed to produce 1,000 for homologation, to make it race legal, yet demand went far beyond that and 2,391 were assembled.

1992

Inspired by its North American racing history, Porsche produced a limited production 911 America Roadster, honoring the modest open cars from 1952 encouraged by American distributors Max Hoffmann and Johnny von Neumann.

It resembled a Turbo-Look Carrera 2 Cabriolet with fenders widened to accommodate 7x17 front wheels with 205/50ZR17 front tires and 9x17 rear wheels carrying 255/40ZR17s. The five-spoke wheels were developed for the international Porsche Carrera Cup series run throughout Europe. Front and rear brakes were similar to those large discs first used on the 917 race cars of the late 1960s competing at Le Mans. Front rotors were 12.68 inches in diameter and the rears were 11.77. The America Roadster sold for $87,900 with five-speed manual transmission or $91,050 with the Tiptronic. In the cockpit, besides a theft-coded digital display stereo cassette radio with six speakers, drivers could take advantage of a six-function computerized driver information center providing such information as instantaneous and average fuel economy, average speed, and distance to empty fuel tank.

Porsche made few changes, and only minor ones at that, to the Carrera 2 and 4 and to the 911 Turbo as well. Once again European customers benefited from more liberal vehicle codes and a lucky 80 individuals purchased an ultra-limited run of 911 Turbo S models. These 3.3-liter cars developed 376 SAE net horsepower, weighed just 2,844 pounds and were capable of 180 mph top speeds.

1993–1994

Porsche reintroduced a Speedster at the Detroit automobile show as a 1994 model. It was available either with the manual five-speed or Tiptronic four-speed automatic transmission. The company also brought out its new RS America (manual only). Mid-year, the company released its new 3.6-liter Turbo after a half-season interruption. Continuing in production were the Carrera 2 and 4 in their three body versions (closed, open and Targa), and the one-year-old America Roadster.

The 1994 Speedster was different from the limited run 1989 version or their predecessors from the mid-1950s. The new car, based on the Carrera 2 chassis, was fitted with Carrera 2 luxury including electric windows. The seats however, were thin, lightweight racing-type buckets. The top, more old than new, was raised or lowered by hand. Once retracted, it was stowed beneath a composite-material tonneau cover. It was introduced at $66,400 with the five-speed manual gearbox. It was available only on the standard C2 body; no Turbo-Look wide-body was offered.

The 1993 RS America was billed as a lower-priced 911 with the emphasis on performance and handling through its pure sports suspension, lighter weight, and limited option selection. Standard Recaro seats were covered in corduroy; sound-deadening material was deleted, as was the back seat; unadorned inner door panels had no map pockets or door handles. Opening was accomplished by pulling a simple nylon strap like the early 911 R and other racing models. The RS America was offered with only five options: air conditioning, manual sun roof, a limited slip differential, metallic paint, and a basic AM/FM cassette sound system. The car was equipped with the M030 sport suspension package and unassisted steering. Available as a coupe only, with a large, fixed rear spoiler, it was priced at $54,800, and sold only in the United States.

The new Turbo was announced in the United States at both the Los Angeles and Detroit auto shows in January 1993 as a 1994 model. Based on the Carrera 2 and 4 3.6-liter

Type 964 bodies, the Carrera 2 and 4 designation, were indistinguishable. A Carrera 2 Cabriolet sold for $70,690 while the C4 went for $82,215. Only the Carrera 2 was offered with the optional Tiptronic dual-function four-speed transmission. *Porsche Cars North America*

The 1992 911 Turbo coupe weighed in at 3274 pounds. However, with 315 horsepower and 332 lb-ft of torque, the 3.3-liter engine provided enough power to get the 911 Turbo to 60 miles per hour in just 4.8 seconds and to a top speed of 168 mph. *Porsche Cars North America*

engine, the turbocharged/intercooled version fired with 7.5:1 compression ratio and produced 355 horsepower at 5500 rpm. It covered 0-60 mph at 4.7 seconds and was capable of 174 mph. The new Turbo ran on 8x18 wheels up front with 225/40 ZR18 tires and 10x18s in back with 265/35s. Porsche reinforced the clutch but made no changes to the gear box or brakes for this new car, an indication of how much over-engineered many of Porsche's mechanical elements really were. The 3.6-liter Turbo was introduced at $99,000.

Beginning in 1993, Porsche Cars North America (PCNA) provided warranty coverage to make ownership of a "pre-owned" Porsche as trouble-free as possible. These warranties were available on any car built in

1986 or later with less than 125,000 miles on it. It was good for one year with unlimited mileage. It covered all major engine components and systems, complete transmission, constant velocity joints, axle shafts and torque tube(s), and much more. It is one of the reasons that Porsches since 1986 also rank well in star ratings. Driving pleasure is much enhanced with a warranty in the glove box.

In September 1993, Porsche recognized 30 years of producing 911s and announced that nearly 351,000 of the 911 and its variants had been produced in those three decades.

Porsche carried over the America Roadster until the end of 1993 model year but carried on with the RS America and the 911 Speedster through 1994. Prices held firm

Inspired by—and taking its name from—Porsche's 1952 U S. market special, designers and engineers basically worked from the platform of the C2 cabriolet to produced the limited edition open car. The America Roadster sold for $87,900 with the manual five-speed gear box. Its appearance was referred to as "turbo-look" because of its adoption of the wider rear track and ended wheel wells. *Porsche Cars North America*

The emphasis was on performance and handling with the RS America, through its standard-equipment sport suspension, lighter weight, and very limited option selection. Available only as a Coupe, the Recaro seats were covered in corduroy, the rear seats were replaced with a parcel shelf, most sound deadening material was removed. The rear wing was fixed and large. It was clearly inspired by and derived from the 1973 Carrera 2.7 RS. *Porsche Cars North America*

Introduced mid-year 1993, the 964-platform Speedster was a more luxurious version of its 1989 and 1954 predecessors. Strictly a two-seater like the Spartan RS America, the Speedster, however, offered a broad array of C2 luxury fittings and options. Even so, its slim top was hand-operated. *Porsche Cars North America*

even with significant, if sometimes indiscernible changes, especially in the Carrera 2 and 4. Beside the obvious addition of new colors from which to chose, below the surface the Carreras were stiffer, due to new chassis reinforcements and the use of thicker gauge metal in several key areas.

Porsche Credit Corporation, the financial arm of PCNA, introduced the Porsche Preferred Lease, including pre-owned 1991 through 1994 models. As with the warranty, this was a way of enticing new customers who might be unable to afford current new prices but whose business arrangements allow them to take advantage of leasing's financial and tax advantages.

1995

Porsche brought its 1995 911 Carrera to North American in early 1994. The car was heavily revised and improved under the skin and slightly so outside. Its in-house designation was the Typ 993. In terms of nomenclature, the Carrera 2 became the Carrera while the C4 continued but with numerous changes. Only Coupe and Cabriolet models were offered, the Targa discontinued in advance of a new version coming for 1996.

Porsche reexamined the entire drivetrain of the C4, looking for places to increase strength and reduce weight. Its stated goal was to further improve handling, to make it closer to those of the rear-drive Carrera and to bring these cars closer in weight despite the addition of all-wheel drive components. The engineers managed to remove 165 pounds, bringing the C4 to within 110 pounds of the two-wheel drive Carreras. As a result, acceleration performance and top speed are identical.

Porsche replaced the electro-hydraulic center differential of the previous C4 with a new, maintenance-free viscous-center clutch running in silicone fluid to control power distribution from front to rear wheels. It responds to power, rpm and temperature differences to vary the amount of slip between front and rear axles. If both rear wheels spin, the center clutch diverts more power to the front wheels. The electro-hydraulic rear differential also was replaced by a simpler mechanical locking rear

The 1989 Speedster was offered on both standard body and also on the "Turbo Look" body as an option. More than 90 percent of those were built on the wider body. No such option was offered for 1994 however, the composite-material tonneau cover was reintroduced to provide weather protection for the rear parcel shelf. *Porsche Cars North America*

The same engine offered for two years on C2 and C4 models of the 964 chassis arrived for the Turbo, introduced at both the Los Angeles and Detroit auto shows in January 1993. The slight increase in bore and stroke and raising the compression from 7.0 to 7.5:1 resulted in 40 more horsepower. The "tea tray" rear wing housed the air-to-air intercooler. *Porsche Cars North America*

end. It now provided 25 percent lock-up on acceleration and 40 percent while coasting or braking (compared to the previous unit's 100 percent under deceleration). This new system yielded "built-in" understeer in abrupt load changes, for example, lifting off the throttle in a turn. (This "plowing sensation" is exactly the opposite of Porsche's

Butzi Porsche's simple, pure lines, caught in golden light photography, reveal a clean, elegant form that his successors Tony Lapine and Harm Lagaay respected through their successive terms as chief of design. The subtly evolved Type 964 in the foreground barely hints at the enormous engineering and technological differences below the surface. *Porsche Cars North America*

Known internally as the Type 993, the new Carreras further integrated "family identity" in the front and rear end treatments, in which their similarity to the 928 and 968 was a carefully developed undertaking. New composite filament headlights lay flatter against the body, yet provide more piercing illumination. *Porsche Cars North America*

legendary tail-happiness. It was one more step toward making the car enjoyable and predictable for a broader audience.)

The new viscous-center clutch and rear differential instantaneously sent power to the wheels with the most traction. The rear end work was aided by Porsche's new Automatic Brake Differential (ABD). ABD was standard equipment on the C4 and is optional on the Carrera. If, despite the action of the mechanical limited slip unit (which after all, has only 25 percent lock-up), wheel spin was detected at one of the rear wheels, the ABD diverted power to the other side. Primarily a traction aid for starting on slippery surfaces, the system became inactive above 44 mph. Driving with ABD was different from driving with a conventional differential or any other traction control system because this one did not reduce engine power. It sensed rear wheel spin and applied rear wheel brakes as needed to provide the maximum amount of traction, reducing the force at the tire contact patch to the limit of what the surface will sustain. With the C4, more of the power was automatically transferred to the front drive. Maximum traction at all times was what it was all about.

For the Carrera (formerly the Carrera 2), the wonderful double function automatic transmission returned as the Tiptronic S. (This automatic was still available only for the rear-wheel drive Carrera.) While gear selection was still controlled on the center console, it also could be operated in manual mode from a pair of rocker switches in the steering wheel spokes, very similar to existing Formula One racing technology. In addition, engineers remapped the shift points and the transmission's five shift programs to improve performance, fuel economy, and riding and driving comfort. Compared to the 1994 C2, the Tiptronic S spent a greater proportion of its time with the torque converter clutch locked. The remapping also more accurately triggered downshifts in automatic mode by braking, ensuring that proper gear selection was made for subsequent cornering.

For both Carrera and C4, Porsche had a new six-speed manual transaxle. It improved fuel economy, although engineers lowered the gearing in fourth and fifth, which resulted in better throttle response at higher speeds. At the other end, new dual cone synchronizers for first and second gears reduced shift effort by 30 to 40 percent.

The 3.6-liter Carrera engine was extensively redeveloped, the goals being to reduce moving mass within the engine, thereby increasing power, optimizing fuel consumption, improving serviceability, and reducing manufacturing cost. Engineers decreased valve train mass using lighter valves with thinner stems, lighter valve springs, washers and retainers, and lighter rocker arms. They located the hydraulic valve lifters in the tips of the rocker arms, completely eliminating the need for periodic valve adjustment. They changed to lighter connecting rods and pistons, having reworked the crankshaft counter weights, which resulted in increased stiffness, they revised the crankshaft

pulley and deleted the vibration damper. They revised the dual exhaust system to reduce back pressure yet decrease noise, accomplishing these two seemingly contradictory goals using acoustic design principles; and they went to composite valve covers, timing chain covers, and intake manifold. As a result, engine output increased to 272 horsepower at 6100 rpm and 243 lb-ft of torque at 5000 rpm. Both Carrera and C4 claimed top speeds of 179 mph. Acceleration to 60 mph took 5.5 seconds in the C4 and 5.6

The now, five-speed, dual-function clutchless manual/automatic transaxle for the Carrera introduced a new wrinkle beginning in 1995. The S-version introduced steering wheel shifting, accomplished by two small toggles on the spokes of the steering wheel at about 10 and 2; rocking toward the + brought an up shift, - brought the transmission down a gear. *Porsche Cars North America*

The new six-speed manual transmission and the Automatic Brake Differential (ABD) are standard in this technological mix. A maintenance-free viscous clutch controls power distribution between front and rear axles. The ABD is supplemented at rear by a conventional rear locking differential that builds in predictable understeer in certain severe handling maneuvers. *Porsche Cars North America*

Reintroduced for 1996, the Targa has come a long way since Butzi Porsche introduced a stainless steel roll-over bar as a method of introducing additional stiffness to Porsche 911s without roofs. Now, the roof, a light-sensitive piece of glass, slides back inside the rear window. *Porsche Cars North America*

It is an engineering tour de force, one more among many from a company that seems to delight in technical challenges. With the roof open, there is less wind noise and buffeting than if one drove with a side window open. Yet, closed up, weather sealing is complete. The Targa was introduced for $70,750 with the manual six-speed. *Porsche Cars North America*

in the Carrera 6-speed while the quarter mile needed 13.9 in the Carrera and 14.0 seconds in the C4.

Holding the car to the road, Porsche revised the front suspension and completely redesigned the rear, using a new multi-link, sub-frame mounted system furthering the Weissach suspension first developed for the 928. Under cornering forces, the camber of the rear wheels changed to improve grip: the outside rear wheel toed in, the inside wheel toed out. This new suspension permitted lateral acceleration in excess of 1.0g on high traction surfaces and allowed five percent higher slalom speeds than the 1994 models.

At front, additional use of aluminum reduced unsprung weight, and along with other subtle changes, it improved wheel control, straight-line and braking stability (under adverse conditions) and reduced steering wheel kickback on rough roads while further refining road feel.

The brake system also was extensively revised, introducing the new Bosch ABS 5 three-channel anti-lock system, incorporating cross-drilled rotors; larger, thicker front rotors with a 45 percent increase in front brake pad swept area.

Finally, the car body received extensive changes while still maintaining the shape outline that Butzi Porsche created more than 30 years earlier. Ellipsoid headlights were integrated into the ever-present stove pipe

The Turbo Look is back. Rear track swelled 1.3 inches and overall width grew 2.5 inches between the Carrera 4 and its more aggressive successor, the 4S. Standard rear tires were 285/30ZR18s, wider even than previous C4 options. The 4S was offered only as a Coupe. *Porsche Cars North America*

fenders; rear quarter windows and the back window were fitted flush; the extendible rear spoiler was enlarged and reshaped; the underbody sheathing was revised to improve aerodynamics, and dozens of small details were improved. Inside, a new Digital Sound Processing system offered a ten-speaker full-function sound system for Coupes (eight speakers in Cabriolets), which digitally delayed the signal to individual speakers to produce the desired acoustic image. Designers and engineers provided a new steering wheel, door panels with increased storage and better speaker location, new seats with flatter seams and improved thigh support, and 20 percent more storage volume in the front trunk.

Perhaps the most astonishing news for 1995 was that, despite the literally hundreds of developments, improvements, and upgrades, the prices were unchanged or even reduced from 1994. The Carrera coupe still was listed at $51,900. The C4 Coupe went down from $78,450 to $65,900. The C4 Cabriolet was returned to the lineup at $74,200 while the Carrera Cabriolet was reduced from $74,190 for 1994 to $68,200 for 1995.

1996

As if there wasn't enough new for 1995, Porsche introduced three vehicles to the U.S. market for 1996 that sent magazine writers and Porsche enthusiasts into a frenzy. Besides retaining the recently heavily revised Carrera and C4 Coupe and Cabriolet, the company launched a new Targa with a retractable glass roof joined by a muscular Carrera 4S with a squat, wide Turbo-appearance, and a new all-wheel drive Turbo, clearly mechanically inspired by the previously unobtainable 959.

The new Targa featured an arched glass roof, tinted for privacy and treated to block out 100 percent of the ultra-violet rays. The two-section roof slid open. The smaller front piece rose to become a wind deflector while the larger rear section rolled back and was stowed inside the rear glass. On the Targa, first introduced in 1965 and produced through 1994, was a removable roof-panel that was mounted between the windshield and the wide B-pillar. Early Targas had a removable, foldable plastic rear window while later models used solid glass with built in defogging. Because of attention to air flow, the new Targa with its roof open was quieter inside than a Coupe with its sun roof open. The new glass-roofed Targa was introduced at $70,750.

The Carrera 4S adopted not only Turbo front, rear, and side body panels but also the same vented, four-piston disc brakes. It was powered by the standard Carrera 282 horsepower boxer engine using the Varioram induction system consisting of variable-length intake pipes and separate, differently tuned air intake systems. Sliding sleeves and flaps operated through various engine speed ranges, the result being increased torque and power

Introduced at $105,000, it was often the case that dealers added on substantial premiums to buyers interested in the newest generation Turbo. After all, with all-wheel drive and 400 horsepower, it was nine-tenths of the unobtainable Type 959 for less than half the price. This was a car that makes lottery investments seem rational. *Porsche Cars North America*

Carrera 4 (C4: 1990–1995), Carrera 2 (C2: 1990–1994), Carrera (1995)

Engine
Design:..........................Air-cooled flat (opposed) six-cylinder
Bore x stroke, mm/inches:....................100x76.4 / 3.94x3.01
Displacement, cc/cubic inches: ....3601 / 219.7
Valve operation:.................(1990) single overhead camshaft, chain driven, solid lifters; two spark plugs per cylinder
Compression ratio: ....(1990)11.3:1
Carburetion:
1990–1994 ....Digital Motor Electronics (DME) fuel injection
1995–1995..DME fuel injection with dual ignition systems with two-stage resonance induction and hot film air flow sensors
BHP (Mfr.):
1990–1994 ....247 @ 6100
1995–1995 ....272 @ 6100

Chassis & Drivetrain
Frame:
1990–1991 ....Unitized, steel
1992–1995..........................Unitized, fully-galvanized steel
Component Layout:
C4 (1990–1991) ....Rear engine, all-wheel drive with differential clutch actuation
C2...Rear engine, rear wheel drive
C4 (1992–1994).......Rear-engine, electronically controlled, hydraulically actuated full-time all-wheel-drive with automatic front-to-rear and side-to-side torque split
C4 (1995–1995) ....Rear engine, six-speed transaxle, full-time all-wheel drive with limited slip differential and automatic brake differential traction system
Transmission:
1990–1994...................Five-speed manual (C4 & C2)
1991–1995 ....Four-speed Tiptronic C2 only
1995–1995..Six-speed manual
Axle ratio:
C4 (1990–1995)...3.44:1 (manual)
C2 (1991–1994) ....3.67:1 Tiptronic
C2 (1992–1995)..............3.33:1 (manual) 3.56:1 Tiptronic
Rear suspension: C4..........................Independent with cast aluminum semi-trailing arms, coil springs, stabilizer bar
Front suspension: C4 ....Independent struts with lower wishbones,coil springs, stabilizer bar

General
Wheelbase, mm/inches: ....2272 / 89.4
Track: Front, mm/inches:
C4 & C2: (1990–1993) ....1380 / 54.3
C4 (1994–1995) ....1434 / 56.5
Rear, mm/inches:
C4 & C2: (1990–1993) ....1374 / 54.1
C4: (1994–1995) ....1493 / 58.8
Brakes:.................Hydraulically power-assisted, dual circuit, four piston, fixed calipers, anti-lock system
Tire size, front & rear:
1990–1993...............................205/55ZR16 / 225/50ZR16
C4 (1994–1994) ....205/50ZR17 / 255/40ZR17
Wheels, front & rear:
1990–1993..6Jx16; 8Jx16
C4 (1994–1994) 7Jx17; 9Jx17
Weight:
C4 coupe (1990–1992):..3252
C4 coupe (1993)..3362
C4 coupe (1994)..3340
C2 coupe (1990–1992):..3031
C2 coupe (1993–)
C2 coupe (1991–1992):..........................3097 with Tiptronic
C2 coupe (1993–).......................................Body builder

through the 2500 to 4500 rpm engine mid range. This translated to more comfortable everyday driving in traffic due to the engine's broader pulling power. The Carrera 4S was listed at $73,000, available as a Coupe only.

After 21 years of continued development and racing experience, the 1996 Turbo brought to U.S. buyers the phenomenal performance potential of the 959 from a decade earlier, yet at half the price, $105,000 for the 911 versus about 200,000 1987 dollars for the 959. A six-speed transmission, standard in Carrera and C4 models and introduced a decade earlier in the 959, was the only gearbox for the Turbo. But unlike the 959s, all six gears are road gears. The lowest gear in the 959 was a creeper gear, really meant for international rally conditions for extricating the car from sand, mud or snow. The previous Turbo developed 355 horsepower and weighed 3,284 pounds; this new Turbo weighed 3,307 pounds, just 33 more than the previous model (even with its all-wheel drive and other equipment). It was only 337 pounds more than the 959; it had 400 horsepower compared to the 959's 450, yet this

new car was a "real world" automobile. The 959 made no compromises in body material or structural materials, and as a result, any repair was extremely costly. The Turbo, on the other hand, could realistically be used as a daily driver. In an environmentally responsible stance, Porsche engineers created the new Turbo engine to meet U.S. emissions standards several years away.

At the 1996 Los Angeles Auto Show, Hans Riedel, Porsche AG Board Member for Marketing, announced that the company had experienced a 50 percent sales increase, to 17,900 units, in 1995. This he attributed not only to continuing to produce a unique product but also one that was now manufactured much more efficiently. He expressed the company's concern that the sports car market has decreased by 50 percent between 1991 and 1996, and hinted that, as a result, "Porsche will not *just* build uncompromising sports cars but offer other exciting concepts that: fit the Porsche image; tap 'best potential' segments in the automotive market; and broaden Porsche's 'footprint' in our sports car core business. These concepts are beyond

---

911 America Roadster (1992–1993)
911 Speedster (1993–1994)
RS America (1993–1994)

Engine
Design:.......................Air-cooled, flat (opposed) six-cylinder
Bore x stroke, mm/inches:....................100x76.4 / 3.94x3.01
Displacement, cc/cubic inches: ....3299 / 219.7
Valve operation: ....Single overhead cam, chain
driven, solid lifters.
Compression ratio: 11.3:1
Carburetion: ....DME fuel injection and ignition systems
BHP (Mfr.):..247 @ 6100

Chassis & Drivetrain
Frame:.....................................Unitized, full-galvanized steel
Component Layout: ....Rear engine, rear wheel drive
Transmission:.......................Five-speed manual transaxle or
Tiptronic dual function four speed
(manual only RS America)
Axle ratio:.................................3.33:1 manual; 3.56 Tiptronic
Rear suspension:........................Independent with aluminum
alloy semi-trailing arms, self-stabilizing
toe-characteristics, coil springs, stabilizer bar
Front suspension: ....Independent MacPherson struts
with aluminum alloy lower control arms,
coil springs, stabilizer bar

General
Wheelbase, mm/inches: ....2272 / 89.4
Track: Front, mm/inches:
    America Roadster..1435 / 56.5
    RS America, Speedster.....................................1374 / 54.1
Rear, mm/inches:
    America Roadster..1494 / 58.8
    RS America, Speedster.....................................1374 / 54.1
Brakes: ....Hydraulically power-assisted
dual circuit four piston aluminum alloy
fixed calipers, anti-lock braking system
Tire size: front & rear:
America Roadster,
 RS America, Speedster:.............205/50ZR17 / 255/40ZR17
Wheels, front & rear:
    America Roadster.....................................7Jx17; 9Jx17
    RS America, Speedster..................................7Jx17; 8Jx17
Weight:
    America Roadster: ....3164 manual; 3230 tiptronic
    RS America 2954
    Speedster................................3031 manual; 3097 tiptronic

---

drawing board stage and will dramatically change Porsche as a company in the near future." (He was speaking at the time of a joint marketing project with Mercedes-Benz in which Porsche dealers would distribute the top-end M-class sport utility as a Porsche-badged and assembled vehicle. Mercedes' dealers were displeased and by the end of January 1997, the plan had collapsed.)

Riedel's near future is, of course, the coming model year, 1998, when Porsche will introduce its water-cooled 911/964-993 successor, the Typ 996. It is, of course, an uncompromising sports car. Artist renderings and spy photos already have indicated what it will look like. People who have driven the Boxster have an inkling of what its engine will be like.

Cynics and skeptics who decry change are already wailing over the end of air-cooled Porsche engines. Those who care are running to dealers to buy the last of the air-cooled Porsches. Yet a number of seasoned Porsche observers caution that it's important to remember that these new cars were designed and engineered by the same people who brought the 993 to the market. Each successive 993-based vehicle was a better car than the one immediately before it. There's no reason to believe the new Typ 996 will not continue that trend.

Carrera Coupe, Cabriolet (1996),
911 Carrera Targa (1996–1997),
911 Carrera S (1997)

Engine
Design: ....Air-cooled flat (opposed) six cylinder
Bore x stroke, mm/inches: ....100x76.4 / 3.94x3.01
Displacement, cc/cubic inches: ....3601 / 219.7
Valve operation: ....Single overhead camshaft, chain driven, hydraulic lifters.
Compression ratio: 11.3:1
Carburetion: ....DME fuel injection with dual ignition systems, with Varioram three-stage resonance induction and hot film air flow sensors, electronically controlled
BHP (Mfr.): ....282 @ 6300

Chassis & Drivetrain
Frame: ....Unitized, fully galvanized steel
Component Layout: ....Rear engine, rear wheel drive
Transmission: ....Six speed manual transaxle or four speed Tiptronic S dual function transaxle
Axle ratio: ....3.44:1 manual; 3.56;1 Tiptronic
Rear suspension: ....Independent multi-link with LSA, self-stabilizing toe characteristics, stabilizer bar
Front suspension: ....Independent MacPherson struts with aluminum alloy lower control arms, coil springs, stabilizer bar

General
Wheelbase, mm/inches: ....2272 / 89.5
Track: Front, mm/inches:
  Coupe, Targa ....1405 / 55.3
  Carrera S ....1411 / 55.6
Rear, mm/inches:
  Coupe ....1444 / 56.9
  Targa ....1474 / 58.0
  Carrera S ....1504 / 59.3
Brakes: ....Power-assisted, dual circuit, four-piston aluminum alloy fixed caliper, anti-lock braking system
Tire size, front & rear:
  Coupe: ....205/55ZR16 / 245/45ZR16
  Targa and Carrera S: ....205/50ZR17 / 255/40ZR17
Wheels, front & rear:
  Coupe: 7Jx16; 9Jx16
  Targa and Carrera S: 7Jx17; 9Jx17
Weight:
  Coupe ....3064 manual, 3120 Tiptronic
  Targa ....3130 manual, 3186 Tiptronic
  Carrera S............................3198 manual, 3254 Tiptronic

911 Carrera 4S (1996–1997), 911 Carrera 4 Cabriolet (1996–1997)

Engine

Design: ....Air-cooled flat (opposed) six cylinder
Bore x stroke, mm/inches: ....100x76.4 / 3.94x3.01
Displacement, cc/cubic inches: 3601/219.7
Valve operation: ....Single overhead camshaft, chain driven, hydraulic lifters
Compression ratio: 11.3:1
Carburetion: ....DME fuel injection with dual ignition systems, with Varioram three-stage resonance induction and hot film air flow sensors, electronically controlled
BHP (Mfr.): ....282 @ 6300

Chassis & Drivetrain

Frame: ....Unitized, fully galvanized steel
Component Layout: ....Rear engine, full-time all-wheel-drive with limited slip differential and automatic brake differential (ABD) traction system
Transmission: ....Six speed manual transaxle
Axle ratio: 3.44:1
Rear suspension: ....Independent multi-link with LSA, self-stabilizing toe characteristics, stabilizer bar
Front suspension: ....Independent MacPherson struts with aluminum alloy lower control arms, coil springs, stabilizer bar

General

Wheelbase, mm/inches: ....2272 / 89.5
Track: Front, mm/inches:
    Cabrio ....1405 / 55.3
    4S ....1411 / 55.6
Rear, mm/inches:
    Cabrio ....1474 / 58.0
    4S ....1504 / 59.3
Brakes: ....Power-assisted, dual circuit, four-piston aluminum alloy fixed caliper, anti-lock braking system
Tire size, front & rear:
    Cabrio ....205/50ZR17 / 255/40 ZR17
    4S ....225/40ZR18 / 285/30ZR18
Wheels, front & rear:
    Cabrio 7Jx17; 9Jx17
    4S 8Jx18; 10Jx18
Weight:
    Cabrio 3175
    4S 319
    Targa (1996–1997) ....3186 Tiptronic

911 Turbo 3.3 (1991–1992), 911 Turbo 3.6 (1994)

Engine

Design: ....Air-cooled flat (opposed) six-cylinder with KKK exhaust turbocharger
Bore x stroke, mm/inches:
    (1991–1992) ....97x74.4 / 3.82x2.93
    (1994) ....100x76.4 / 3.94x3.01
Displacement, cc/cubic inches:
    (1991–1992) 3299/201.3
    (1994) 3601/219.7
Valve operation: ....Single overhead camshaft, chain driven, hydraulic lifters
Compression ratio:
    (1991–1992) 7:0:1
    (1994) 7.5:1
Carburetion: ....Bosch K-Jetronic fuel injection with air-to-air intercooler
BHP (Mfr.):
    (1991–1992) ....315 @ 5750
    (1994) ....355 @ 5500

Chassis & Drivetrain

Frame: ....Unitized, fully galvanized, steel
Component Layout: ......Rear engine, rear-wheel drive, with torque-controlled, variable-ratio limited slip differential
Transmission: ....Six speed manual transaxle
Axle ratio: ....3.44:1 manual
Rear suspension: ....Independent with aluminum-alloy semi-trailing arms, coil springs, self-stabilizing toe characteristics, stabilizer bar
Front suspension: ....Independent MacPherson struts with aluminum alloy lower control arms, coil springs, stabilizer bar, negative steering roll radius

General

Wheelbase, mm/inches: ....2272 / 89.5
Track: Front, mm/inches:
    (1991–1992) ....1435 / 56.5
    (1994) ....1442 / 56.8
rear, mm/inches:
    (1991–1992) ....1494 / 58.8
    (1994) ....1488 / 58.6
Brakes: ....Power-assisted, dual circuit, four-piston aluminum alloy fixed caliper, anti-lock braking system
Tire size, front & rear: 205/50ZR78, 255/40ZR17
Wheels, front & rear: 7Jx17, 9Jx17
Weight: ....3274 lbs

911 Turbo (1997); 911 Turbo S (1997)

Engine
Design: ....Air-cooled flat (opposed) six cylinder with dual exhaust turbochargers
Bore x stroke, mm/inches: ....100x76.4 / 3.94x3.01
Displacement, cc/cubic inches:.........................3601/219.7
Valve operation:.........................Single overhead camshaft, chain driven, hydraulic lifters
Compression ratio:.....................................8.0:1
Carburetion:.......................DME fuel injection with hot film air flow sensor
BHP (Mfr.):...Turbo 400 @ 5750
Turbo S 424 @ 5750

Chassis & Drivetrain
Frame:................................Unitized, fully galvanized, steel
Component Layout: ....Rear engine, full-time all-wheel-drive with limited slip differential and automatic brake differential (ABD) traction system
Transmission: ....Six speed manual transaxle
Axle ratio: ....3.44:1 manual
Rear suspension:.............Independent multi-link with LSA, self-stabilizing toe characteristics , stabilizer bar.
Front suspension: ....Independent MacPherson struts with aluminum alloy lower control arms, coil springs, stabilizer bar.

General
Wheelbase, mm/inches:....................................2272 / 89.5
Track: Front, mm/inches: ....1411 / 55.6
Rear, mm/inches:..1504 / 59.3
Brakes: Power-assisted, dual circuit, four-piston aluminum alloy fixed caliper, anti-lock braking system
Tire size, front & rear: 225/40ZR18, 285/30ZR18
Wheels, front & rear: 8Jx18, 10Jx18
Weight:..3307 lbs

Never content, Porsche provided the wide, sure-footed stance of the 911 Turbo and Carrera 4S to buyers of the rear-wheel drive version beginning in 1997. Introduced at the New York Auto Show, the new S-model offers all the options of the normal Carrera, including Tiptronic S steering-wheel shifting. Suggested retail was $63,750. *Porsche Cars North America*

Imagine times when 400 horsepower in an all-wheel drive, 3300-pound car was inadequate? Porsche had an answer, however fewer than 200 of you were able to acquire the 424 horsepower 3300 pound Turbo S. This legitimate successor to the Type 959 sold for $150,000. Considering Porsche's technological advances in the decade since the 959 inspired lust in enthusiasts' hearts, this new Turbo S was undoubtedly an even better automobile. A more pronounced chin spoiler and a bi-plane-wing rear spoiler, as well as the *turbo s* designation on the rear deck, helped identify the car. *Porsche Cars North America*

1997

Porsche added a rear-drive version of the wide-bodied S, the Carrera S, for the 1997 model year. Buyers could order the S with either the six-speed manual or five-speed Tiptronic S. Among its most distinctive features were its split, body-colored air inlet grille in the rear spoiler and the name *Carrera S* in steel grey script on the engine cover. Engineers fitted the Carrera S with 17-inch Carrera Cup wheels as standard equipment, adding Porsche crests to the wheel centers. Rear hubs rode on 31 mm spacers to widen the track. That wider bodywork limited the car's top speed to 168 mph, 3 mph slower than the standard Carrera body. Porsche sold the Carrera S for $73,650, a price that was $650 higher than the all-wheel-drive C4S model at $73,000. The C4S and the rest of the model line held their prices unchanged from 1996.

1998

The final model year for the 993 series saw no changes to bodies, engines, running gear, or options. Porsche introduced a more potent Turbo, the Turbo S, selling for $150,000 compared to $105,000 for the Turbo. Engineers fitted the S with twin K-24 turbochargers and performed several electronic tweaks to the Motronic engine management system. Engine output reached 424 horsepower for U.S. models, 450 for those in the rest of the world. The larger turbochargers and the all-leather and carbon-fiber interior reportedly added about 65 pounds to the vehicle weight, taking the normal Turbo at 3,307 pounds up to roughly 3,372 pounds. Porsche manufactured a total of 345 Turbo S models, some appearing in the late 1997 model year. The company ended production of the 993 models in July 1998, having manufactured more than 72,500 of the cars.

This 1998 Carrera S adopted the distinctive front-end treatment of the 911 Turbo. As Porsche introduced the new water-cooled 996, it kept the air-cooled 993 Targa, Turbo, Carrera S, and 4S in production.

One distinctive feature of the Carrera S and 4S models was the divided grille on the engine lid. These two models also used Turbo wheels and tires. Using the Turbo body—without the wing—gave the back the wider wheel track as well.

Buying Notes

At the 1996 Los Angeles Auto Show, Hans Riedel, Porsche AG board member for marketing, announced that the company had experienced a 50 percent sales increase in 1995 to 17,900 units. He attributed this not only to continuing to offer a unique product but also one that the Zuffenhausen assemblers manufactured much more efficiently. He expressed the company's concern that the sports car market fell by half between 1991 and 1996, and hinted that as a result, "Porsche will not *just* build uncompromising sports cars but offer other exciting concepts that fit the Porsche image, tap 'best potential' segments in the automotive market, and broaden Porsche's 'footprint' in our sports car core business. These concepts," he added, "are beyond drawing board stage and will dramatically change Porsche as a company in the near future."

He was speaking at the time of the joint marketing project with Mercedes-Benz where Porsche dealers would distribute a top-end M-class sport utility as a Porsche-badged and -assembled vehicle. Please see Chapter 18 for the story.

Riedel's "near future" was the coming model year, 1998, when Porsche introduced its water-cooled 911/993 successor, the Typ 996. It proved to be a somewhat compromised sports car. But the choices Porsche made were smart and shrewd. As successful as the 993 series was, the 996 brought tens of thousands of first-time Porsche buyers into the family.

Cynics and skeptics who decried change already were wailing over the end of air-cooled Porsche engines. Those who cared ran to dealers to buy the last of the air-cooled Porsches. Yet Porsche's final air-cooled series, the 993, was not without problems. The 993

Porsche gave the Carrera S and 4S models distinctive oval gearshift knobs and painted the bezel on the hand brake as well as the instrument trim rings and door sills steel gray. Inner door panels were a textured black leather.

The flat-six 3.6-liter engine developed 285 horsepower, making use of the innovative VarioRam induction system. Acceleration from 0 to 62 mph took 5.3 seconds.

Carrera S models used 17-inch "Cup" wheels carrying 205/50 ZR 17 tires on the front and 255/40 tires on the rear. Optional wheels included 17-inch "Targa" wheels and 18-inch Turbo wheels.

engines carried over the 964 dual-distributor system, driven by a rubber belt. If this belt breaks, the engine runs badly because one distributor is working while the other has stopped on one plug, firing it repeatedly. This could burn a hole in a piston or cylinder wall. If the engine begins to run badly, shut it off immediately.

The 993 engine valve guides wear, allowing lubricating and cooling oil to seep along the valve stem and into the engine. Combustion burns this oil, leaving a sooty residue on exhaust valves and emissions control equipment like the secondary air injection pump used to quickly heat catalytic converters. Burnt oil residue can block the pump and can plug entire exhaust runners. Monitor systems will trigger "fault codes" but often not before much of the system is blocked. Such an engine would not pass smog certification tests in most states requiring them. Removing this residue is very costly.

Engine valve covers can leak. Distributor caps and rotors can fail. The engine wiring harness was improperly insulated, so engine heat could fry wires. Flywheel seals (the rear main engine seal) can leak. The gear selector shaft seal can leak. The steering rack can leak.

With the cabriolet, be certain the Cabriolet Top Service Action has been performed.

The 993s are the most preferred model for many enthusiasts and loyalists. As the last of the air-cooled engines, they offered the engine sound many people prefer. They are handsome and nimble, fun to drive, and a pleasure to own *if* you get a good one. Be sure to have a thorough pre-purchase inspection performed before buying any Porsche and especially a 993 or later model. Expect to pay $200 to as much as $750 for this inspection. What you learn will help you make an intelligent purchase and could save you much more.

Chapter 16

986 Boxster

★	1997–2000 Boxster
★1/2	2000 Boxster S
★1/2	2001–2002 Boxster
★★1/2	2001–2002 Boxster S
★★1/2	2003–2004 Boxster
★★1/2	2003–2004 Boxster S
★★★1/2	2003 50th Anniversary Commemorative
★★1/2	2005–2006 Boxster
★★★1/2	2005–2006 Boxster S
★★★1/2	2007–2008 Boxster
★★★1/2	2007–2008 Boxster S
★★★1/2	2009 Boxster
★★★★	2009 Boxster S

1989

By 1989, Porsche had three distinct model lines with virtually no common parts, a legacy of Ernst Fuhrmann who commissioned cars to replace the 911. By this time, Fuhrmann had retired, and engineer Horst Marchardt had risen through Porsche's ranks to manage new-car development, answering to engineering director Ulrich Bez. Marchardt had joined Porsche in 1960 as a graduate engineer, and he assisted Helmuth Bott in developing the 901/911. Under Bez, a new strategic philosophy emerged, seeking additional applications for any research and development program. Commonality of parts between car lines would reduce manufacturing costs.

The most expensive part of new automobiles is the front end, which requires crash-testing. This area contains the steering, the instrument panel, and all controls for driving, heating, air-conditioning, entertainment, and navigation, as well as door frames and the doors themselves. Marchardt envisioned not merely common parts but common assemblies: He wondered if Porsche could share chassis development—design, testing, crashing, and parts sourcing—over two separate car models. With this idea barely more than a concept, October 1991 served as a pivotal time for Porsche.

1991

Design director Harm Lagaay attended the Tokyo Motor Show with Arno Bohn, Porsche's new chairman, who was a businessman but not a car guy. Bohn asked Lagaay why other manufacturers showed futuristic concepts but Porsche did not?

"Just ask me," Lagaay replied. Bohn asked, and Lagaay started the process from his hotel room that evening, challenging his designers visiting the show and those back at the studio in Weissach. A fax machine in his room ran all night as his staff forwarded their ideas. Lagaay awoke to find a roll of concept sketches.

At breakfast, Lagaay presented his favorite, and Bohn approved. Lagaay launched the project but alerted only those who could authorize a small budget. Few people in Weissach knew about it.

Meanwhile Horst Marchardt had accepted a Porsche board seat two weeks before the Tokyo show. His idea of making two different cars using the same front end had become a plan, and as a board member he moved it forward. Along with Bohn's show car, Lagaay found himself assigned to design two new car lines as well. One updated the 911/993, and the second would be an entry-level car below the 911. The plan to make two cars with one face was born. In early 1992, Lagaay, desiring a variety of ideas, staffed three studios with two designers each, working side by side on full-size concepts, one on the entry-level Typ 986, another on the 911 Typ 996.

From the design concept car in 1993 through its entire production run, the Boxster has only been a roadster with a steel body on a welded central box structure. The production car grew substantially in size from the concept because of safety and engine cooling considerations.

Arno Bohn had authorized Grant Larson's proposal for a show car. The inspiration for his show car, he explained a decade later, came from the RSK, the 550 Spyder successor. "We wanted to do a car," Larson explained, "that was not so futuristic that it would be uncomfortable to look at but also not retro, a car that defies a definition of time or style trend." As that project moved forward, Lagaay teamed Larson, an American from Milwaukee with a degree in automotive design from the Art Center College of Design in Pasadena, California, with Pinky Lai, a Chinese native of Hong Kong who had earned an industrial design degree in Rome and an automobile design degree at the Royal College of Art in London. Larson split his time finishing the show car and working with Lai on the new production cars. In the end, Lagaay chose their ideas, and both men started creating two cars from the same front end.

Lagaay took Larson's show car to Detroit. In those days, the organizers allocated space based on U.S. sales. Porsche got a small, dark corner because show management reckoned the company was on its last legs. Management was nervous. The night before the introduction, U.S. distributor Fred Schwab organized a so-called "crisis meeting." They wrote down every difficult question they could anticipate: "What will Porsche do when it goes bankrupt? What happens to American customers when you are finished and gone?"

The press conference was packed. Every journalist wanted to witness what might be Porsche's last auto show in North America as an independent or as an automaker at all.

"There were hundreds of journalists," Harm Lagaay recalled years later. "All our people had prepared their answers to all these terrible questions. And when Fred Schwab finished his remarks, he asked if anyone had questions."

"What's under the cover?" That was the first and only question that ever got out. The answer was Larson's show car, named the "Boxster" in a marathon brainstorming session by designer Steve Murkett who combined the Boxer nickname for the flat-six engine with the word "Speedster." The car was an instant and huge hit. Journalists loved it. Newspapers, magazines, and television shows featured it. Detroit-area

Among the Boxster's clever innovations were its integral dual-hoop roll bars. Porsche offered standard seats (shown here) and sport seats with greater side support for the car.

The Boxster's mid-engine provided the car with exemplary handling. The aerodynamic drag on this cleanly styled body was just 0.31. The base model's water-cooled flat-six developed 204 horsepower.

dealers worked the stand through the next week and recorded deposits from people who demanded they be first on a waiting list even though no one could promise the car would reach production.

After the media left the stand, Lagaay phoned the studio. The car had rekindled interest in Porsche. The company was not dead; it had this great Boxster. While Larson was thrilled, it didn't lessen the challenge he and Lai faced back home. Their styling themes for the 986 and 996 weren't working. Lai and Larson were days away from scrapping their concepts and starting fresh. Complicating things, the Boxster was a tiny show car while the 986 was midsized and the 996 had to be a full-size 911. Lagaay suggested the two men take the Boxster design and enlarge all the proportions 20 percent to make the new 986, then share the show car front-end treatment with the 996. With the popularity of the Boxster and the warm reception Wendelin Wiedeking and others had in Detroit, Lagaay argued he might find money to solve the aerodynamic problems that plagued Lai with the 996 body.

These new cars were no less challenging for the engine and chassis developers. Porsche engineers knew that future

standards for noise and noxious emissions complicated their efforts to offer a stronger, faster, and more fuel-efficient engine than the company's previous model.

For the 986, Porsche's project manager for the Boxster-line powertrain and supervisory board member Jürgen Kapfer devised one of the company's most innovative flat-sixes. Some engineers believed no further improvement was possible for these engines. Others

Porsche brought out a base Boxster and a more potent Boxster S when the company introduced the car in 1997. The 2000 Boxster S, shown here, used a newly introduced water-cooled 3.2-liter flat six that developed 252 horsepower. *Photo courtesy Porsche Cars North America*

For 2000, Porsche gave the Boxster soft-top a new fabric headliner to further insulate the car from wind noise and temperature variations. Boxster S models also used twin exhaust tips rather than the large single tip found on base models. *Photo courtesy Porsche Cars North America*

Just visible at the far right is a new lockable glove box, a first for the Boxster, introduced for 2003. The car was available with either Porsche's six-speed manual gearbox or the five-speed Tiptronic. *Photo courtesy Porsche Cars North America*

advocated four-valve technology. In experiments with aluminum four-valve cylinder heads, a group of engineers nearly melted the heads at 3500 rpm. "This led to the radical discussion to have water cooling," Kapfer explained. "Our philosophy was to take what was good from the old and determine what to make better." All that survived was the flat-six configuration and the 118 mm cylinder bore centers.

Kapfer's engineers devised a two-piece block cast that split vertically and bolted together. They used forged-steel "cracked" connecting rods. A laser beam scored a point midway down the circle on the rod's big end. Freezing made it brittle. A machine pulled it, making a rough separation along the laser-scored line. The irregular surfaces mated together around the forged-steel crankshaft more securely than traditional machined surfaces and worked almost as if they still were one piece. Engineers fitted aluminum main bearings after concluding cast-iron ones weighed too much.

The engine's integrated dry sump lubrication was a Kapfer team innovation. Unlike a true dry sump with a separate tank, this system integrated a tank into the engine block but separated from the crankshaft. "The target," Kapfer explained, "was to not have a separate oil tank, to facilitate meeting emission and noise standards. Still,

the car had to be drivable like a classic Nine-Eleven on a racetrack." To do that, engineers devised "oil flaps," baffles within the tank that restrained the sloshing that occurs during high-speed cornering.

Weissach developed a truly interchangeable cylinder head. These four-valve, single-plug, three-cylinder heads used cam-drive duplex chains and were completely interchangeable, saving time in design and assembly, and costs by casting and assembling just one style of head. Chains on one end drove one bank of cams from the engine front; the other bank drove from the engine rear. Rotate one 180 degrees, and it worked on the opposite bank. Cup tappets opened the valves, and conical springs closed them. Kapfer's engine used automatic hydraulic valve adjustment and had automatic chain tensioners. His target was no maintenance.

Cooling a centrally placed, fully enclosed engine presented substantial obstacles. Kapfer's engineers adopted a racer-style cross-flow system forcing coolant from the exhaust side to the intake side around the cylinders in an open-deck design. Matching temperatures around each cylinder ensured full and consistent combustion, important in minimizing emissions. The engine displaced 2,480 cc with a bore of 85.5 mm and stroke of 72 mm. It developed 201 SAE net horsepower.

Porsche gave the 2003 Boxster an updated front-end treatment, incorporating two functional air intakes as well as reshaping those ahead of the rear wheels. With standard engine improvements, the base Boxster could reach a top speed of 157 mph while the S could hit 164. *Photo courtesy Porsche Cars North America*

1997

As the two cars raced toward production, the similarity of the front ends troubled Larson. "We hoped that all the carry-over parts between the Boxster and the Nine-Eleven would be invisible. But the fact was that it was just the whole front of the car. They had the same front fascia and exactly the same bumper for several months during development. The only thing that was different on the cars was the windscreen was shorter on the Boxster."

"We had this funny little late night discussion with Harm Lagaay," Larson continued. "'Harm, we've got a big problem here. The cars are identical.' I thought a year later when we introduced the Nine-Eleven, we would have had a hard time selling the new Nine-Eleven with the mask of the Boxster on it.

"He said, 'Yeah, you're right. But not on the Nine-Eleven. We'll change the Boxster.' It was just weeks before the final cutoff point when we're supposed to deliver data. That was the turning point in the Boxster that it would at least get its own front bumper. They had to share the same headlamps, but that was cost-and-investment driven." Harm Lagaay recalled their origin. They came from assembly.

"They need to be able to mount the headlamp in twenty seconds," he explained.

"Push it in, fix it in place. Twenty seconds. So we came up with these five functions in one piece: main beam, dipped beam, fog lamp, turn signal, light washer. It was a typical Porsche business decision."

Following lavish dealer and media launch programs, sales took off better than Porsche had hoped. This required the company to find extra factory production capacity even with adding a second work shift at Zuffenhausen. A large factory in Valmet on Finland's southwest coast became available.

The Boxster steadily improved over time. For 1998, Porsche introduced door-mounted side airbags as standard equipment. An optional child-seat detection system deactivated the passenger airbag when owners fitted a special child seat. In anticipation of major improvements coming for 2000, Porsche changed little for 1999.

The innovative engines were not always successful. Sometimes intermediate shaft

The 2003 Boxster engine still displaced 3.2 liters. However Porsche fitted its VarioCam technology into this model. This increased output to 260 horsepower, which resulted in 0-to-62-mph acceleration in 5.7 seconds. *Photo courtesy Porsche Cars North America*

The Boxster is an extremely efficient package that provides storage space in front and behind the passenger compartment. For 2003, styling changed slightly, but under-the-skin—especially in the mid engine compartment—improvements included adding the VarioCam continuously variable valve-and-cam-timing system. *Photo courtesy Porsche Cars North America*

Model year 2005 introduced the second-generation Boxster roadster with new headlights, new parking and side-marker lights, new front air intakes and chin spoiler, and a new front deck lid. New 17- and 18-inch wheels and tires appeared as well. *Photo courtesy Porsche Cars North America*

bearings failed, and other times, the cast-in/fused-in cylinder liners failed. These jammed rapidly moving parts with catastrophic results. Because of this, early Boxsters sell for prices that seem inappropriately low for a Porsche. However, many of these early cars have found a huge following among weekend enthusiasts who appreciate their excellent handling around tight autocross circuits laid out around pylons.

2000

The Boxster "S" version arrived with an all-new integrated dry-sump engine. This 3.2-liter powerplant developed 252 brake horsepower and propelled the car to 60 in 5.9 seconds and to a top speed of 162 miles, or 260 kilometers, per hour. The S version came with a tighter suspension mounted on 17-inch wheels, and a new air inlet at the front accommodated a third radiator for cooling. Porsche improved the standard model as well, increasing displacement of its engine from 2.5 to 2.7 liters. With 220 brake horsepower available, the car accelerated from 0 to 60 mph in 6.6 seconds and reached a top speed of 155 mph.

A year later, for 2001, technology took another leap on the Boxsters as electronic throttle linkages reached the car line. "Fly by wire throttle linkage," engineering chief

Jürgen Kapfer explained, "offers no friction, and they don't break. All signals go directly to the motor management system, which instantly calculates timing, fuel flow, and all other factors." The "system," Motorola's Motronic ME 7.2, accompanied the 911's stability management PSM to the Boxster lineup. Models remained unchanged through 2002.

For 2003, the entire Boxster lineup experienced a facelift. Grant Larson supervised a new nose and tail, and he reconfigured the side air inlets. New engine management from

The 2005 Boxster and Boxster S benefited from attention to air flow management. Porsche engineers completely closed up the undercarriage of the car. This and other adjustments resulted in a drop in aerodynamic drag coefficient from 0.31 to 0.29. *Photo courtesy Porsche Cars North America*

The base Boxster 2.7-liter engine developed 240 horsepower, an increase of 12 over the previous generation. Output of the 3.2-liter S engine increased from 260 to 280 horsepower. Base Boxsters rode on 17-inch wheels mounted with 205/55 ZR17s at the front and 255/50s in the back. The S used 18-inch wheels with 235/40 ZR tires on the front and 265/40s on the rear. *Photo courtesy Porsche Cars North America*

the Motronic ME 7.8 system boosted base model output to 225 SAE net horsepower and the S up to 258.

Porsche produced a commemorative 50th-anniversary Boxster honoring the 1953 550 Spyder, limiting production to 1,953 copies. Painted GT Silver Metallic, the cars got a special dark brown "Cocoa" interior. Equipped with the S engine and chassis package, the cars were capable of 165 mph top speeds.

2005

While Boxster and Boxster S versions remained unchanged through 2004, Porsche introduced the second generation of each model for 2005. New headlights pulled the fog lamps out of the combined pod, lowered them, and situated them nearer the "corners" of the car. Rear lights changed as well, adopting a fixture using 18 light-emitting diodes (leds) for the center high-mounted stop light.

Porsche redesigned the convertible top, providing greater visibility, larger side windows, and better accommodation for taller drivers. The new front end greatly improved aerodynamic efficiency, dropping the Boxster's coefficient of drag from 0.31 to 0.29. Reshaped A-pillars, Carrera GT–style mirrors, a new rear spoiler, and a full-length undertray reduced the drag, increased the top

speeds, and improved high-speed stability on both the base and S models.

Enlarging the side air intakes, air filters, intake manifolds, and exhaust systems helped Porsche engineers derive more power from the 2.7- and 3.2-liter engines. The base engine developed 240 SAE net horsepower while the S engine produced 280. A new electronic monitor inside the engine measured the quantity of oil and replaced the traditional dipstick.

Both the Boxster and the Boxster S got a standard variable-ratio rack-and-pinion steering system. Porsche Active Suspension Management, PASM, introduced on the 2005 911/997 models, was optional on the Boxsters, along with the Sport Chrono Package. The company made its enhanced Porsche Stability Management (PSM) system standard on both versions. Boxsters rode on 17-inch wheels, and the S traveled on 18s; 19-inch wheels and tires were available for either model.

Porsche stiffened the car's structure by incorporating a new extra-strength structural-steel front section that enhanced occupant safety in a frontal crash. Coincidentally, this new structure enlarged foot wells and the front storage compartment as well.

Porsche introduced new interiors with the second-generation launch for 2005. These remained unchanged for 2007 models, with S versions resembling more closely their 911 siblings, including available Sport Chrono S packages (with the accompanying cowl-mounted clock). *Photo courtesy Porsche Cars North America*

Late-afternoon light shows off the second-generation styling changes apparent on these 2007 models. The front of the base Boxster (left) and the rear of the Boxster S reveal front, side, and rear panel changes that improve fuel economy and high-speed stability. *Photo courtesy Porsche Cars North America*

Stylists completely redesigned the interior, covering the dashboard, interior door panels, and sides of the center console in a more durable material that looked like leather, while real leather covered the gearshift lever, steering wheel trim, handbrake lever, and door handles. Three optional steering wheels and the standard assortment tilted and telescoped to fit a wider variety of driver and passenger physiques as they sat cradled in either of four seating choices, all derived from the new 911/997 model.

For 2006, Porsche added standard-equipment two-stage air-bag technology. An optional tire-pressure monitoring system appeared for the first time on the Boxster and S. The Porsche Communications Management (PCM) system incorporated an "electronic logbook" to automatically record mileage, trip length, start and destination point addresses, date, and time. Porsche *Exclusiv* offered a new SportDesign exterior trim option.

Big news for 2007 was in engine improvements. By adding VarioCam Plus, Weissach's innovative system that controls the intake-side camshaft (VarioCam) and valve-lift

(Plus), the Boxster gained 5 horsepower, taking peak output to 245 SAE net. The Boxster S with VarioCam Plus grew in displacement from 3.2 to 3.4 liters, with 295 SAE net horsepower output. Optional Tiptronic S transmissions incorporated new hydraulics and electronics to improve responsiveness and offer variable shift programs. Optional tire pressure monitors became standard for 2007. Buyers of the Boxster and S models could order 19-inch, 911 Turbo, forged-alloy, two-tone wheels.

In 2008, the base Boxster models earned Ultra Low Emissions Vehicle (ULEV) certification, and the S model achieved a Low Emission Vehicle (LEV) rating. Yet power output remained unchanged in both vehicles. The oil change interval increased to 12,000 miles—or one year—and the spark plug life increased to 36,000 miles. New optional, lightweight, deeply contoured, folding sports bucket seats arrived with adjustable backrests.

2009

For 2009, Porsche introduced the second "second generation" of the Boxster at the Los Angeles Auto Show. The direct-fuel-injection engine and the transmission topped the list of most talked-about improvements. The new 2.9-liter engine in the base model (now with

Dramatic light illuminates the handsome interior of the 2007 Boxster. Boxster designer Grant Larson often said his inspiration for the roadster came from Porsche's 1960 RS60 racers, one of which was in the background near the windows in this photo. *Photo courtesy Porsche Cars North America*

Boxster (1997–2009)

Engine

Design............Water-cooled flat (opposed) 6-cylinder
Bore & Stroke, mm/inches:
  1997–1999......................... 85.5x72.0 / 3.37x2.83
  2000–2008..........................85.5x78.0 / 3.37x3.07
  2009-2010.....................................89x78 / 3.5x3.1
  2000–2006 S,
    2004–2005 S 50th.............93.0x78.0 / 3.66x3.07
  2007–2008 S.......................96.0x78.0 / 3.78x3.07
  2009–2010 S..................................97x78 / 3.8x3.1
Displacement, cc/cd:
  1997–1999...................................... 2,480 / 151.3
  2000–2008...................................... 2,687 / 163.9
  2009–2010...................................... 2,893 / 176.5
  2000–2006 S................................... 3,179 / 193.9
  2007–2008 S................................... 3,387 / 206.7
  2009–2010 S................................... 3,436 / 209.7
Valve operation ....Double overhead camshafts, four
    valves per cylinder, chain driven.
    Hydraulic lifters with VarioCam variable
    valve timing system.
Compression ratio:
  1997–2006 Boxster and S 11.0:1
  2007–2008...11.3:1
  2007–2008 S..11.1:1
  2009-2010..11.5:1
  2009–2010 S..12.5:1
Fuel feed:
  1997–2008 Boxster and S .... DME fuel injection
    and ignition system
  2009–2010 Boxster and S .... Direct fuel injection
HP (SAE net) (mfr):
  1997–1999..201 at 6,000
  2000–2002..217 at 6,400
  2000–2002 S.....................................248 at 6,250
  2003–2005..225 at 6,300
  2003–2005 S.....................................256 at 6,200
  2006...240 at 6,400

  2006 S...280 at 6,200
  2007–2008..245 at 6,500
  2007–2008 S.....................................295 at 6,250
  2009–2010..255 at 6,400
  2009–2010 S.....................................310 at 6,400

Chassis & Drivetrain

Frame..........................Unitized, fully galvanized steel
Component layout...................Mid-engine, rear drive
Transmission:
  1997–2008............ Manual five-speed transaxle or
    Tiptronic five-speed dual function
    automatic transaxle
  2009–2010..............Manual six-speed transaxle or
    PDK seven-speed dual-function
    automatic transaxle
Axle ratio:
  1997–1999........3.89:1 manual / 4.21:1 Tiptronic S
  2000–2005........3.56:1 manual / 4.02:1 Tiptronic S
  2006–2008...........3.75:1 manual / 4.38:1 Tiptronic
  2009–2010 ....3.88:1 manual / 3.25:1 PDK
  2000–2002 S.....3.44:1 manual / 3.73:1 Tiptronic S
  2003–2005 S.....3.44:1 manual / 3.09:1 Tiptronic S
  2006 S...............3.88:1 manual / 3.91:1 Tiptronic S
  2007–2008 S.....3.89:1 manual / 4.21:1 Tiptronic S
  2009–2010 S...............3.89:1 manual / 3.25:1 PDK
Front suspension ..... Independent MacPherson struts
    with aluminum alloy lower control
    arms, longitudinal and transverse link,
    coil springs, dual-tube gas-filled
    shock absorbers, anti-roll bar
Rear suspension ...... Independent MacPherson struts
    with aluminum alloy lower control
    arms, lateral and trailing links coil
    springs, dual-tube gas-filled shock
    absorbers, anti-roll bar

General

Wheelbase, mm/inches...........................2,415 / 95.2

Track:

front, mm/inches:

1997–2005 .... 1,465 / 57.7
2006–2010 .... 1,490 / 58.7
2000–2005 S .... 1,455 / 57.3
2006–2010 S .... 1,486 / 58.5

Rear, mm/inches:

1997–2005 .... 1,528 / 60.2
2006–2010 .... 1,534 / 60.4
2000–2002 S .... 1,508 / 59.4
2003–2005 S .... 1,514 / 59.6
2006–2010 S .... 1,528 / 60.2

Brakes .... Power-assisted, dual-circuit
four-piston aluminum alloy monoblock
fixed caliper anti-lock braking system

Tire size: front, rear

1997–2005 .... 205/55ZR16, 225/50ZR16
2006–2010 .... 205/55ZR17, 235/50ZR17
2000–2005 S 205/50ZR17, 225/40ZR17
2004–2005 S 50th 225/40ZR18, 265/35ZR18
2006–2010 S 235/40ZR18, 265/40ZR18

Wheels: front, rear

1997–2005 .... 6Jx16, 7Jx16
2006–2008 .... 6.5Jx17, 8Jx17
2009–2010 .... 7Jx17, 8.5Jx17
2000–2005 S 7Jx17, 8.5Jx17
2004–2005 S 50th 7.5Jx18, 9Jx18
2006–2010 S 8Jx19, 9Jx18

Weight:

1997–1999 .... 2,822 manual / 2,951 Tiptronic
2000–2002 .... 2,722 manual / 2,882 Tiptronic
2003–2005 .... 2,822 manual / 2,954 Tiptronic
2006 .... 2,855 manual / 2,987 Tiptronic
2007–2008 .... 2,877 manual / 3,009 Tiptronic
2009–2010 .... 2,943 manual / 3,009 PDK
2000–2002 S .... 2,849 manual / 2,937 Tiptronic
2003–2005 S .... 2,904 manual / 2,992 Tiptronic
2006 S .... 2,965 manual / 3,053 Tiptronic
2007–2008 S .... 2,987 manual / 3,075 Tiptronic
2009–2010 S .... 2,987 manual / 3,042 PDK

For 2009, Porsche introduced special editions styled and "dressed" by its industrial- and product-design arm Porsche Design. The ultra-limited-edition roadsters used either the base 2.9-liter, 255-horsepower, water-cooled flat six or the new direct-injection, 3.4-liter, 310-horsepower engine, available with the new PDK transmission. *Photo courtesy Porsche Cars North America*

a standard six-speed transmission) produced 255 horsepower, while the 3.4-liter S engine developed 310 SAE net horsepower. The long-anticipated PDK transmission arrived. This revolutionary double-clutch gearbox provided seven forward gears, which improved performance and fuel economy by 11 percent over previous manual gearbox ratings and 16 percent over the Tiptronic S–equipped car. EPA highway numbers rose to 26.3 mpg with the 2.9-liter base model and 25.5 with the 3.4-liter S. Acceleration from 0–60 mph fell from 5.8 seconds for the manual and 6.7 seconds for the Tiptronic 2.7-liter base model to 5.6 and 5.5 seconds, respectively, for the new 2.9-liter Boxster. The run from 0 to 60 mph in the 3.4 Boxster S improved from 5.1 for the manual and 5.8 for the Tiptronic S to 5.0 and 4.9 for the PDK. From the outside, the cars were more recognizable, with new front and rear body panels, larger halogen headlights with a "two-tube" appearance reminiscent of the Carrera GT, and new LED rear lights.

Chapter 17

996, 997

1999–2004 Typ 996	
★★1/2	1999–2001 Carrera
★★	1999–2001 Carrera 4
★★1/2	2000 911 Millennium
★★1/2	2001 Carrera S, 4S
★★★★	2001 Turbo, GT2
★★1/2	2002–2004 Carrera 4
★★1/2	2002–2004 Carrera 4S
★★1/2	2002–2004 Targa
★★★★	2002–2004 Turbo
★★★★1/2	2002–2004 GT2
★★★★	2003–2004 GT3
★★1/2	2004 40th Anniversary
★★★	2004 Carrera 4, 4S
★★★★	2004 Turbo

2005–2009 Typ 997	
★★★	2005–2008 Carrera
★★★1/2	2005–2008 Carrera S
★★★★	2005 911 Turbo S
★★★	2006–2008 Carrera 4
★★★1/2	2006–2008 Carrera 4S
★★★1/2	2007–2008 Targa 4, 4S
★★★★	2007–2008 GT3
★★★★1/2	2008 GT3 RS
★★★★1/2	2007–2009 Turbo
★★★★★	2008–2009 GT2
★★★★	2009 Carrera 4
★★★★1/2	2009 Carrera S, 4S

1991–1998: Two Cars, One Face

In one studio, Porsche designer Grant Larson and the engineers working on styling hurried to complete the Boxster show car for the Detroit auto show. In another, he and Pinky Lai struggled with a larger task. New car line development manager Horst Marchardt had decided to create two models at once by sharing front-end structures. Marchardt planned to make more efficient use of the huge investment in design, engineering, assembly, and crash-test prototypes by sharing those costs between two car lines. Whether he intended both cars to look nearly identical is uncertain, however styling director Harm Lagaay and designers Larson and Lai took that as part of their brief as well. One model was Larson's production Boxster, and the other was Lai's new 911, the radically new Typ 996.

Weissach had worked toward making the previous generation Typ 993 water-cooled. But Porsche needed the car at dealers sooner than development times for a new engine allowed. Now Lai and Larson had to incorporate radiators and plumbing into their designs, factors that changed the shapes and forms of their ideas. Adding to their challenge was Porsche's dire financial condition. Sales of the 993 were barely adequate to finance an entirely new treatment of the 911. The two designers could not get their styling themes to work on the 986 and 996. Worse, the Boxster concept was a tiny car while the 986 was midsized and the 996 was the full-size

911. Not only was the appearance troubling them, aerodynamic concerns on the new 911/996 were impossible to solve.

"We were not allowed to even think of a moving spoiler by the platform team," Lai recalled. "They had a very tough bean counter at the time in their department. He showed up every day." Lai knew his car body had to meet the aerodynamic target, so his concepts grew taller at the rear end. One day in the wind tunnel, Lai and an engineer cut one of the grille louver panels and put it on backward. Suddenly the aerodynamics changed. Lai argued that it wasn't a moving spoiler, it was a moving grille, something not as expensive as a moving spoiler.

Then the Boxster concept stole the show at Detroit. Overnight, new life and new energy flowed throughout Porsche. Worries that

Toyota, Mercedes-Benz, BMW, or an American company would buy them evaporated.

Lagaay suggested that the two men take the Boxster design and enlarge all the proportions 20 percent to make the new 986. Share the front end treatment with the 996. After the Boxster's success at Detroit, Lagaay argued he might find some money for a "moving grille."

The Boxster appeared in 1997 and was so successful the factory went to second shifts and then took on an additional production facility in Finland to keep up with demand. When Porsche's new 996/911 appeared, engineers and designers had worked out a new engine, new platform, new suspension, new interior, and new creature comforts that drew in thousands of first-time Porsche buyers. Some hardcore purists felt betrayed—the car was heavier, wider, and more civilized, with more creature comforts than they felt upheld the heritage. But Porsche's board and its marketing managers knew that purists didn't buy a new 911 every year. If Porsche waited for them, it could go out of business. It had to compete against Mercedes-Benz and BMW, Corvette and Jaguar, and even Ferrari for customers.

Engine and chassis engineers faced equally daunting challenges. Tighter standards for noise and noxious emissions made it harder to provide a stronger, faster, and more fuel-efficient engine than the 993. One vocal group of engineers believed four-valve technology was the answer. But the heads lost cooling fins because of the complex valvetrain; engineers testing prototype aluminum four-valve cylinder heads learned they were melting them at 3500 rpm. Water-cooling, first seen as one possibility, became the only possibility.

Engineers working in tandem with the Boxster team conceived a block cast in two pieces that split vertically and bolted together. A complex system incorporated a chain-driven intermediate shaft below the crankshaft that ran four more chains to drive intake and exhaust valves.

Weissach developed an integrated dry sump system for both engines. Unlike a true dry sump with a separate tank, this system used a tank integrated into the engine block but separated from the crankshaft. This eliminated tubing and the separate oil tank, which helped meet emission and noise standards while ridding the cars of a source of troublesome oil leaks. Yet the cars had to be drivable on a racetrack; engineers created "oil flaps," baffles inside the sump that restrained the sloshing that occurred in high-speed cornering.

Weissach developed a truly interchangeable cylinder head that was identical for either three-cylinder bank. These four-valve, single-plug heads put cam-drive chains at one end and fit either left or right cylinder bank. This saved time in design and assembly, and reduced costs to mold and manufacture a single head. Cup tappets opened the valves, and conical springs closed them. Engineers adopted hydraulic valve adjustment and incorporated automatic chain tensioners. Their goal was a no-maintenance engine. Cooling these engines presented other challenges.

"Water cooling," Stefan Knirsch explained, "allowed us to get higher performance because of better cooling of the cylinder head." Knirsh had joined Porsche in 1996 as these new engines reached pre-production phases. He was the troubleshooter for the start of production for both Boxster and 996 engines. "The

One of the first things Porsche customers noticed at the 996 introduction was its strong resemblance to the 986 Boxster that Porsche had brought out the year before. It grew from a concept called "Two cars/one face," which represented a method of reducing development costs of the most expensive part of the car, the front end.

Designing the first water-cooled 911, the Typ 996, presented huge challenges to stylist Pinky Lai. He had to incorporate a larger engine as well as all the water-cooling hardware in a car that carried on the heritage.

Where the previous-generation 993 had been more spartan in its interior, Porsche targeted owners of Mercedes-Benz, BMW, and other sports luxury models as new buyers and raised the comfort and luxury level accordingly. The new dimensions required to accommodate water-cooling hardware provided more elbow room in the passenger compartment.

robustness of these heads against knocking is much better. So our ignition angle is earlier. This helps in fuel economy, and it helped in power output. The only drawback," he went on, "was additional mass, the twenty liters of water and all the parts."

Pinky Lai's 996 body concepts, in his efforts to meet aerodynamic and anti-lift targets, had elevated the tail. Engineers welcomed the height because it provided them space for the new engine. It displaced 3,387 cc with bore and stroke of 96 mm and 78 mm. Four-valve cylinder heads fit easily since air circulation around cooling fins no longer mattered. Design engineers reverted to a single-spark-plug ignition. Porsche rated the new engine at 296 SAE net horsepower. Engineers tuned intake and exhaust manifolds not only for flow efficiency but also for the sound they produced. Water-cooling further reduced engine mechanical noises and improved heating and defrosting capabilities. Porsche and Getrag had to design a new six-speed transmission that not only could handle the additional power but could accommodate much more for 996 variations that would follow. The Tiptronic S transmission offered five speeds.

The cars accelerated toward production. The similarity of the fronts troubled Larson.

"We hoped that all the carry-over parts between the Boxster and the Nine-Eleven would be invisible. But the fact was that it was just the whole front of the car. Look at them and you can tell that they had the same front fascia and exactly the same bumper for several months during development. I thought a year later when we introduced the Nine-Eleven, we would have had a hard time selling the new Nine-Eleven with the mask of the Boxster on it."

1998–1999

Porsche took a big gamble with its Boxster and 996. Giving the two cars front end styling so nearly identical validated Horst Marchardt's engineering, design, and financial estimates. Yet the timing of introductions sent a confusing message to enthusiasts and journalists. The 996, introduced as a 1998 model in Europe, was the company flagship, yet it appeared too much like the entry-level product introduced a year earlier. Lagaay acknowledged nearly a decade later that they should have strived for greater differentiation.

In terms of performance, handling, interior comfort, and sophistication, few people had any complaints. Acceleration to 60 mph came in 4.6 seconds. Porsche quoted a top speed of

Both 996 coupes and cabriolets remained unchanged in their second year. European customers got access to a new 996 Turbo, but that vehicle didn't arrive in the United States until the 2001 model year. Porsche purists lamented the loss of the traditional front fender forms that had hugged the headlights nearly to the windshield.

174 mph. Cabriolets appeared in mid-April 1998, in time for Porsche Cars North America's full line introduction to U.S. buyers.

All-wheel-drive C4 models had accounted for more than 20 percent of 964 sales, and that hit 30 percent with the 993s. All-wheel-drive C4 996 models appeared in Europe in October 1998 and the following spring in

For 2000, Porsche sold the 996 cabriolet for $74,970 while the coupe retailed for $65,590. The all-wheel-drive Carrera 4 coupe listed for $71,020 while the C4 Cabrio went for $80,400. Porsche commemorated the passing of Y2K with a new Millennium Coupe, for $89,000.

the States. Buyers could order a C4 with the Tiptronic transmission.

Porsche's stability management system, PSM, distinguished C4 models from rear-drive Carreras. Bosch developed the system, and Weissach engineers adapted it to the 996. It expanded the capabilities of anti-lock braking, ABS, by applying brakes electronically to a single wheel when conditions of excessive under- or oversteer affected cornering stability.

2000–2004

The 996 forms had swelled seductively when the Turbo appeared in Europe in 2000 and in the United States for 2001. Chassis engineers put all-wheel drive underfoot to keep the Turbo's 420 SAE net horsepower efficiently on the ground. Transmission engineers who had heavily reinforced the Tiptronic to handle C4 purposes had done so to accommodate Turbo power as well for the first time. Acceleration from 0 to 60 mph took less than 4 seconds, and top speeds exceeded 190 mph. A misread of U.S. Department of Transportation height regulations forced early 2001 models to wear black triangular front bumperettes. Porsche

The 911 Turbo reached U.S. shores in the summer of 2000, introduced as a 2001 model. U.S. Customs agents and Department of Transportation personnel held up the cars, claiming front bumper height was too low, so Porsche quickly added small front bumperettes mounted even with the top of the license plate.

and the U.S. DOT clarified things before year-end, and the extensions disappeared from subsequent imports.

Styling introduced its second-generation headlights on the Turbo, and the new fixtures spread across the full 996 line in second-generation 2002 models. The C4S Turbo-look wide rear body betrayed a performance upgrade across the entire 996 line: Engineers lengthened piston stroke from 76 mm to 82.8, enlarging displacement to 3,596 cc. New VarioCam Plus valve timing technology helped boost output to 320 SAE net horsepower. This system varied intake-side camshafts (VarioCam) and intake-side valve operation (Plus). A rear-drive GT2 appeared, accompanying the 911 Turbo at the peak of Porsche performance. This new coupe offered enthusiasts 456 SAE net horsepower in a car weighing 220 pounds less than the Turbo. (This engine configuration got a second life in mid-2002 as the Turbo S package.)

Porsche revised the Targa for 2002. Reliability problems and warranty claims against jammed glass roofs led engineers to rethink the system. Sustained high-speed driving caused lift that stressed the welds of

roof members mounted on top of the reinforced 993 Cabriolet bodies. Body engineers turned the mounts inside out for the 996. An assembly-line robot inserted the new roof through the windshield opening of a strengthened, modified, and decapitated Coupe body before welding it in place from the inside. Lift tendencies helped seal the seams more tightly.

The twin-turbo, 3.6-liter, opposed, six-cylinder engine was a different version from the one used in the normally aspirated Carrera 2 and Carrera 4 models. It developed 420 horsepower.

The Turbo, with its wider rear track, produced a more aggressive stance even when standing still. Acceleration from 0 to 62 mph took 4.2 seconds, and Porsche quoted a top speed of 190 mph. The car sold for $111,000.

Few changes marked the 2003 model year. Porsche's website indicated that throughout the 911 lineup, the standard radio became a digital receiver with in-dash CD players. For racing enthusiasts, Porsche introduced the GT3 Coupe late in the model year, based on an earlier version not available to U.S. customers. This normally aspirated, rear-wheel-drive model developed 380 SAE net horsepower. For 2004, Porsche celebrated the 40th anniversary of the 911 with a commemorative model run of 1,963 cars. Slight tuning tweaks boosted output to 345 SAE net horsepower, 30 more than standard 911 Carrera models. A new mechanical rear-axle differential lock enhanced acceleration and handling. The rear-wheel-drive 911GT2 coupe appeared with 477 SAE net horsepower, Porsche composite ceramic brakes, a top speed of 198 mph, and acceleration from 0 to 62 mph that took just 4 seconds. In addition, the company offered Cabriolet versions of the C4S and Turbo models.

Over the years from introduction in 1998 to the final 996 Turbo Coupes and Cabriolets, the car evolved. It became the best-selling 911 model up to that time as Porsche delivered more than 170,000. It engaged first-time Porsche buyers and turned them into Porsche enthusiasts. The 996 moved Porsche from barely surviving to fully thriving.

Early 996 engines were not without problems. However, Porsche quickly replaced those that failed under its warranty. There was little warning, and there still is no real means to determine which engine might fail. Anyone considering buying a 996 at this time should include an aftermarket extended warranty as part of their car's purchase. Replacing an engine out of warranty cost about $15,000 in parts and labor in 2009. Innovative independent repair facilities like Callas Rennsport in Torrance, California, and a few others around the United States are developing techniques to repair these engines. Until late 2008, however, this was impossible, since Porsche had not released engine drawings.

2005–2008 Typ 997

The 911 heritage provided as many challenges to engineers and designers as it offered guidelines. The characteristic front fenders still retained a form that, as Ferry Porsche first dictated to Erwin Komenda, allowed the driver to see where the front wheels were located. The 911/964/993/996 lineage carried on Butzi Porsche's iconic angled-down roofline. The car still defined itself with the rear engine that dictated its shape, form, handling, sound, and appeal.

European customers got access to the glass-roof Targa as a 2002 model, but buyers in the United States waited until 2003. Fully retracted, the glass panel offered 4.8 square feet of open sky above drivers' and passengers' heads.

"Designing to fit the Nine-Eleven heritage is a big challenge," Grant Larson said. "My goal," Larson continued, "was to make the car look more technical, more precise, more agile." The work he did defined the car. While the final tweaks with engineers enhanced aerodynamics, reducing the drag coefficient from 0.30 for the 996 to 0.28 for the new coupe, the original concept was more revolutionary.

Larson's first sketches showed a familiar form with taller, wider tires. For engineers, this choice carried consequences: The tires intensified loads so greatly under cornering, acceleration, and braking that the stresses literally destroyed preliminary running prototypes in 2001. It forced body, chassis, and suspension engineers to redesign much more of the car than they anticipated. For the unibody of the 996, they had developed techniques to weld and glue components. These methods had increased body rigidity by 8 percent. Additional reinforcement and adhesives for the 997 resulted in a 40 percent improvement in chassis stiffness.

Porsche boasted that the new 997 was 80 percent changed from the 996. More than half of that hid beneath the surface. Not a single suspension piece was interchangeable. This clashed with Wendelin Wiedeking's often-repeated goal of commonality of parts, but new designs proved simpler to manufac-

ture and easier to install. The 20 percent that remained unchanged included expensive elements like the roof panel, the interior rear seats, and the 3.6-liter engine block, crankshaft, and pistons.

Nineteen-inch wheels forced power-train engineers to rework gearboxes. Larger rolling circumferences required shorter final drive gears to best use engine torque and horsepower. Weissach engineers addressed concerns in the manual and Tiptronic transmissions. They developed a new six-speed manual gearbox with torque and horsepower capacity to spare. Engineers raised gearshift pressure and increased stall speed on the five-speed Tiptronic. This gave drivers faster starts from a standstill, more powerful and spontaneous acceleration, and quicker shifts, especially in lower gears with the dual-function automatic.

From the start, body and platform structural engineers developed a Cabriolet ahead of the Coupe. Under August Achleitner, Porsche's director of product line management for the Carrera, Weissach engineers spent more time thinking about the car before designing it and welding the first parts. Prior to supervising the 997, Achleitner had managed new car concepts and packaging for all Porsche vehicles from 1989 through 2000. The 997 was largely his creation.

The glass roof—unlike a cloth convertible top—could be opened or closed at any speed because the top roof panel slid down inside the rear window. However, body reinforcing and roof hardware added 154 pounds to the weight of the Targas over the coupes.

The 3.6-liter, water-cooled engine, introduced on 2002 models, developed 320 horsepower. This was sufficient to push the Targa to a top speed of 177 mph and from 0 to 62 mph in 5.2 seconds—identical to the cabriolet acceleration.

The GT3 was perhaps one of the most desirable 996s ever produced. Deeply satisfying to drive, with just enough visual cues to make other Porsche owners slightly envious, the 996 GT3 was a car that was equally comfortable on the track or on the daily commute.

Improvements that engineers made to the Cabriolet strengthened the Coupe as well. To stiffen the Cabriolet body, engineers devised a so-called third load path for passive safety. This transferred forces of an impact through the top of the door to the back of the car. A strong beam inside the sheet metal extended across the top of each door starting at the base of the A-pillar at the instrument panel. This was the point at which the door beam connected, making a very rigid torsional-, bending-, and stiffness-load passage from the front fenders to the rear of the car. This also fortified the passenger compartment in a front, side, or rear end crash. It kept the compartment from folding in on itself, as may happen in other open cars in high-speed accidents. It provided the new 997 Cabriolet with 5 percent greater torsional stiffness and 9 percent more flexing stiffness than the 996 Cabrio.

The new car gave engineers a chance to revisit ideas that had come up before

Porsche designers, engineers, and aerodynamicists worked every surface of the car—and every detail of its superb 380-horsepower, 3.6-liter engine—to obtain maximum performance and driver satisfaction. The car sold for $99,000.

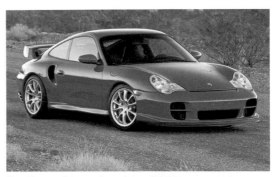

For those drivers for whom 380 horsepower was not enough (or Turbo was too "gentrified"), Porsche offered the GT2. Introduced in 2002 with 456 horsepower, by the time the company manufactured this 2004 model, the engine developed 477.

Porsche created a rule when it introduced the 993 turbo that required any Porsche with more than 400 horsepower to use all-wheel drive. With the GT2, it discarded that stipulation because its designation—GT2—represented a racing category in which all-wheel drive was not legal.

but that management had shelved. One of these ideas that engineers brought back for the 997 was the Porsche Active Suspension Management, PASM. In the mid-1990s, technology was not advanced enough to do what engineers had in mind. Achleitner's commitment to 19-inch wheels and tires on the Carrera S motivated Porsche to raise the technology to meet its standards.

"For some people the 996 was a little too soft at first," Achleitner said. There was no 996 GT3, Turbo, or C4S yet. "*We* knew what was coming, but we took this feedback and decided that the 997 should be a little more muscular, a little bit sportier." This required a balance; Porsche didn't want to lose customers it had won from Mercedes-Benz and BMW. These were buyers who never would have bought a 993. That car had been too harsh, loud, or uncomfortable for them.

How would they achieve this balance? What makes a car faster? How do you make the car smoother and more comfortable without sacrificing sportiness? The PASM system met many of these challenges. Aside from the 959, which many inside Porsche still considered to be a run of 337 prototypes, this 997 was the first time Porsche offered an electronic spring and damper system. In the Cabrio, this was an industry first.

The interior was not spartan. Unlike "Sport" versions of the 959, this car came with no roll cage installed, and it did offer leather seats, a radio, and climate control. The 2004 GT2 sold for $191,700.

The GT2 was nearly 250 pounds lighter than the Turbo and was capable of a top speed of 195 mph. Acceleration from 0 to 62 mph was 4.0 seconds. It was, however, a very difficult car to drive fast.

Porsche introduced its second water-cooled 911 series in 2004 in Europe and 2005 for U.S. customers. Designers acknowledged criticism of the compound headlight fixtures on the 996 and returned to a more traditional oval shape with the new car.

Virtually everything was new in the 997. As with earlier versions, when buyers ordered the Tiptronic S transmission, Porsche also mounted finger shifters on the steering wheel as well as the center console. This S model also had the Sport Chrono Plus option.

Bringing technology and its resulting performance to the road required a multifaceted assault. Powertrain manager Stefan Knirsch was part of the 20-member group making concept studies outlining their goals.

"You always want more power in the next generation of any Porsche," he said. He and his staff came up with intake and exhaust modifications to the familiar 3.6-liter 996 engine that added 5 horsepower to reach 325 SAE net horsepower for the "base" Carrera. This engine carried over the VarioCam Plus valve management system comprising two interacting switching cup tappets on the intake side of the engine, driven by two cams of varying size on the intake camshaft.

Enlarging cylinder bore from 96 mm to 99 (but retaining stroke at 82.8 mm) brought the new S engine displacement to 3,823 cc, 3.8 liters. It developed 355 SAE net horsepower. The new Carrera coupes reached 60 mph in 4.8 seconds (5.2 for the Cabriolet), and 4.6 seconds for the S (but 4.9 seconds for the S Cabriolet). Porsche quoted top speeds of 177 mph and 182 mph respectively. This was the first time since 1977—with 2.7-liter and 3.0-liter engines—that Porsche offered two normally aspirated engines simultaneously.

While little changed from the design concept of the 996 engines, these Carrera and Carrera S powerplants apparently have suffered none of the catastrophic failures that plagued early 996 models.

Porsche introduced the 997 Carrera and Carrera S coupes in the United States as 2005 models. Through the model year, it continued manufacturing and selling 996 Turbo S Coupes and Cabriolets. Cabriolet versions of the 997 Carrera and Carrera S reached dealers worldwide in April 2005 as 2006 models. The first all-wheel-drive models arrived in showrooms in midsummer, with Targas, Turbos, GT3s, GT2s, and other variations following through 2006 and into 2007 and 2008.

Except for its back seat, the 997 interior was nearly all new, the work of interior designer Anke Wilhelm and interior chief Franz-Josef Siegert. In the late 1990s, Harm Lagaay hired in Siegert, and he brought in a staff of designers to do only interiors and still others to attend to the details—the jewelers, as he called them. Wilhelm's and Siegert's instrument pod seemed familiar to Porsche owners, and Uli Sauter's graphics were quickly comprehensible to those driving a Porsche for the first time. The 996 interior had been the most comfortable and user friendly of any previous model. The 997 improved on that and offered four seat options, satisfying most backs and occupant shapes.

The legacy of the Porsche Cabriolet went back generations. Porsche had carried over the same convertible roof from the 1983 911 SC through the 3.2 Carreras and on through the 964 series. From Tony Hatter's efforts to improve the 993 Cabrio roof came Lai's forms with the 996 and then Larson's with the 997. Roughly 40 percent of all 997s for 2005/2006 were Cabriolets, and about 50 percent of those went to the United States. The solid, fixed-glass back window with an electric defogger was one of many selling points, something introduced at the 996 facelift in 2002 and slightly enlarged with the 997. Unlike any 996, at speeds up to 31 mph the 997 driver could raise or lower the roof while moving. That process, including dropping and raising side windows, took 20 seconds in either direction.

Because the roofline could not exactly mimic that of the Coupe, engineers tweaked rear spoiler performance. The spoiler rose another 20 mm higher on the Cabriolet than on the Coupe to provide more aerodynamic

For the first time in many years, Porsche offered two power variations for the 911, the base Carrera and Carrera S. The appearance and the engineering of the car were directly influenced when early concept sketches showed it with 18-inch wheels.

effect. The subtly higher wing was not the only effect that top-down Porsche drivers noticed. As with 996 models, audio volume changed with road speed. However, opening the roof reconfigured the audio systems graphic equalization and front-rear speaker mix automatically. Front-rear balance moved forward something like 9 inches, and the system boosted bass and treble levels.

Porsche created a limited edition for 2006 honoring the 50th anniversary of the Porsche Club of America. The company limited manufacture to just 50 examples, one for each year. Cars were painted "Azure California Blue," a variation on Azure Blue, the color long associated with PCA.

Porsche used the Club Coupe as the platform on which to launch its X51 performance package. Larger throttle bodies, modifications to cylinder heads and exhaust valves, improved air flow, a sport exhaust system, and other modifications raised output to 381 horsepower and dropped 0-to-60 times to 4.4 seconds.

996 Carrera, 4, 4S (1999–2005)

Engine
Design............Water-cooled flat (opposed) 6-cylinder
Bore & Stroke, mm/inches:
    1999–2001 .... 96x78 / 3.77x3.07
    2002–2005 .... 96.0x82.8 / 3.78x3.26
Displacement, cc/cd:
    1999–2001 ....3,387 / 206.7
    2002–2005 ....3,596 / 219.4
Valve operation ....Double overhead camshafts, four
    valves per cylinder, duplex chain
    driven. Hydraulic lifters with VarioCam
    variable valve timing system.
    2002–2005 ....VarioCam Plus
Compression ratio...11.3:1
Fuel feed ...... DME sequential multipoint fuel injection
HP (SAE net) (mfr):
    1999–2001 ....296 at 8,000
    2002–2005 ....315 at 6,800

Chassis & Drivetrain
Frame.......................... Unitized, fully galvanized steel
Component layout........Manual six-speed transaxle or
    Tiptronic S five-speed dual
    function automatic transaxle
Axle ratio:
    1999–2002 .... 3.44:1 manual / 3.68:1 Tiptronic
    2002–2005 .... 3.44:1 manual / 3.37:1 Tiptronic
Front suspension ... Independent with "disconnected"
    light-alloy wishbones, MacPherson
    struts with coil springs, dual-tube
    gas-filled shock absorbers, anti-roll bar
Rear suspension .... Independent on five wishbones
    per side, light-alloy transaxle with LSA
    (Lightweight, Stability, Agility) system,
    coil springs, single-tube gas-filled
    shock absorbers, anti-roll bar

General
Wheelbase, mm/inches........................... 2,350 / 92.5
Track:
    front, mm/inches:
      1999–2001 ....1,455 / 57.3
      2002–2005, Carrera, 4 ....1,465 / 57.7
      2002–2005 4S Coupe........................1,465 / 57.7
      2004–2005 4S Cabriolet.....................1,47 / 57.9

    Rear, mm/inches:
      1999–2005, Carrera, 4 ....1,500 / 59.0
      2002–2005 4S Coupe........................1,528 / 60.2
      2004–2005 4S Cabriolet....................1,528 / 60.1
Brakes .... Power-assisted, duel-circuit four-piston
    aluminum-alloy monobloc fixed caliper
    anti-lock braking system.
    2004–2005 4S................Optional Porsche Ceramic
    Composite Brakes (PCCB)
Tire size: front, rear:
    1999–2005 Carrera, 4 ....205/50ZR17, 255/40ZR17
    2002–2005 4S................225/40ZR18, 295/30ZR18
Wheels: front, rear:
    1999–2005 Carrera, 4 ....7Jx17, 9Jx17
    2002–2005 4S................................8Jx18, 11Jx18
Weight:
    1999–2001 Coupe ....2,904 manual /
    3,003 Tiptronic
    1999–2001 Cabriolet.......................3,069 manual /
    3,168 Tiptronic
    1999–2001 4 Coupe ....3,025 manual /
    3,124 Tiptronic
    1999–2001 4 Cabriolet....................3,190 manual /
    3,289 Tiptronic
    2002–2004 Coupe ....2,959 manual /
    3,080 Tiptronic
    2002–2005 Cabriolet.......................3,135 manual /
    3,256 Tiptronic
    2002–2005 Targa ....3,113 manual /
    3,234 Tiptronic
    2002–2004 Coupe ....2,959 manual /
    3,080 Tiptronic
    2002–2005 Cabriolet.......................3,135 manual /
    3,256 Tiptronic
    2002–2005 4S........ 3,234 manual / 3,355 Tiptronic
    2004–2005 4S........ 3,443 manual / 3,564 Tiptronic

Similar to the two generations of Targa that came before, 993 and 996, the more recent 997 version once again utilized a large retracting piece of tinted glass. Unlike previous models, the 997 version was available only on the all-wheel-drive platform as Targa 4 or Targa 4S.

The exhaust sound was more aggressive with the Cabrio, too. Porsche wanted its customers to hear the engine. It reminded some drivers of the 993 more than a water-cooled 996. Because of America's relaxed exhaust-noise standards, U.S. buyers got the loudest exhausts of any 997 purchaser.

As Porsche prepared a new Targa for introduction, the company again studied its customers. The company found an audience for this model that "desired exclusivity and valued distinctive design, were connoisseurs of automobiles rather than racers, and were safety conscious." A single decision—to offer the Targa only on the C4 and C4S platform—immediately resolved many questions about what the new version should be. The 1.7-inch (44 mm) wider rear end provided the aggressive and dynamic form that engineers and stylist Mathias Kulla had in mind. Porsche's engineers and marketers understood that these owners routinely used their cars year-round in climates with snow, so the C4 drive system made further sense. Engineers recalibrated the actual suspension as well as the virtual electronic one.

The rear window served as a functioning hatchback as well. Two gas pressure shocks held the glass up to allow easier access to the 8.1-cubic-foot rear luggage space. With the roof open, a wind deflector reduced wind noise and turbulence so much that it was possible to use the black-fabric sunscreen even while driving.

The large roof provided the same 4.8-square-foot opening that the 996 version offered. Porsche reconfigured the retractable glass, however, using two pieces sandwiched rather than a single thicker piece. This change saved 4.2 pounds in weight at the top of the car.

Carrera 4 and Carrera 4S engine specifications remained unchanged for the 2007 model year. Output for the 3.6-liter base engine was 325 horsepower while the 3.8-liter S developed 355 horsepower. Porsche charged $99,700 for the Targa 4 and $110,900 for the Targa S models.

By increasing anti-roll-bar diameters, they limited body roll in cornering. Lowering the spring rates kept the ride suitably compliant for those whose attendance at track days was limited to the spectator side of the fence. They shifted PASM calibration slightly toward the moderate-to-softer end of its range of sport-to-soft.

The glass-roof Targa started life as a great but troubled idea in 993 models in 1996. The system, produced by Webasto, began on a convertible body. With the 996, Porsche stopped mounting the roof *on* the car and moved the roof *into* the car body through the windshield before the marriage (the point in assembly at Zuffenhausen at which workers bring the chassis up underneath the body and mate the two together) to bolt it in place with 16 interior bolts. The entire structure added 132 pounds to the car's weight. Of this, 17.6 pounds was additional reinforcement to the platform.

The C4S, in its own right and as the basis for the Targa, had been so thoroughly tamed beyond even its 996 predecessor that anticipated heavy front-end sensations never

This was the most powerful 911 that Porsche had offered up to this point: 530 horsepower out of its 3.6-liter, twin-turbocharged, water-cooled flat-six engine. This gave the GT2 a top speed of 204 mph and 0-to-62-mph acceleration of just 3.7 seconds.

Typical of Porsche styling and engineering, the car did not scream about its potential. Because it was designed and executed as the production version of a race group, Porsche designed the body shell structure to accommodate a roll cage, and mounting points were pre-installed in the body.

996 Turbo, GT2, GT3 (2001–2005)

Engine

Design.............................Water-cooled flat (opposed) 6-cylinder, twin turbochargers, twin intercoolers

Bore & Stroke, mm/inches........ 100x76.4 / 3.94x3.00

Displacement, cc/cd..............................3,600 / 219.7

Valve operation ....Double overhead camshafts, four valves per cylinder, duplex chain driven. Hydraulic lifters with VarioCam Plus variable valve timing system. Twin turbochargers, twin intercoolers

Compression ratio:
  2001–2005 Turbo, GT2.....................................9.4:1
  2004–2005 GT3..11.7:1

Fuel feed .... DME sequential multipoint fuel injection, ignition

HP (SAE net) (mfr):
  2001–2005 Turbo ....414 at 6,000
  2002–2003 GT2....................................456 at 5,700
  2004–2005 GT2....................................476 at 5,700
  2004–2005 GT3....................................375 at 7,400

Chassis & Drivetrain

Frame...........................Unitized, fully galvanized steel

Component layout.......... Rear engine, all-wheel drive. Cardan shaft, viscous clutch

Transmission...............Manual six-speed transaxle or Tiptronic S five-speed dual function. Manual six-speed transaxle only

Axle ratio.................3.44:1 manual / 2.89:1 Tiptronic

Front suspension ....Independent with "disconnected" light-alloy wishbones, MacPherson struts with coil springs, dual-tube gas-filled shock absorbers, anti-roll bar

Rear suspension ....Independent on five wishbones per side, light-alloy transaxle with LSA (Lightweight, Stability, Agility) system, coil springs, single-tube gas-filled shock absorbers, anti-roll bar.

General

Wheelbase, mm/inches:
  2001–2005 Turbo ....2,350 / 92.5
  2002–2005 GT2, GT3 ....2,355 / 92.7

Track:
  Front, mm/ inches:
    2001–2005 Turbo ....1,465 / 57.7
    2002–2005 GT2 ....1,495 / 58.9
    2004–2005 GT3 ....1,485 / 58.5
  Rear, mm/inches:
    2001–2005 Turbo............................1,522 / 59.9
    2002–2005 GT2 ....1,520 / 59.8
    2004–2005 GT3 ....1,495 / 58.9

Brakes:
  2001–2005 Turbo, GT3..................Power-assisted, dual-circuit ventilated and drilled, four-piston aluminum alloy monobloc fixed caliper anti-lock braking system. Optional Porsche Ceramic Composite Brakes (PCCB)
  2002–2005 GT2.............. Ventilated, drilled ceramic composite, six-piston fixed aluminum alloy monobloc calipers, PCCB

Tire size: front, rear
  2001–2005 Turbo 225/40ZR18, 295/30ZR18
  2002–2005 GT2, GT3 .....235/40ZR18, 315/30ZR18

Wheels: front, rear
  2001–2005 Turbo 8Jx18, 11Jx18
  2002–2005 GT2.........................8.5Jx18, 12Jx1
  2004–2005 GT3...........................8.5Jx18, 11Jx18

Weight:
  2001–2005 Turbo Coupe.................3,388 manual / 3,487 Tiptronic
  2004–2005 Turbo Cabriolet.............3,652 manual / 3,740 Tiptronic
  2002–2005 GT2, GT3 ....3,168 manual

---

appeared. Porsche derived and developed the C4 964, introduced in 1989, with an increasing U.S. market in mind. It tended to understeer when drivers pushed it too hard. This was a comfortable response for most Americans, and Porsche engineers settled for this reaction. In the 993 they compensated.

This car produced handling characteristics that were more rear-dominant, reminiscent of earlier two-wheel-drive 911s. With the 996 and 997 C4 and C4S, turn-in was crisp, precise, predictable, and dependable. Too much exuberance produced a seeming "no muss, no fuss" response in the car.

Porsche began shipping its all-wheel-drive 997 C4 and C4S models to the United States in November 2005 as 2006-model-year cars. The Turbo and the GT3 first appeared at Geneva in February 2006. The 3.6-liter engine, designed by Hans Mezger originally for the racing GT1 models and incorporating a true dry-sump oil system, developed 480 SAE net horsepower in the Turbo. Acceleration to 62.5 mph took 3.9 seconds, and Porsche quoted its top speed as 193 mph. The Tiptronic version of the all-wheel-drive Turbo was quicker at reaching 62.5 mph, taking just 3.7 seconds. The Turbo Cabriolet arrived in September 2007 and boasted nearly identical performance figures, a longtime goal for Weissach's engineers. The GT3 and its wilder-looking sibling, the GT3 RS, with their normally aspirated version of the Mezger dry-sump flat-six, achieved 415 horsepower, giving owners acceleration to 60 mph in 4.1 seconds and a top speed of 193 mph.

With the race-car-derived Carrera GT out of production, the GT3 RS was as near as a Porsche buyer could get to a race car with a license plate on it. For 2007, Porsche also offered its GT2, a rear-drive, 530-horsepower 911 that reached 204 mph. It was the

Porsche introduced the 997 GT3 to the world's automotive press at a racetrack outside Paris. A group of European Carrera Cup champions delighted in flinging the cars through glorious drifts, to the delight of engineers Roland Kussmaul and Andreas Preuninger, who stood watching, beaming like proud parents.

company's first production street-legal 911 to exceed 200 mph. The large horsepower jump came about by using twin turbochargers and a newly designed expansion intake manifold. The car, weighing 3,175 pounds, reached 62.5 mph in 3.6 seconds. Ironically, because the GT2 was another Porsche homologation

Subtle changes differentiated the appearance of first-generation 997s from the second-generation models. Ultra-low-profile 19-inch wheels and tires filled the wheel wells, and designers incorporated a strip of light-emitting diodes (LEDs) as daylight running lights.

997 Carrera, S, 4, 4S (2005–2010)

Engine

Design ....Water-cooled flat (opposed) 6-cylinder. Integrated dry sump

Bore & stroke, mm/inches:
2005–2008 Carrera, 4.............96.0x82.8 / 3.78x3.26
2005–2006 S, 4S...................99.0x82.8 / 3.90x3.28
2007–2008 S, 4S ....99.0x82.8 / 3.90x3.26
2009–2010 Carrera, 4.............97.0x81.5 / 3.82x3.21
2009–2010 S, 4S.................102.0x77.5 / 4.02x3.05

Displacement, cc/cid:
2005–2008 Carrera, 4..................3,596cc / 219.4cid
2005–2008 S, 4S......................3,824cc / 233.4 cid
2009–2010 Carrera, 4.................3,614cc / 220.5cid
2009–2010 ....3,800cc / 231.9cid

Valve operation:
2005–2010 Carrera,
4, S, 4S......................Double overhead camshafts, four valves per cylinder, duplex chain driven. Hydraulic lifters with VarioCam Plus variable valve timing system
2009–2010 .... Direct Fuel Injection

Compression ratio:
2005–2008 Carrera, 4......................................11.3:1
2005–2008 S, 4S...11.8:1
Carrera, 4, S, 4S 12.5:1

Fuel feed:
2005–2008 .... DME sequential multipoint fuel injection and ignition, solid-state distributor system, six ignition coils
2009–2010 ....Motronic with six coils, sequential multipoint fuel injection

HP (SAE net)(mfr):
2005–2008 Carrera, 4...........................325 at 6,800
2005–2008 S, 4S..................................355 at 6,600
2009–2010 Carrera, 4...........................345 at 6,500
S, 4S ....385 at 6,500

Chassis & Drivetrain

Frame...................Monocoque galvanized steel body

Component layout:
2005–2010 Carrera, S ....Rear engine, rear-wheel drive
2005–2008 4, 4S ....Rear engine, all-wheel drive, Cardan shaft, viscous clutch;
2009–2010 4, 4S ....Rear engine, all-wheel drive, electromagnetically operated multiplate front differential clutch

Transmission:
2005–2010, 2005–2006 ....Manual six-speed transaxle
2007–2008 .... Tiptronic five-speed dual-function automatic transaxle
2009–2010 ....PDK seven-speed dual function transaxle

Axle ratio:
2005–2010, 2009–2010 ......3.44:1 manual and PDK
2007–2008 ....3.56:1 Tiptronic S

Front suspension:
2005–2008 ....Independent MacPherson spring strut axle, track control arms, longitudinal arms and spring struts, single-sleeve gas-charged shock absorbers.
2009–2010 ....Twin-sleeve gas pressure shock absorbers.
2005–2010 S, 4S............................... Active control

Rear suspension:
2005-2008 .... Independent five-arms configuration. Coil springs, single-tube gas-charged shock absorbers.
2009–2010 ....Cylindrical coil springs, coaxial inner single-sleeve gas-charged shock absorbers.
2005–2010 S, 4S............................... Active control

General

Wheelbase, mm/inches ....2,350 / 92.5

Track:
Front, mm/inches:
2005–2006 ....1,486 / 58.5
2007–2010 Carrera, S ....1,486 / 58.5
2007–2010 4, 4S................................1,488 / 58.6
Rear, mm/inches:
2005–2006 Carrera, 4 ....1,534 / 58.5
2005–2010 S, 2005–2007 4S ....1,516 / 59.7
2007–2010 Carrera ....1,534 / 60.4
2007–2010 4, 4S................................1,548 / 60.9

Brakes.............. Power-assisted dual-circuit four-piston aluminum monobloc calipers, cross-drilled and inner-vented rotors, anti-lock braking system. Optional PCCB.
2009–2010.................Integrated anti-lock control and Porsche Stability Management (PSM)

Tire size, front/rear:
2005–2006 ....235/40ZR18, 265/40
2007–2008 Carrera.......... 235/40ZR18, 265/40ZR18
2007–2008 4, S 235/40ZR18, 295/30ZR18
2007–2008 4S 235/35ZR19, 305/30ZR19
2009–2010 Carrera, 4...... 235/40ZR18, 265/40ZR18
2009–2010 S, 4S............. 235/35ZR19, 295/30ZR19
Wheels, front/rear:
2005–2006 Carrera, 4.........................8Jx18, 10Jx18
2005–2006 S, 4S...............................8Jx19, 11Jx19
2007–2008 Carrera...........................8Jx18, 10Jx18
2007–2008 4 ....8Jx18, 11Jx18
2007–2008 S, 4S...............................8Jx19, 11Jx19
2009–2010 Carrera, 4.....................8Jx18, 10.5Jx18
S, 4S 8Jx19, 11Jx19
Weight:
2005–2008 Carrera, 4......................... 3,075 manual
2005–2008 S, 4S................................. 3,131 manual
2007–2008 Carrera Coupe.................3,164 Tiptronic
2007–2008 S Coupe ....3,219 Tiptronic
2007–2008 4 Coupe .... 3,197 manual,
3,285 Tiptronic
2007–2008 Carrera Cabriolet.............. 3,263 manual,
3,351 Tiptronic
2007–2008 4 Cabriolet .... 3,384 manual,
3,472 Tiptronic
2007–2008 4 Targa............................ 3,329 manual,
3,417 Tiptronic
2007–2008 4S Coupe .... 3,252 manual,
3,340 Tiptronic
2007–2008 S Cabriolet....................... 3,318 manual,
3,406 Tiptronic
2007–2008 4S Cabriolet..................... 3,439 manual,
3,527 Tiptronic
2007–2008 4S Targa .... 3,384 manual,
3,472 Tiptronic
2009–2010 Carrera Coupe.......3,186 manual or PDK
2009–2010 Carrera Cabriolet.............. 3,307 manual,
3,373 PDK
2009–2010 4 Coupe ....3,307 manual, 3,421 PDK
2009–2010 4 Cabriolet .....3,428 manual, 3,494 PDK
2009–2010 4 Targa...........3,373 manual, 3,439 PDK
2009–2010 S Coupe ....3,208 manual or PDK
S Cabriolet ....3,329 manual, 3,395 PDK
4S Coupe ....3,263 manual, 3,329 PDK
4S Cabriolet ....3,450 manual, 3,516 PDK
4S Targa............................3,395 manual, 3,461 PDK

The most significant interior change was also the subtlest: A new shifter on the console and the steering wheel designated this Carrera S was equipped with the new seven-speed PDK Porsche Double Clutch transmission. The PDK cut shift time by 60 percent under hard acceleration.

model and the category was rear-wheel-drive only, acceleration to 62.5 mph was faster in the all-wheel-drive Tiptronic Turbo than in the rear-wheel-drive GT2. All cars in Porsche's 2007 lineup adopted the previously optional tire-pressure monitoring system as standard equipment.

For 2008, Porsche continued its efforts to lessen its carbon "footprint" in the world by increasing oil-change service intervals from 7,500 miles to 12,000 miles. This reduced the frequency of harmful vapors entering the atmosphere. Spark plugs got a boost as well, to a four-year or 36,000-mile replacement requirement.

2009

Porsche introduced significant changes under the skin in 2009 while making only subtle modifications to the body. Engine designers and engineers adopted direct fuel injection for all Porsche 911–model normally aspirated engines, and they introduced a long-awaited seven-speed, double-clutch, "manu-matic" *Porschedoppelkopplungsgetriebe* (PDK) transmission. To completely and finally rid the 997 of intermediate shaft bearing failure, engineers redesigned the 911 engine to drive overhead camshafts without this additional shaft. New casting technology eliminated the

997 Turbo, GT2, GT3, GT3 RS (2007–2010)

Engine

Design............................Water-cooled flat (opposed) 6-cylinder, dry sump.

GT2.............. Twin turbochargers, twin intercoolers

Bore & stroke, mm/inches ....100x76.4 / 219.7

Displacement, cc/cid..............................3,600 / 219.7

Valve operation:

2007–2008 Turbo........... Dual overhead camshafts, four valves per cylinder, duplex chain driven. Hydraulic lifters with VarioCam Plus variable valve timing system

2007–2010 Turbo,
2009–2010 GT2 ....Twin turbochargers, two intercoolers. Variable turbine geometry

Compression ratio:

2007–2010 Turbo, GT2....................................9.0:1

2007–2008 GT3...12.0:1

Fuel feed:

2007–2008 Turbo, GT3................... DME sequential multipoint fuel injection and ignition solid-state distributor system, six ignition coils

2009–2010 Turbo, GT2....... Motronic with six coils, sequential multipoint fuel injection

HP (SAE)(mfr):

2007–2010 Turbo...............................480 at 6,000

2007–2008 GT3................................415 at 7,600

2009–2010 GT2................................530 at 6,500

Chassis & Drivetrain

Frame....................Monocoque galvanized steel body

Component layout:

2007–2010 Turbo, GT2, GT3 ....Rear engine, all-wheel drive

2007–2008 Turbo...............................Cardan shaft

2007–2010 Turbo, GT2............. Electromagnetically operated multi-plate front differential clutch

Transmission..................Manual six-speed transaxle, Tiptronic S five-speed dual function transaxle (2007–2010 Turbo only)

Axle ratio..........................3.44:1 manual or Tiptronic

Front suspension .... Independent MacPherson spring strut axle, track control arms, longitudinal arms and spring struts, twin-sleeve gas-charged shock absorbers, active control (PASM)

Rear suspension .... Independent, five-arms configuration, coil springs, single-sleeve gas-charged shock absorbers, active control (PASM). Split-track control arms (GT3 RS)

General

Wheelbase, mm/inches:

2007–2010 Turbo, GT2........................2,350 / 92.5

2007–2008 GT3...................................2,355 / 92.7

2007–2008 GT3 RS............................2,360 / 92.9

Track:

Front, mm/inches:

2007–2010 Turbo............................1,490 / 58.7

2009–2010 GT2 ....1,515 / 59.7

2007–2008 GT3 ....1,497 / 58.9

Rear, mm/inches:

2007–2010 Turbo............................1,548 / 60.9

2009–2010 GT2 ....1,550 / 61.0

2007–2008 GT3 ....1,524 / 60.0

GT3 RS...................................... 1,558mm / 61.3

Brakes:

2007–2010 Turbo, GT2...........Power-assisted dual-circuit six-piston (front) / four-piston (rear) aluminum monobloc calipers, cross-drilled inner-vented rotors. Optional PCCB. Porsche Stability Management (PSM).

2007–2008 GT3............................. Traction control

Tire size, front/rear.............235/35ZR19, 305/30ZR19

Wheels, front/rear:

2007–2008 Turbo 8Jx19, 11Jx19

2007–2008 GT3............................8.5Jx19, 12Jx19

2009–2010 Turbo 8.5Jx19, 11Jx19

2009–2010 GT2............................8.5Jx19, 12Jx19

Weight:

2007–2010 Turbo Coupe................. 3,494 manual, 3,572 Tiptronic

2007–2010 Turbo Cabriolet............. 3,649 manual, 3,726 Tiptronic

2007–2008 GT3.............................. 3,075 manual

GT3 RS.. 3,031 manual

2009–2010 GT2.............................. 3,175 manual

Both the brand-new base 3.6-liter and the brand-new Carrera S 3.8-liter engines introduced direct fuel injection with the 2009 models. This system, with other improvements, increased power output over the previous 3.6 by 20 horsepower to 345 and by 30 horsepower in the S to 385. Fuel economy also improved between 6 and 8 percent.

Rear taillights changed shape again and incorporated LEDs as back-up illumination. The new Carrera rode on 18-inch wheels with 235/40ZR18 front tires and 265/40s on the rear. The S used 19-inch wheels with 235/35ZR19s in front and 295/30s in back.

chance for cylinder wall failure as well. The highly sophisticated direct fuel-injection system sprayed microscopic amounts of gasoline into the cylinder through the head between the intake valves so that the fuel—cooled and condensed by meeting the outside air at the last instant—vaporized inside the cylinder. This permitted more responsive monitoring of fuel feed demands, and all these improvements resulted in a 6.2 percent increase in output from the base Carrera 3.6-liter engine—from 325 to 345 SAE net horsepower In the 3.8-liter S this jumped 8.5 percent, from 355 to 385 SAE net horsepower. Engineers further improved and recalibrated the VarioCam Plus intake valve timing-and-lift system. As a result, these two engines improved fuel economy as well, using 6.4 percent less gasoline than 2008 models. The

new PDK transmission further improved fuel economy by 12.5 percent over the previous Tiptronic S gearbox. Finally, because of reduced emissions as well as decreased fuel consumption, the Carrera and S models were both qualified for the Low Emissions Vehicles category two (LEV-II) by the U.S. Environmental Protection Agency.

The company continued to offer six-speed manual transmissions for base and S models, although they rated lower fuel-economy ratings, 18 and 25 mpg against 19 and 27 for PDK-equipped cars. While Porsche expected to sell as many as half its production with PDKs, engineers involved in the project assured journalists at the in-troduction that the company always would offer manual transmissions because racers demanded them.

Chapter 18

Cayenne

★★1/2	2003 Cayenne S
★★★	2003 Cayenne Turbo
★★	2004 Cayenne
★★1/2	2004 Cayenne S
★★★	2004 Cayenne Turbo
★★	2005 Cayenne
★★1/2	2005 Cayenne S
★★★	2005 Cayenne Turbo
★★	2006 Cayenne
★★1/2	2006 Cayenne S
★★★	2006 Cayenne Turbo
★★1/2	2007 Cayenne
★★★	2007 Cayenne S
★★★1/2	2007 Cayenne Turbo
★★★★1/2	2007 Cayenne Turbo S
★★★	2008 Cayenne
★★★1/2	2008 Cayenne S
★★★★	2008 Cayenne Turbo
★★★★	2008 Cayenne GTS
★★★	2009 Cayenne
★★★1/2	2009 Cayenne S
★★★★	2009 Cayenne Turbo
★★★★★	2009 Cayenne Turbo S
★★★★	2009 Cayenne GTS

1995–2002

Few vehicles in automobile history have provoked such a spirited response from an existing customer base as Porsche heard when it announced it would develop and sell a sport utility vehicle named the Cayenne. For the company to "sell out," to cater to America's love of SUVs, was regarded as the worst pandering any purist could envision. That the development, marketing, audience, and purpose for the vehicle had little to do with the United States was a story that took several years to emerge.

The early 1990s were a challenging period of time for Porsche. While the 986 Boxster and 911/996 development moved forward, Wendelin Wiedeking convinced the supervisory board to adopt a growth strategy, to capture interest and sales in emerging economies. But growth in which direction was the question.

Porsche was known throughout the world as a predominant sports car producer. Yet sports cars required paved roads, and many countries with burgeoning economies had few of those. Mercedes-Benz, Range Rover, Toyota, Nissan, and of course American manufacturers sold vehicles that were more utilitarian into these markets, vehicles with all- or four-wheel drive and higher ground clearance.

Wiedeking assigned Horst Marchardt to determine suitable products. Marchardt tapped an engineer named Klaus-Gerhard Wolpert to work with a handful of others to investigate options. Wolpert had joined Porsche in 1984 and worked mostly for outside clients like Volkswagen, Ford, Chrysler, Mercedes-Benz, and Audi. This had given him a broad perspective. For Volkswagen he did the Passat and Golf Synchro prototypes. He worked routinely on electronically controlled chassis systems, anti-lock brakes, four-wheel steering, and air suspension control systems. He helped engineer the 959 and the Paris–Dakar Rally entries with Helmuth Bott. By the end of the 1980s he was responsible for every electronically controlled chassis system at Porsche. He and others worked "undercover" for nearly a year.

"We were looking at brand segments," Wolpert explained, "the small sports car segment, small convertibles, the sport utility segment. We did a lot of consumer tests, marketing tests, and in the end, we decided to invest into the SUV segment.

Porsche went from two doors (or sometimes three with hatchback front-engine cars) to five with its initially controversial Cayenne. The company introduced it in 2002 in Europe. Porsche developed the vehicle jointly with Volkswagen after determining its next sensible market was for a Porsche vehicle for developing nations. *Photo courtesy Porsche Cars North America*

The SUV segment is, worldwide, still the area with the most growth. In the early 1990s, especially in the exclusive upper end, there was no real competition."

Porsche faced huge research and development costs. It hoped to find a cooperating partner with whom engineers could produce similar but different vehicles. Mercedes-Benz had sold a boxy, utilitarian, Austrian-made Gelandewagen mostly for European customers, with a few sneaking across the Atlantic to U.S. customers. Mercedes' parent Daimler-Chrysler was planning an all-new, more stylish vehicle, having announced plans to construct a $300 million plant in Alabama to assemble the sport utility vehicle. While Porsche and Daimler executives crafted licensing and other legal details, engineers and designers began sharing ideas, concepts, sketches, and data. Then, as negotiations neared completion, a member of Daimler-Chrysler's board proposed that in exchange for D-C's contribution to the end product, they would accept Porsche stock—sources say it was around 5 percent—in compensation. Porsche management and manufacturing staffs had worked hard to launch the turnaround that would begin with the Boxster. Wiedeking refused to compromise their future. The meeting ended within minutes, and collaboration stopped that day.

Porsche's supervisory board considered continuing alone, but development costs were daunting. Porsche proposed the idea to Volkswagen, who accepted. Porsche would produce a Cayenne, VW its Toureg.

"Volkswagen was a very self-confident company," designer Steven Murkett said. "They knew exactly how to design cars. They knew what they wanted. Porsche in late 1997 was not there. The Boxster had been out a year. We were still seen as the sports car company that was struggling to save itself."

Murkett started at Porsche in September 1983. During the slow times that followed, he busied himself sketching, creating, and inventing. He had won two international design competitions, first with a six-passenger hybrid and then with a Smart-sized urban vehicle. He had done the production version of the 959 and then the 964. Now he had to translate "Porsche-Ness," the form-language all enthusiasts and customers knew and loved, into something utilitarian.

"The Cayenne was a very controversial car to work on back then," he said. "Many of my colleagues were quite happy to not

Porsche scattered production of the Cayenne across central Europe. A plant in Bratislava, capital of the Slovak Republic, manufactured the bodies; engines came from Zuffenhausen; and Porsche did final assembly at an ultra-modern facility it built in Leipzig, Germany. The Cayenne S sold for $55,900 in the United States. *Photo courtesy Porsche Cars North America*

As was typical of its products, front and rear seats were covered in leather. Rear seats split 60/40; with the seats raised, the Cayenne provided 19 cubic feet of storage capacity. With the seats down, the interior swallowed 62.5 cubic feet of cargo. *Photo courtesy Porsche Cars North America*

The twin-turbo V-8 developed 450 horsepower. Maximum turbo boost reached 1.6 bar (23 psi) during hard acceleration. This was sufficient to move the 5,190-pound vehicle to a 165 mph top speed and provide acceleration from 0 to 62 mph in 5.6 seconds. Fuel economy suffered. *Photo courtesy Porsche Cars North America*

work on it. 'Who wants an SUV Porsche anyway?' It was easier for the Volkswagen people because the step from a Passat Combi to a Toureg was not as big a step. But from a Nine-Eleven to a Cayenne was a big step."

Defining that big step, delineating its boundaries, was the job Klaus-Gerhard Wolpert tackled. "From the technical . . . the product point of view," he explained, "we wanted to make a sporty SUV for daily use as every Porsche is. Today you can drive with a Nine-Eleven for shopping as well as on a racetrack. That was a target for this new vehicle: It had to be a sporty vehicle, not just a car for going through a field or on a rocky mountain."

To learn those distinctions, Wolpert put his project managers into vehicles from all of the competitors for months on end, using the vehicles as their daily drivers and rotating them every season. "If you drive a car in every situation," he said, "winter, summer, to the opera or carrying kids . . . you know it. We bought them all. Jeep Grand Cherokee, Range Rover, ML, later the BMW. If you drive it and use it, you can see a lot of small details. Seating position, comfort. How you use a switch, what is the position of the switch? After three, six months, you have a good overview of what is

best in this category. Then you can think about what you can do better than your competitors or what you can make different? What is *not* Porsche? Our background was with sports cars. The next step was to define what *was* our sporty SUV."

Porsche routinely established targets in performance and among its competitors.

In the Cayenne's first year, Porsche offered a turbocharged, 4.5-liter V-8 and a normally aspirated version of the engine. While performance always was a Porsche concern, designers and engineers worked hard on the concept to provide comfort and safety for all passengers. *Photo courtesy Porsche Cars North America*

The family resemblance was clear, and it was intentional. Porsche sensed from the start that adding a sport utility vehicle to its lineup would not be popular with its purist base. Yet the vehicle acquitted itself with surprising agility on paved roads and exceptional passenger comfort on or off the highway. *Photo courtesy Porsche Cars North America*

Though not standard equipment, these Porsche Design cases certainly ended up on many owners' wish lists. The Cayenne was a true "utility" vehicle, handling kids, pets, luggage, and cargo, and towing trailers with equal ease. The Turbo sold for $88,900 in the United States. *Photo courtesy Porsche Cars North America*

Acceleration times, top speeds, fuel economy, and CO_2 emissions all got specific attention. Engineers concluded they must start with both a normally aspirated V-8 and the same engine with a turbocharger. Eighteen months into the development process they added a V-6. The turbo was an easy decision: No other vehicles in the marketplace offered that performance level.

The marketing and product research surveys told them, however, that not every buyer in so very broad a market range desired high performance. Some customers were interested in driving a Cayenne off-road. The V-6 slotted into this starting segment.

"Due to the fact that Volkswagen has a lot of V-6 engines," Wolpert continued, "we decided to do our own with special characteristics, a different induction system, combustion improvements, and the exhaust system gas exchange so we have a significant power difference from what Volkswagen offers."

Engineers broke new ground to develop a chassis capable of the performance that enthusiasts and longtime customers expected of any Porsche. The question that took longer to resolve was what the new model would look like.

"We had design models that looked like a Hummer with a fastback," Steve Murkett said, laughing. "We had cars that looked like Nine-Elevens with four-doors that were up on their toes, with high ground clearance and huge wheels. We had some cars that were really racy-looking with very low roofs. These were influenced by Paris–Dakar, by the Baja buggies."

To accompany this Cayenne Turbo and its normally aspirated V-8 sibling Cayenne S, Porsche introduced a more modestly powered 250-horsepower, 3.2-liter V-6. This Turbo remained at the top of the lineup, most easily recognized by additional cooling intake grilles and "power bulges" sculpted into the engine hood. *Photo courtesy Porsche Cars North America*

Cayenne S and Turbo (2003–2004)

Engine
Design:
  S .... Water-cooled 8-cylinder V-engine,
                   90 degrees, dry sump lubrication
  Turbo .... Twin turbochargers, intercooler
Bore & Stroke, mm/inches .... 93.0x83.0 / 3.66x3.27
Displacement, cc/cd .... 4,511 / 275.3
Valve operation .... Double overhead camshafts,
                  four valves per cylinder, chain
                  driven. Hydraulic lifters with
                  VarioCam variable valve timing
Compression ratio:
  S 11.5:1
  Turbo 9.5:1
Fuel feed .... DME fuel injection and ignition system
HP (SAE net) (mfr):
  S .... 340 at 6,000
  Turbo .... 450 at 6,000

Chassis & Drivetrain
Frame .... Unitized, fully galvanized steel
Component layout .... Front engine, four-wheel drive
Transmission .... Tiptronic S 6-speed transmission
Axle ratio:
  S .... 4.10 Tiptronic
  Turbo .... 3.70 Tiptronic S

Front suspension .... Independent, wide-based
                  aluminum-and-steel upper and lower
                  A-arms and links, coil springs over
                  tubular shock absorbers, anti-roll bar.
                  Optional air-adjusted suspension.
Rear suspension .... Independent, multi-link axle,
                  steel-and-aluminum links, coil springs
                  over tubular shock absorbers, anti-roll bar.
                  Optional air-adjusted suspension.

General
Wheelbase, mm/inches .... 2,855 / 112.4
Track:
  front, mm/inches .... 1,662 / 64.8
  Rear, mm/inches .... 1,662 / 65.4
Brakes .... Power-assisted dual-circuit
                  six-piston (front) four-piston (rear)
                  aluminum monoblock calipers,
                  ventilated rotors, anti-lock brake system
Tire size: front, rear 255/55R18, 255/55R18
Wheels: front, rear 8Jx18, 8Jx18
Weight:
  S .... 4,949 Tiptronic
  Turbo .... 5,192 Tiptronic

"We got additional help from F. A. Porsche, Butzi," Murkett explained. "Butzi had always been an SUV enthusiast. It was his—and his brothers'—enthusiasm that helped convince the family when Wiedeking decided that the company needed this car. It was *their* enthusiasm that made the deal go through."

It became a mixed blessing then because Butzi got very involved. He wanted his design firm to do its own model.

"That was a moment," Murkett recalled. "We've got this design department and we've been working for months and years on this, and now F. A. Porsche is going to come along with the family advantage and he's going to design the damned thing for us! He has the legacy; he did the Nine-Eleven. . . ."

Butzi's staff at Porsche Design in Zell am See, Austria, went to work. It was, as Murkett characterized it, a product-design approach.

"He wanted the car to have really simple shapes. His car would quite possibly have been the most radical approach to the motorcar that the industry ever had. But quite possibly it would have scared the daylights out of half the industry and most of the public!" In the end, a design competition, judged by marketing bosses and the board of directors, resolved the question. They never learned which car was whose, but Murkett's concept carried the vote.

"We won. Flat out. But there is no doubt of his contribution to the simplicity of the Cayenne, which was something that made it a little bit difficult for some people to accept at the beginning. It doesn't have all the little muscles and edges, the functional-looking edges that BMW's X-Five or an ML has. That was Butzi's thing: Keep it simple. Don't put unnecessary lines or details on the car."

One of the features of the Cayenne that made it an exceptional off-roader was its optional air suspension. Basic configuration of the vehicle offered long up-and-down wheel travel of more than 8 inches in the front and 9 in back. The optional air system, shown here on a base V-6, provided a maximum ground clearance of 10.75 inches. *Photo courtesy Porsche Cars North America*

Porsche introduced the Cayenne for 2003 with a normally aspirated Cayenne S and the Cayenne Turbo. The shapely vehicle had undergone extreme testing, the most rigorous of any Porsche vehicle ever because once the Cayenne excelled at its on-road capabilities, the engineers felt challenged to make it a superior off-roader. One test involved driving it into a small river and shutting off the engine. Test drivers waited two minutes, restarted the engine, and drove out. They drove prototypes across Siberia and Mongolia. They accumulated nearly 1 million miles testing prototypes—not only off-road but on highways, then to a racetrack for 1,200 miles at high speeds, then back to the wilderness, then to the track, then back on public roads again.

The Cayenne shared common parts below the cockpit with Volkswagen's Toureg, including the heating box and air conditioning, seat structure (the only structure shared), some of the suspension body controllers, and some of the engine controllers. But the cars have different "B" and "C" pillars (the center and rear pillars), different roofs

This Turbo's high ground clearance made it look somewhat ungainly, yet the active suspension worked just the opposite on paved roads. At 62 mph, the suspension automatically lowered the car 1 inch and brought it down a further 0.5 inch at 130 mph. *Photo courtesy Porsche Cars North America*

Porsche's Communication Management (PCM) system was optional on all Cayenne models, including this Turbo. PCM included a CD player, a GPS navigation system, a trip computer, and the further option of a GSM telephone system. An off-road navigation function recorded the route driven on an electronic map, allowing the Cayenne to backtrack along the same way it had driven. *Photo courtesy Porsche Cars North America*

Only discreet badging, a slightly different grille treatment, four large tailpipes, and standard 20-inch SportTechno wheels betrayed the potency this new Cayenne offered. Porsche fitted it with its most powerful engine up to that time, the 4.5-liter twin turbo that developed 521 horsepower. This got the Turbo S from 0 to 62 mph in 5.2 seconds and took the vehicle to a top speed of 168 mph. *Photo courtesy Porsche Cars North America*

Because of its higher performance capabilities, Porsche fitted larger brake rotors, 380mm front and 358mm rear, instead of the usual 350mm discs all around. The brakes required larger calipers as well. *Photo courtesy Porsche Cars North America*

and cockpits. The gearboxes are the same, but the Cayenne uses different software. There is a Porsche drivetrain.

The first-generation, 4.5-liter V-8s developed 340 SAE net horsepower with the normally aspirated engine and 450 horsepower with the turbocharged version. Permanent all-wheel drive split traction 62 percent to the rear and 38 percent up front. The six-speed Tiptronic transmission coupled to an electronically controlled locking differential, a low-range gearbox, and an automatic braking differential (ABD). The Porsche Stability Management System (PSM) controlled vehicle stability. An optional air-suspension system offered six settings with ground clearance on the road from as low as 6.2 inches (157 mm) for loading to as much as 10.7 inches (273 mm) off-road.

Six-piston fixed calipers grabbed hold of 350 mm front discs and 330 mm rears to stop the car. The Cayenne S reached a top speed of 150 mph (242 kph) and accelerated from 0 to

The Turbo S buyer also got an upgraded interior. Every Cayenne fitted dual hand grips on the center console. Between these were drivetrain and suspension selector knobs. For all models, Porsche split torque 38 percent to the front, 62 to the rear for normal conditions. A multi-plate clutch allowed the driver to redirect as much as 100 percent of the torque to the front or rear depending on conditions. *Photo courtesy Porsche Cars North America*

Cayenne, Cayenne Turbo (2005–2006)

Engine

Design:

Cayenne.......... Water-cooled 6-cylinder (8-cylinder, Turbo) V-engine 75 degrees (90 degrees, Turbo), dry sump lubrication

Turbo .... Twin turbochargers, intercooler

Bore & Stroke, mm/inches:

Cayenne............................ 84.0x95.9 / 3.31x3.78

Turbo .... 93.0x83.0 / 3.66x3.27

Displacement, cc/cid:

Cayenne... 3,189 / 194.6

Turbo .... 4,511 / 275.3

Valve operation .... Double overhead camshafts, four valves per cylinder, VarioCam variable valve timing system.

Compression ratio:

Cayenne.. 11.5:1

Turbo 9.5:1

Fuel feed .... DME fuel injection and ignition system

HP (SAE net) (mfr):

Cayenne... 247 at 6,000

Turbo ....450 at 6,000

Chassis & Drivetrain

Frame.......................... Unitized, fully galvanized steel

Component layout........Front engine, four-wheel drive

Transmission................. Manual 6-speed, Tiptronic S 6-speed (Tiptronic S only, Turbo)

Axle ratio....................... 3.44 manual / 4.56 Tiptronic (3.70 Tiptronic, Turbo)

Front suspension:

Cayenne......................... Independent, wide-based aluminum-and-steel upper and lower A-arms and links, coil springs over tubular shock absorbers, anti-roll bar. Air-adjusted suspension.

Turbo ....Porsche Active Stability Management (PASM)

Rear suspension:

Cayenne..................... Independent, multi-link axle, steel-and-aluminum links, coil springs over tubular shock absorbers, anti-roll bar

Turbo ....Porsche Active Stability Management (PASM)

General

Wheelbase, mm/inches.........................2,855 / 112.4

Track: front, mm/inches:

Cayenne...1,647 / 65.2

Turbo ....1,647 / 64.8

Rear, mm/inches:

Cayenne...1,670 / 65.8

Turbo ....1,662 / 65.4

Brakes............. Power-assisted dual-circuit six-piston (front) four-piston (rear) aluminum monoblock calipers, ventilated rotors, anti-lock brake system

Tire size: front, rear

Cayenne...........................235/65R17, 235/65R17

Turbo 255/55R18, 255/55R18

Wheels: front, rear

Cayenne..................................... 7.5Jx17, 7.5Jx17

Turbo 8Jx18, 8Jx18

Weight........................ 4,762 manual, 4,785 Tiptronic (5,192 Tiptronic, Turbo)

---

62 mph (100 kph) in 7.2 seconds. The turbocharged model reached 62 mph in 5.6 seconds and topped out at 165 mph (266 kph).

The six-cylinder variation appeared in 2004, joining the V-8 Cayenne S and Turbo. The base Cayenne used a 24-valve, 3,289 cc engine that developed 247 SAE net horsepower. Acceleration from 0 to 60 mph took 9.5 seconds, and the vehicle reached a top speed of 133 mph. Later that model year, Porsche offered the S model with a six-speed manual transmission (though not in the United States until model year 2005 for both V-6 and Cayenne S V-8 models). For 2005, Porsche also added an electronically latching rear tailgate as standard equipment and offered optional XM or Sirius satellite radio.

Upgraded electronics marked the major changes for 2006. All three models received an "electronic logbook" to record mileage, journey length, date, and time. An upgrade to the Porsche Communication Management

Cayenne, Cayenne S, Cayenne Turbo, and Cayenne Turbo S (2007–2009)

Engine

Design............... Water-cooled 6-cylinder (8-cylinder, S, Turbo, Turbo S) V-engine, 75 degrees (90 degrees, S, Turbo, Turbo S)

Bore & Stroke, mm/inches:
2007 .... 84.0x95.9 / 3.31x3.78
2008–2009 .... 89.0x96.4 / 3.50x3.80
2007–2009 S, Turbo,
    Turbo S............................. 93.0x83.0 / 3.66x3.27

Displacement, cc/cid:
2007 ....3,189 / 194.6
2008–2009...3,598 / 2,129.6
2007 S, Turbo, Turbo S ....4,511 / 275.3
2008–2009 S, Turbo,
    Turbo S..4,806 / 293.3

Valve operation ....Dual overhead camshafts, four valves per cylinder, VarioCam Plus variable valve timing system.

Compression ratio:
2007 ....11.1:1
2008–2009..12.25:1
2007 S...11.5:1
2007–2008 Turbo, 2007 Turbo S....................9.5:1
2008–2009 S...12.5:1
2008–2009 Turbo...10.5:1
2009 Turbo S... 10-5:1

Fuel feed:
2007–2009 Cayenne........ MED electronic, six coils, Direct Fuel Injection, E-Gas electronic throttle
2007 S, Turbo S......................... DME fuel injection and injection system
2007–2008 Turbo .... DME fuel injection and injection system
2008–2009 S, Turbo,
    Turbo S.......................SDI electronic, eight coils, Direct Fuel Injection, E-Gas electronic throttleHP

HP (SAE net) (mfr):
2007 .... 250 at 6,000
2008–2009...290 at 6,200
2007 S..340 at 6,000
2007–2008 Turbo ....450 at 6,000
2007 Turbo S.....................................521 at 5,500
2008–2009 S......................................385 at 6,200
2008–2009 Turbo ....500 at 6,000
2009 Turbo S.....................................550 at 6,000

Chassis & Drivetrain

Frame ....Unitized, fully galvanized steel
Component layout........Front engine, four-wheel drive
Transmission:
2007–2009 Cayenne,
    2007 Cayenne S ....Manual 6-speed, Tiptronic S 6-speed
2007–2009 S, Turbo,
    Turbo S......................... Tiptronic S 6-speed only

Axle ratio:
2007 .... 4.10 manual / 4.56 Tiptronic
2008–2009 .... 3.70 manual / 3.55 Tiptronic
2007 S........................ 3.70 manual / 4.10 Tiptronic
2007–2008 Turbo, 2007 Turbo S.......3.70 Tiptronic
2008–2009 S, Turbo, Turbo S ....3.55 Tiptronic

Front suspension:
2007–2009 Cayenne.......... Independent, aluminum track control arm top, spheroidal-cast track control arm bottom. Steel spring, struts with lateral-force compensation through coil springs offset from shock absorber axis. (Porsche Dynamic Chassic Control (PDCC) active anti-roll, 2008–2009.)
2007 S........... Independent, wide-based aluminum-and-steel upper and lower A-arms and links, coil springs over tubular shock absorbers, anti-roll bar. Air-adjusted suspension.
2007 Turbo S..... Independent, double track-control arm configuration with subframe; aluminum track control arm top, spheroidal-cast track control arms bottom, full pneumatic spring struts with integrated shock absorbers. Porsche Automatic Stability Management (PASM).
2007–2008 Turbo .... Independent, wide-based aluminum-and-steel upper and lower A-arms and links, coil springs over tubular shock absorbers, anti-roll bar. Porsche Active Stability Management System (PASM).
2008–2009 S, Turbo.......... Independent, aluminum track control arm top, spheroidal-cast track control arm bottom. Steel spring, struts with lateral-force compensation through coil springs offset from shock absorber axis. (Porsche Dynamic Chassis Control (PDCC) active anti-roll, S.) (Porsche Active Suspension Management (PASM) on demand, Turbo.)

2009 Turbo S..............Independent, aluminum track control arm top, spheroidal-cast track control arm bottom, onto subframe. Steel spring, struts with lateral-force compensation through coil springs offset from shock absorber axis. Porsche Active Suspension Management (PASM) on demand.

Rear suspension:

2007–2009 Cayenne.......... Independent, aluminum track control arm top, spheroidal-cast track control arm bottom. Steel spring, struts with lateral-force compensation through coil springs offset from shock absorber axis. (Porsche Dynamic Chassis Control (PDCC) active anti-roll, 2008–2009.)

2007 Turbo S.............. Independent, multi-link axle, steel-and-aluminum links, coil springs over tubular shock absorbers, anti-roll bar. Air-adjusted suspension.

2007–2008 Turbo .... Independent, multi-link axle, steel-and-aluminum links, coil springs over tubular shock absorbers, anti-roll bar. Optional air-adjusted suspension.

2008–2009 S, Turbo.......... Independent, aluminum track control arm top, steel-plate track control arm bottom. Steel spring, struts with lateral-force compensation through coil springs offset from shock absorber axis. (Porsche Dynamic Chassis Control (PDCC) active anti-roll, S.) (Porsche Active Suspension Management (PASM) on demand, Turbo.)

2009 Turbo S.............Independent, aluminum track control arm top, steel-plate track control arm bottom, onto subframe. Steel spring, struts with lateral-force compensation through coil springs offset from shock absorber axis. Porsche Active Suspension Management (PASM) on demand.

General

Wheelbase, mm/inches..........................2.855 / 112.4
Track:
  front, mm/inches:
    2007–2009.......................................1,655 / 65.2
    2007–2009 S, 2007–2009
      Turbo, 2007 Turbo S.....................1,647 / 64.8
    2009 Turbo S...................................1,641 / 64.6
  Rear, mm/inches:
    2007–2009.......................................1,670 / 65.8
    2007–2009 S, 2007–2009
      Turbo, 2007 Turbo S.....................1,662 / 65.4
    2009 Turbo S...................................1,656 / 65.2
Brakes............. Power-assisted dual-circuit six-piston (front) four-piston (rear) aluminum monoblock calipers, ventilated rotors (cross-drilled, 2009 Turbo S), anti-lock brake system
Tire size: front, rear
    2007–2009.........................235/65R17, 235/65R17
    2007–2009 S, Turbo..........255/55R18, 255/55R18
    2007, 2009 Turbo S............275/40R20, 275/40R20
Wheels: front, rear
    2007–2009.................................7.5Jx17, 7.5Jx17
    2007–2009 S, Turbo..........................8Jx18, 8Jx18
    2007, 2009 Turbo S........................9Jx20, 10Jx20
Weight:
    2007–2009.............. 4,762 manual, 4,784 Tiptronic
    2007 S..................... 4,895 manual, 4,939 Tiptronic
    2008–2009 S...................................4,950 Tiptronic
    2007, 2009 Turbo S........................5,192 Tiptronic
    2007–2009 Turbo............................5,192 Tiptronic

Porsche introduced its Panorama Roof option in 2005. This consisted of one fixed and three movable glass panels and provided as much as 15 square feet of open area, roughly four times what the standard sunroof provided. The system allowed 15 variations for ventilation or visibility. *Photo courtesy Porsche Cars North America*

In the United States, Porsche introduced its second-generation Cayenne lineup with restyled front ends featuring new, smaller headlight modules and LED light bars for turn signals. All 2008 models incorporated new engines with direct fuel injection (DFI) for improved fuel economy, reduced exhaust emissions, and increased horsepower output. *Photo courtesy Porsche Cars North America*

(PCM) system allowed owners to play MP3-encoded CDs through the CD unit and add a mobile telephone to the system. Extended Navigation let a driver trace a route back to a starting point even when roads or trails used did not appear on the system's internal maps. This was vital when exploring unmarked off-road terrain or using new suburban streets that had not yet been mapped.

Model year 2007 brought a new benchmark to the SUV world when Porsche introduced the Cayenne Turbo S. The twin-turbocharged and dual-intercooled 4.5-liter V-8 developed 521 SAE net horsepower at 5500 rpm. Acceleration from 0 to 62 mph took just 5.2 seconds, and Porsche established the top speed at 167 mph. The Porsche Active Stability Management System (PASM) helped keep the vehicle in control at all times. Brakes were up to the challenge, with 380-mm (14.96-inch) front rotors and 358-mm (14.09-inch) rear rotors, running inside 20-inch wheels at 186-mph-rated 275/40R20 tires.

The Cayenne GTS introduced in 2008 was conceived as Porsche's "sportiest" SUV, with 405 horsepower from its normally aspirated, 4.5-liter, DFI V-8 engine. The GTS came standard with a six-speed manual transmission and sold for $69,300 in the United States. *Photo courtesy Porsche Cars North America*

Subtle styling cues for the GTS came from its most potent stablemate, the Turbo S. Porsche fitted the new model with 21-inch wheels mounted with 295/35R21 tires. With the optional Tiptronic S six-speed transmission, the GTS returned 16.9 mpg. *Photo courtesy Porsche Cars North America*

Cayenne models evolved for 2008 as Steve Murkett gave the vehicle bodies facelifts. Under the hood, new engines took advantage of direct fuel injection technology and VarioCam Plus variable valve control to improve performance and fuel economy and reduce carbon-dioxide emissions. The new 4.8-liter V-8 offered 500 SAE net horsepower in the Cayenne Turbo model and 385 brake horsepower in the normally aspirated Cayenne S model. A new V-6 engine of 3.6 liters displacement developed 290 horsepower for the Cayenne. With the six-speed manual, the V-6 reached 60 mph in 7.5 seconds. The S made that speed in 6.4 seconds, and the new Turbo got to 60 mph in just 4.9 seconds. New to these models as well was Porsche's Dynamic Chassis Control, a system incorporating active anti-roll bars that almost completely offset body roll in turns.

To further emphasize the importance of handling in its Cayenne lineup, Porsche introduced the GTS for midyear 2008 as well. Using the same 4.8-liter engine, this configuration developed 405 horsepower, but just as important, engineers set standard ride height 0.8 inches lower than other Cayenne models. New 21-inch alloy wheels supported 295/35R21 tires all around. The GTS came with either a six-speed manual or six-speed Tiptronic S transmission. Acceleration from standstill to 60 mph took just 5.7 seconds with the manual gearbox.

Cayenne GTS (2008–2009)

Engine

Design.............................Water-cooled 8-cylinder V-engine, 90 degrees

Bore & Stroke, mm/inches .... 96.0x83.0 / 3.78x3.27

Displacement, cc/cid........................ 4,806 / 293.3

Valve operation .... Dual overhead camshafts, four valves per cylinder, chain driven. Hydraulic lifters with VarioCam Plus variable valve timing system.

Compression ratio....................................... 12.5:1

Fuel feed ....SDI electronic, eight coils, Direct Fuel Injection, E-Gas electronic throttle

HP (SAE net) (mfr)......................... 405 at 6,500

Chassis & Drivetrain

Frame...................... Unitized, fully galvanized steel

Component layout... Front engine, four-wheel drive

Transmission..............Manual 6-speed, Tiptronic S 6-speed

Axle ratio...............3.70:1 manual, 3.55:1 Tiptronic

Front suspension ..... Independent, aluminum track control arm top, spheroidal-cast track control arm bottom. Steel spring, struts with lateral-force compensation through coil springs offset from shock absorber axis. Porsche Active Stability Management (PASM).

Rear suspension ..... Independent, aluminum track control arm top, steel plate-cast track control arm bottom. Steel spring, struts with lateral-force compensation through coil springs offset from shock absorber axis. Porsche Active Stability Management (PASM).

General

Wheelbase, mm/inches..................... 2,855 / 112.4

Track:

    front, mm/inches............................ 1,659 / 65.3

    Rear, mm/inches .... 1,682 / 66

Brakes.........Power-assisted dual-circuit six-piston (front) four-piston (rear) aluminum monoblock calipers, ventilated rotors, anti-lock brake system.

Tire size:

    front, rear 295/35R21, 295/35R21

Wheels:

    front, rear 10Jx21, 10Jx21

Weight.......................... 4,906 manual or Tiptronic

The Turbo presented an understated if formidable package. Subtle engineering improvements to the 4.5-liter twin turbo raised output to 550 horsepower. This provided acceleration from 0 to 62 mph in just 4.8 seconds and a top speed of 174 mph. Riding on 21-inch SportPlus alloy wheels, the Turbo S sold for $124,800 in the United States. *Photo courtesy Porsche Cars North America*

Two-tone leather treatments were options on the most potent Cayenne yet offered, the Turbo S. Updated electronics, including navigation and audio management, paralleled the finest options available in the Porsche 911 Turbo coupe, with attention to detail remaining a hallmark of the ultimate models. *Photo courtesy Porsche Cars North America*

For 2009, Porsche brought back the ground-pounding Turbo S model using direct fuel injection and VarioCam Plus technology. With 550 horsepower available, performance was as expected: 0–60 took just 4.7 seconds, and the Turbo S topped out at 174 mph. Performance and other specifications remained unchanged for the rest of the 2009 model lineup. Once again, however, user-electronics received an update: The optional Porsche Communication Management System (standard on the Cayenne Turbo and Turbo S) changed from a separate keyboard for inputs to a touch screen that required fewer keys and menus. Bluetooth connectivity offered hands-free cellular phone use and the ability to play music from iPods or USB memory sticks. XM Satellite radio provided real-time traffic updates.

The success of the Cayenne surprised critics. It sold well in the United States and everywhere, and it did better its second year in 2004. Porsche's original plan was to assemble 20,000 each year. In 2005, its third year, Cayenne was Porsche's largest-selling car line with 42,000 vehicles manufactured compared to 40,000 Boxsters and 911s. The market for Cayenne continued to grow, and it has redefined the company in some parts of the world.

"Today," Klaus-Gerhard Wolpert said, "in the emerging markets, China, Russia, India, Cayenne stands for Porsche." In the Middle East in 2001 and 2002, Porsche had sold 400 sports cars. In 2007, sales reached 5,000 vehicles. Porsche's largest-volume dealer in the world was in Dubai. This dealership sold 1,200 Porsches; 85 percent of them were Cayennes.

"In the Arabic states," Wolpert explained, "normally you go somewhere together with friends or a group. You never go out alone. It's not in the culture of the Arabs. If you own a Boxster, it is impossible. You need two Boxsters, and there aren't so many roads.

"In China, while everyone is equal, it is a sign of status if you are driven. To ride in a Nine-Eleven looks as if you go with a friend. And there weren't so many paved roads."

★★★★★	2004
★★★★★	2005
★★★★★	2006

Carrera GT

The Carrera GT represented a new process in creating an automobile as much as a flagship that set performance benchmarks and calmed enthusiast anxiety. The "process" began in 1991 and grew out of V-12 engines for Formula One that Porsche developed for the Footwork Arrows team. These engines failed due to oil starvation in hard cornering. Engineer Herbert Ampferer was in charge of all engine development at Weissach, and he halted the F1 program, temporarily at first. Intense testing fixed the problem, but the engine still was too heavy and underpowered. Ampferer withdrew Porsche permanently, provoking a lawsuit from Arrows. More importantly, it provoked a challenge from Weissach's director Horst Marchardt: Did Porsche have good enough engineers to produce an engine that could win in F1?

There was no hurry to answer: Porsche was out of F1, and so Ampferer and his team made improvements to the V-12 and achieved a very competitive 700-plus horsepower. But Ampferer still felt the engine was too heavy and too long. So he returned a challenge to Marchardt:

"If you need to prove to the management that we can do it, we will make you a new engine if you give us a little bit more time. We will prove to you that we can do a modern Formula One engine, competitive in power, competitive in package, competitive in stiffness, and competitive in reliability." Marchardt gave him funds that allowed his team to develop a new Formula One engine.

It was a very small group, "a handful of engineers," Ampferer recalled, "but not with the target to go to Formula One. Just to prove that Porsche engineers were able to do something like a Formula One engine."

By the end of 1994, he had an engine configured to the "package specifications" (weight, length, width) that a friendly team provided him from their own current car. On a Weissach dynamometer it revved to 14,800 rpm. "This was a V-10 engine," he explained, "with pneumatic valve systems, with variable intake valves, variable exhaust valves, with variable trumpets. All our variables were on that engine."

He ran the cylinder heads in 1994 in a 20-hour durability test at 20,000 rpm. This effectively covered the distance of 10 Formula One races in one day of testing. His team put the entire engine on the dyno and ran it 2 hours, regularly developing 760 horsepower on pump fuel. It was, he concluded, an engine they could use. Marchardt was convinced: Weissach had engineers who could produce an F1 engine. If another opportunity arose. . . . Meanwhile, Ampferer had gained approval to enter Le Mans with GT1 prototypes for 1996, 1997, and 1998.

"What do we do with that V-10 engine?" he asked rhetorically. "Nothing. It was just to prove our engineering capability. We put it into storage." Then one day, he had to talk to Wiedeking after a GT1 won Le Mans in 1998. "What now?" the chairman asked. Ampferer knew that to compete in F1 in 1999 gave them

Porsche racers and enthusiasts alike characterized the Carrera GT interior as being a race car with air conditioning, a great sound system, and a navigation system. Few race cars offered so much leather or a comfortable passenger seat. *Photo courtesy Porsche Cars North America*

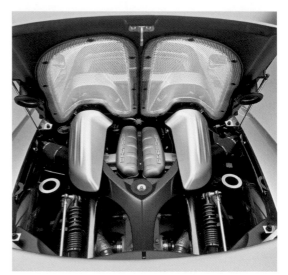

Porsche engineers derived this V-10 from work they had done on V-12 engines for Formula One and a prototype 5.5-liter V-10 for Le Mans 2000. Enlarged slightly to 5.7 liters, this engine developed 612 horsepower, rocketing the car from 0 to 62 mph in 3.9 seconds and from 0 to 124 mph in just 9.9 seconds. *Photo courtesy Porsche Cars North America*

just seven months to design and produce a racer to meet new regulations.

He demurred, feeling that 1999 was too soon on too tight a budget. But 2000? Wiedeking told him to go ahead with design and testing. He would decide later about entering. Ampferer believed he could start with the carbon-fiber chassis from the 1998 GT1 winner and use his V-10 F1 engine. But 3.5 liters was not enough for Le Mans. An engine conceived for a 2-hour F1 sprint was not durable enough for 24 hours.

Ampferer's engineers redesigned the V-10, enlarging displacement from 3.5 to 5 liters. They replaced pneumatic valves with standard spring valves. Other considerations of a modern V-10 engine—the 65-degree V-angle, torsional vibration of the crankshaft and of the cam drive, gearing systems of the cam drive, the cams themselves—remained unchanged. And they built a prototype and tested it extensively on the circuit at Weissach.

"We talked with Wiedeking. He said, 'Nice car, this race car.'" But then he posed questions that would change Porsche's history: "How many times has Porsche won Le Mans?" Ampferer answered: 16. Wiedeking asked who had the next highest number of wins. Ferrari with eight.

"What difference does it make if Porsche goes to Le Mans and wins seventeen times instead of sixteen times? It's another Le Mans win," Wiedeking continued. "What do you think we are as Porsche? Are we *the* sports car manufacturer in the world?"

In early 1999 rumors and stories from other automakers about future products filled the automobile world. The super car genre that Porsche had invented with its 959 had fathered challengers. Ferrari talked about an Enzo. McLaren and Mercedes leaked hints about an SLR. The name Bugatti had resurfaced.

"'We are the sports car manufacturer,' Wiedeking told me, 'and these are sports cars

Designers and engineers achieved virtually even weight distribution. When this was combined with its low center of gravity and its ultra-light/ultra-strong materials, the Carrera GT was capable of high cornering speeds and race-car-like handling. *Photo courtesy Porsche Cars North America*

The Carrera GT stretched 181.5 inches long on its 107.5-inch wheelbase. It stood 45.7 inches tall with the two removable roof panels in place. It weighed 3,042 pounds without fuel or driver.

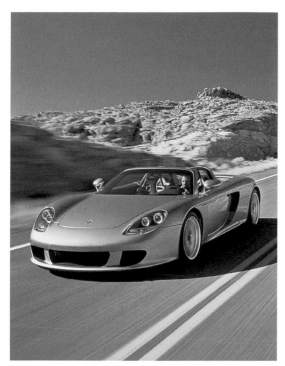

Porsche first showed a version of this car to the public at the Paris auto show in late 2002. It took the company's Le Mans racing technology, adjusted it to the real world of traffic, and put it on the street. Although it was strictly rear-wheel drive, it was as technologically marvelous as the 959 had been 18 years earlier. But this one made money. *Photo courtesy Porsche Cars North America*

they are talking about. So we need a sports car like that. What do you think?' And I had to agree with him. 'Yes, yes sir.'"

But rumors slipped out that Porsche had a car, a Le Mans Prototype Category 1 entry for 2000, LMP2000. Insiders had heard that it was fast but that Wiedeking had killed it. Voices hinted that the SUV project needed money.

"Wiedeking did not change his mind," Ampferer said emphatically. "We got the approval for a Le Mans 2000 car. But he stated from the first minute that we discussed this issue with him. He said: 'Do the car, do the concept. Go to a certain level of the development. But this is no confirmation that you will go to Le Mans in 2000.'

"It was hard, because it was a really good race car," Ampferer said. "We got a new lap record at Weissach. But we never got the approval. On the other hand, having something as a vision in front of me which was a super sports car was good too."

That launched a long consideration phase. What car? What engine? What concept? Answering those questions involved August Achleitner. Achleitner was the packaging manager for the new 911, the man at the time whose department made sure every element necessary for an automobile fit within the confines of designers' concepts. Grant Larson was designing the next 911, the Typ 997, in Porsche's satellite design studio in Huntington Beach in southern California.

223

Porsche's visual heritage is never far from the minds of its designers. This view gives a hint of the legacy designers Grant Larson and Tony Hatter continued from the company's 718RS race cars of the early 1960s. Similar to the 718, the driver sat slightly ahead of the halfway point.

All but essential crash structures were fabricated from carbon-fiber-reinforced plastic. Engineers found a method to produce carbon-fiber pieces to support the engine and rear running gear, and obtained a patent for this new technique of engineering and manufacture.

Design director Harm Lagaay used this studio to isolate his designers from prying eyes and corporate politics.

Achlcitner needed some sketches and ideas for an all-new car, a mid-engine super car. He called Larson and briefed him on what it was about: The sleek racer should become a stylish road car. He created several ideas through February and March of 1999. By May, Horst Marchardt had approved one of his concepts, and Grant divided his time between the 997 and the new super car. He spent seven months tuning the design. At the end, Wiedeking and Lagaay commuted to California every other week to review Larson's model. In early 2000, Marchardt forwarded Wiedeking's approval to move forward on not just one show vehicle but two identical copies.

One had to run so that Walter Röhrl could drive it for a video and for its live presentation at the Paris show. The second was strictly a "push-around" for times when two shows coincided, such as Los Angeles and Detroit around January 1, 2001. For enthusiasts who had been torqued out of shape by announcements of a coming SUV, this car silenced them. A year later in Detroit, on January 8, 2002, Wiedeking announced that Porsche would produce the car called the Carrera GT.

"The Carrera GT was a continuation of everything we had learned in the GT1 chain of cars," designer Tony Hatter explained. Lagaay brought him into the project early. The new road car was based on the LMP2000 prototype, a car that Hatter had worked on using an open carbon-fiber monocoque with a V-8 engine in the back. The assignment was to make a road-worthy sports car out of the LMP2000.

Porsche show cars were rooted in reality. They had to be manufacture-able and return a profit in production. But a direct translation from auto show turntable to the street was not always realistic. Hatter explained that "every single millimeter was completely new and different from the show car to the production model."

Larson's show car had very little machinery behind it. Once Weissach engineers started to work, it became clear they had to change everything from safety to packaging to snow chain clearances to engine cooling. The road car had to have a roof.

Hatter and Norbert Singer took one of the show cars into the wind tunnel. "What came out of the wind tunnel was horrible," Tony recalled. "Air blowing down the side of the car does not automatically turn ninety degrees and go into air scoops. To get the car to cool, those openings at the back had to be

What a still photo can't impart to a reader is the sound this engine produced, like a mid-tone growl from deep in the throat at idle to—as one of the chief development engineers called it—a shrieking *woo-woo-woo* sound as the driver blipped the throttle or shot up through the gears.

The Carrera GT was capable of a published top speed of 205 mph. While tire pressure monitoring was a mandatory safety feature by the time the Carrera GT was designed, another Porsche, the 959, pioneered the technology of reading accurate pressure on the fly. The Carrera GT sold for $440,000 in the United States.

so big that the car would look nowhere near like the show car. Cooling had to go to the front. The radiators on the Carrera GT are at the front, two in the side and the big one in the middle. The air openings behind the doors on the side are for induction air, air conditioning, and air circulating around the engine compartment. When you look at the car, it was just a plumbing exercise."

Cooling the engine became critical. Cooling air easily surrounded racing engines running at full throttle. The Carrera GT had to crawl through traffic. This created a challenge for the material Porsche chose to build nearly the entire car: carbon fiber. Engine compartments baked. Carbon fiber typically did not survive more than 130 degrees Centigrade, about 266 degrees Fahrenheit, the temperature at which most of it was created. The fibers were fine, but resins failed and the part collapsed. Engineers needed something that resisted 180 degrees C, about 356 degrees F. To help, they isolated exhaust pipes and mounted engine-temperature-controlled fans in the compartment to cool the engine, the gearbox oil, and the air conditioner condenser.

The car was mostly carbon fiber, but not its front crash structure. Porsche had vast experience with crash structures in steel. The growing team of engineers (it started

out at 15, and by the time production began it counted 200), reasoned they would make no "experiments" with crash structure. Their suppliers developed a new high-energy-absorption stainless steel that saved some weight. The steel structure offered another benefit to buyers.

"It was made on a simple bending machine. It was bolted through the carbon fiber structure. It could be replaced easily if the customers had a crash. They can easily change the structure with a relatively low cost."

Working with carbon fiber for series production threw Weissach engineers countless first-time challenges. In addition to engine compartment heat management, another challenge was the engine cradle. In an actual race car, designers bolted the engine and transmission directly to the chassis as "stressed members." They mounted rear axles directly to the gearbox, making the rear of the car a large, stiff compound surrounding the engine. Yet this stiffness transferred unacceptably loud engine and road noise to the passenger compartment. Michael Hölscher's engineers had to isolate certain structures, tuning their work to the sounds they knew customers wanted to hear.

Herbert Ampferer had warned the development team, "If we want to do a super sports car, you need a modern racing

Carbon-fiber, magnesium, and aluminum alloys are the usual materials of modern race cars. Add in a few square meters of fine leather and an excellent sound system plus air conditioning and you have the Carrera GT. Many observers have questioned the need for an auxiliary audio system when Porsche installed a 10-cylinder system behind the driver's head.

engine in that. Otherwise it's not a real sports car. A high-revving V-10 with this typical sound . . . 'WooWooWoo' . . . we needed something like that.

"The alternative would have been making something from the Cayenne, a V-8 turbo or something like that. Strong, but not really what enthusiasts love to hear, love to see." They chose the V-10 for the LMP2000 prototype. They took a race car engine suitable for 24 hours and made it durable for 24,000 and more. Still, they had to contend with air-conditioning condensers, a big alternator, and a hydraulic pump.

"Our engine in this car was a real race engine," Michael Hölscher said. Hölscher was project manager for the car. He was a veteran mechanical engineer with experience gained in entire car development and manufacture ranging from Porsche, where he produced E500 Mercedes-Benz automobiles at Zuffen-hausen works, to designing and developing

Audi's RS2 and Opel's Zafira models. The V-10 "was designed for this Le Mans car, and the most important point in the design of a race car engine was to have a low center of gravity," he explained. Flat Boxer engines had exhausts below the cylinders that consumed space, elevating the engine position in the car. V-configurations allowed a lower center of gravity because exhausts sometimes were higher than oil pans.

"But if you had the V and a conventional engine, you had a clutch like a pizza plate," he continued. "This also caused the need to raise the engine. So race cars all had nice small carbon fiber clutches, some not more than one hundred millimeters in diameter [4 inches]. Racing teams threw them away after one race or two." Porsche would not accept having its customers change clutches as often as motor oil.

Hölscher and Ampferer remembered Porsche's success with carbon-reinforced ceramic brakes. They tested countless proto-type composite clutches. At high revs, they burst. Ampferer's engineers had set the V-10's engine rev limiter at 8400 rpm. Porsche typically demanded their clutches survive nearly double that speed for safety reasons, nearly 15,000 in this case. The final version of the ceramic clutches withstood 20,000 rpm. Exceptional wear re-sistance and a working diameter of 6.3 inches proved to be two additional bonuses. With this small diameter, Porsche installed the engine so low it set a world record for crank-shaft height above the pavement of 4 inches at its lowest rotating point, which ended up below the centerline of the driving wheels. The original design of the engine used a rotating countershaft above the driveshaft to transfer engine output to a gearbox. The low position, however, enabled Hölscher, Hatter, and Singer to incorporate air tunnels beneath the car. "This entire composition," Hölscher explained, "allowed us to have a diffuser over the whole width of the rear of the car. That brought us tremendous down force. At top speed, we have about four hundred kilograms [880 pounds] of down force."

The car offered racing-world perfor-mance to street-car customers. It reached a top

Carrera GT (2004–2006)

Engine

Design.........Water-cooled V (68 degree) 10-cylinders
Bore & Stroke, mm/inches.......98.0x76.0 / 3.86x2.99
Displacement, cc/cid............................ 5,722 / 349.8
Valve operation .... dual overhead cams, gear and duplex chain driven, 4 valves per cylinder. VarioCam Plus
Compression ratio...10.5:1
Fuel feed ....DME, 2 Motronic ME 7.1.1
HP (SAE net) (mfr)................................612 at 8,000

Chassis & Drivetrain

Frame....................monocoque, carbon fiber, steel
Component layout....................mid-engine rear drive
Transmission.................................six-speed manual
Axle ratio (manual/Tiptronic)............................4.44:1
Front suspension ....Independent, aluminum double wishbones with pushrod activated spring-and-shock absorber units, progressive oil springs, anti-roll bar

Rear suspension ....Independent, aluminum double wishbones with pushrod activated spring-and-shock absorber units, progressive oil springs, anti-roll bar

General

Wheelbase, mm/inches..........................2,730 / 107.4
Track:
    front, mm/inches................................. 1,612 / 63.5
    Rear, mm/inches ....1,587 / 62.5
Brakes.....................Power-assisted Porsche Ceramic Composite brakes, venitlated and drilled ceramic composite rotors, 6-piston fixed aluminum monobloc calipers
Tire size:
    front, rear .... 265/35ZR19 / 335/30ZR20
Wheels:
    front, rear ....9.5Jx19 / 12.5Jx20
Weight.. 3,091 manual only

---

speed of 205 mph (330 kph), with acceleration to 62.5 mph in 3.9 seconds. The final 5.7-liter version of the V-10 developed 612 SAE net horsepower. Hölscher's engineers installed 15-inch brake rotors inside 19- and 20-inch front and rear wheels in the 3,043-pound two-seater. It sold for $444,400.

But none of this would have satisfied Wendelin Wiedeking had not two other considerations been met. First, the car had to be usable; it had to be the Porsche among the super cars. Second, the car had to have a Porsche feeling and a Porsche look.

Production began for the 2004 model year. Advanced orders and customer interest suggested that Porsche might produce as many as 1,500. Hand-assembled at Porsche's new factory in Leipzig, a small crew of 110 workers turned out 3 cars per day. As with any of its models, Porsche invited custom exterior and interior color choices, though these cars did not get assembled till the end of the run in 2005. When assembly ended, Porsche had manufactured 1,270 production models. The car made money for Porsche, unlike the company's earlier super car, the 959. It generated countless magazine, newspaper, and TV stories, just as the 959 had done. More importantly, the car startled everyone. Loyalists and cynics alike, who feared Porsche had become an SUV maker, were stunned and thrilled.

"I think we learned," Michael Hölscher summed it up, "that it is possible to bring a really special product to the market but one that has very different demands from our big production numbers. How do you deal with it? With suppliers you must have a different approach. But you cannot make such a project one after another. You have to learn how the customers think. They do not buy such a car every year. You must know when the time is right to bring a new drumbeat to the market."

Chapter 20

987 Cayman

★★★1/2	2006–2008 Cayman S Coupe
★★★	2007–2008 Cayman Coupe
★★★★	2009 Cayman S Coupe
★★★1/2	2009 Cayman Coupe

Grant Larson had designed the Boxster concept car and then developed the production version. Almost as soon as it was finished, in typical Porsche fashion, design director Harm Lagaay asked him to begin to think about the second generation. With a small budget, he built a full-scale prototype of a Boxster with a fixed coupe top. But when it came time to follow it through, Larson was occupied designing the 911/996 replacement, the Typ 997, and then the Carrera GT show car. Lagaay asked Pinky Lai to take over the Boxster and its closed version.

Lai joined Porsche in 1989, the first member of the design team that Harm Lagaay brought in from BMW when Ulrich Bez (also from BMW) hired Lagaay. Born in Hong Kong, Lai moved to Rome where he earned an industrial design degree in 1978. A scholarship from Ford in Cologne sent him to London's Royal College of Art where he earned a second degree in 1982 in car design. After two years at Ford, he joined BMW and met Lagaay. His first assignment at Porsche was the exterior and interior of Bez's passion, the four-door Typ 989. By the late 2000s Lai chiefly designed projects for outside clients, however his most recent Porsche was the Typ 987 Cayman. It evolved from the 986 Boxster.

By the time Lai took over the Boxster second generation, Larson's coupe had been pushed back and forgotten. Not yet an official program, this idea had emerged during product discussions on developing Boxster's second generation. The marketing department feared the Boxster as a roadster alone would not survive the competition by the time it reached the market. They compared it to the 911, which had 10 or more variations to offer customers from C2 to Turbo to GT2 to open cars. They worried that even a second-generation Boxster was too weak to compete against the strong competition Porsche expected from other German carmakers, the Japanese, and the Americans.

Larson's proposal was essentially a "three-box" sports car. That represented one end of the spectrum or possibilities. The other end was the "stretched greenhouse." BMW had designed Z1 and Z2 concepts with long greenhouses. Lai recalled a Volvo P1800 in the 1970s with two doors and a long greenhouse.

"Marketing really supported the idea. During the initial stage, they were pushing. I wouldn't wonder if they weren't even funding the initial study. They needed volume and variety to satisfy the customers."

Those ideas had to be realistic as well as convincing. Lai's design group could not go for 19- or 20-inch wheels. The lower body of this car had to fit within the Boxster perimeter. "We could only play around with the greenhouse area and its proportions," he recalled. "How far can you stretch it, how do you position the windscreen, or a new position of the greenhouse?"

Marketing staffers worried that it was unwise to have only Photoshop concepts

The Cayman S grew out of Porsche's perceived need to offer a "closed" Boxster body. Two variations developed during concept phase, and this fastback configuration won the review held for management and Porsche board members. The Cayman and Boxster share a significant number of components.

When stylist Pinky Lai designed the Cayman S, it was with the goal in mind to recognize its Boxster lineage while creating a new coupe that reflected other Porsche coupe designs from the 911. The large back window is a functional hatchback, providing easy access to the 9.2-cubic-foot rear storage area.

to show the board. They funded two new models. One was the original short-greenhouse idea of Larson's. The other was the longer-greenhouse fastback that Lai had developed. Both were called the Boxster Coupe. (The "Cayman" name came much later.) Timing was crucial because Porsche closed for its winter holiday. Worse, Lai knew that if he wanted the board of directors to fund a new development program, they needed to see a three-dimensional model, "something that looks like a real car and then they will sign the check."

The only way this shop could meet Lai's deadline was to work from data, the x-y-z coordinates marking the thousands of points on the car that defined its shape. Time was too short to follow conventional procedures with two-dimensional section drawings to develop a surface to start the three-dimensional model. Lai had advanced this digital process when he did the 996 Turbo program, developing many of its forms on computer.

Porsche's supervisory board had an important meeting scheduled for the spring of 2000. They were deciding, fixing, and freezing long-term development schedules over a decade span. Had the platform team balked at the expenditure, funding for Boxster Coupe models would have slipped

six months, delaying the car two years or longer. The platform team delivered two first-generation Boxsters in raw-body form to the model shop. They sliced off each upper body, packed the lower bodies with modeling material, and began milling the two body versions. The project was essentially Lai's to manage. Harm Lagaay and Horst Marchardt appeared rarely and offered only minor suggestions.

The "see-through" models that arrived were body shell openings to allow viewers to see the crude interiors. They required extensive sanding but fortunately only minor changes. Lai's team upgraded everything for the show and board review. They had carried over passenger compartments from the Boxsters. They improved the interior and cut a lift gate. The luggage area had been just a sketch, but they opened up front and rear trunks so viewers could see them.

"Going from an open car to a closed car also was new in the company. Normally you have a closed car and you chop it and fix it. You always can expect a higher price for the open car. In this case, we were doing the reverse. We were basing the coupe on an open car which was supposed to be more expensive than the coupe. But it was not going to be cheaper than the Boxster because it was a new body! The whole rear end was new."

The interior of the Cayman S was similar to that of the Boxster. Air conditioning was standard, and the seating surfaces were covered with Alcantara in smooth or pebble-grain finish. Standard seats, power adjustable seats, and two types of sport seats were offered.

"I can recall the first directors' show," Lai said. "It was really impressive." With background data from dealers, they had initial cost calculations for taking the whole project into production. Wiedeking was there, and he told everyone, "We have to be profitable. Doing something beautiful is not enough. We have to survive!"

"He mentioned a figure, how many percent, the margin of profitability. 'Give me that margin and I will do it. It's too pretty to kill it.' And that was more or less the end of the presentation," Lai recalled. "Then the financial guys did their tricks. It is their 'art' to create workable figures, and we got the program— finally. We started the official production.

"All the ingredients were there. It was a mid-engine car. We had the opportunity to play around with the greenhouse, the most critical part; it was the major character of the Cayman. You know, if you stretch the backlight a little bit more than it is now, it would be a pure Nine-Eleven.

"The location of the backlight is determined by the transition of the greenhouse to the rear fender. We call it the Mountain and Valley, the ups and downs. That was the sexiest part of the car." In automobile manufacturing terminology, that segment is known as the "one-piece body side."

Lai was willing to work at it, to make some compromises from a styling point of view. But when body engineering's suppliers asked him for "some room to play with," he refused to let them "play" with the rear fender transition into the greenhouse.

The "one-piece body side" started with the rocker panel at the A-pillar behind the front door where assemblers fixed hinges to the door bolt. The front fender screwed onto the body side. Front fenders were never considered body-side in manufacturing. From there, the A-pillar went up to the roof. That is the reason for the two channels. These are the welding points of the body side and roof panel. This incorporates the whole rear fender, up the C-pillar and all the way down to the rocker. On the Cayman this was one piece of stainless steel.

"It's like a monument, a huge sculpture in stainless steel." There was one single operation to stamp it. Workers removed it without rubbing or scratching it. The most difficult area for the stamping was the valley and mountain, called a "negative draw." The draw angle was sideways. The sheet metal had to wrap up to the roof frame and end with a flange. The rocker sill had flanges that turned in and up. The mold makers had to work a certain draw angle that did not create any rubbing of the mold.

Porsche launched the car in 2006 only at the S level. The company fitted the 3.4-liter engine developing 295 horsepower. The car sold for $58,900 in the United States.

For 2007, Porsche supplemented the Cayman S with a base-model Cayman using the company's 2.7-liter, 245-horsepower flat-six engine. Dealers sold this for $49,400 while the 3.4-liter, 295-horsepower S retailed for $58,900. *Photo courtesy Porsche Cars North America*

Lai characterized the aerodynamics on the car as "a nightmare. It was a less-favorable greenhouse aerodynamically than the Nine-Eleven." They carried over the Boxster's rear trunk so they could use its spoiler mechanism. "We didn't think the Boxster telescoping wall type of spoiler would be very appealing on this car," he explained. "What about the double-plane spoiler of the Turbo? If it worked on the Turbo, it should work there as well, maybe not as efficiently as the Turbo because that one was longer."

"We gave the Cayman its own identity. The spoiler was an element that people identify as a Boxster or not a Boxster. We had to create a new animal. Although we were using the bones and a lot of parts borrowed from the Boxster, the goal was for the customer to get a unique vehicle. The Cayman was about giving support to the Boxster as a model line." Porsche's Boxster already had set a benchmark for competitors. Other carmakers could approach the Boxster on paper, but on a fast track, the Boxster ran away. Porsche did not want to see potential customers go elsewhere because they wanted a closed sports car with a proper coupe body. Porsche did not have it, and they already had lost customers. Lai's 996 designs had been about survival. This 987 was about keeping customers satisfied.

For 2006, Porsche introduced the Cayman with its more powerful and larger-engine-displacement, 3.4-liter, 295-horsepower S package. A base Cayman appeared for 2007, using a 2.7-liter flat six that developed 245 SAE net horsepower. With this engine, the car reached a top speed of 160 mph (258 kph). Acceleration from 0 to 62.5 mph took 6.1 seconds. The S achieved a top speed of 171 mph and needed just 5.4 seconds to reach 62.5 mph (100 kph). Porsche's integrated dry-sump lubrication from the Boxster engine carried over to Cayman versions as well. The Cayman S appeared with the Porsche six-speed manual gearbox or the optional five-speed Tiptronic S. The base Cayman used Porsche's five-speed manual gearbox, while the six-speed unit and the Tiptronic were options. Both manual transmissions incorporated short-throw shift action and connected to the engine through dual-mass flywheels and hydraulic clutches.

Front and rear MacPherson struts made best use of the space in the platform and ensured exceptional handling. Porsche's stability management (PSM) system was standard, while the active suspension management system (PASM) was optional on both models. Base cars rode on 17-inch wheels and tires, and the S fitted 18s. Four-piston, monobloc, aluminum brake calipers grasped

The Cayman, with its 245-horsepower, 2.7-liter engine accelerated from 0 to 62 mph in 5.8 seconds and on to a top speed of 160. Environmental Protection Agency (EPA) fuel ratings were 20 mpg city/29 highway. The 295-horsepower S reached 62 mph in 5.1 seconds and topped out at 171. EPA numbers were 18/26. *Photo courtesy Porsche Cars North America*

Cayman, Cayman S (2009–2009)

Engine

Design...........................Water-cooled flat (opposed) 6-cylinder, integral dry sump

Bore & Stroke, mm/inches:
2006 S	93.0x78.0 / 3.66x3.07
2007–2008	85.5x78.0 / 3.37x3.07
2007–2008 S	96.0x78.0 / 3.78x3.07
2009	88.9x78.7 / 3.50x3.10
2009 S	96.5x78.7 / 3.80x3.10

Displacement, cc/cd:
2006 S	3,179 / 193.9
2007–2008	2,687 / 163.9
2007–2008 S	3,386 / 206.7
2009	2,893 / 176.5
2009 S	3,436 / 209.7

Valve operation.............Double overhead camshafts, four valves per cylinder, chain driven. Hydraulic lifters with VarioCam variable valve timing system.

Compression ratio:
2006 S	11.0:1
2007–2008	11.3:1
2007–2008 S	11.1:1
2009	11.5:1
2009 S	12.5:1

Fuel feed:
2006–2007	DME fuel injection and ignition system
2008	DME, six coils, sequential multipoint fuel injection
2009	DME, six coils, Direct Fuel Injection

HP (SAE net) (mfr):
2006 S	208 at 6,200
2007–2008	245 at 6,500
2007–2008 S	295 at 6,250
2009	265 at 7,200
2009 S	320 at 7,200

Chassis & Drivetrain

Frame..........................Unitized, fully galvanized steel

Component layout..................Mid-engine, rear drive

Transmission:

2006 S....................Manual five-speed transaxle or Tiptronic S five-speed dual-function automatic transaxle

2007–2008......Manual five- or six-speed transaxle, or Tiptronic S five-speed dual function automatic transaxle

2007–2008 S...........Manual six-speed transaxle or Tiptronic S five-speed dual-funtion automatic transaxle

2009 Cayman, S...........Manual six-speed transaxlc or PDK seven-speed dual-function automatic transaxle

Axle ratio:
2006 S	3.88:1 manual / 3.91:1 Tiptronic
2007–2008	3.75:1 M5, 3.88:1 M6, 4.38:1 Tiptronic
2007–2008 S	3.88:1 manual, 4.16:1 Tiptronic
2009	3.875:1 manual, 3.25:1 PDK
2009 S	3.889:1 manual, 3.25:1 PDK

Front suspension..... Independent, spring strut wheel guidance, wheels suspended on track control and longitudinal arms, spring struts with twin-sleeve gas-pressure shock absorbers. Optional PASM.

11.7-inch front rotors on the base Cayman and 12.5-inch discs on the S. Both models shared 11.8-inch rotors at the rear. Porsche's ceramic composite brake system (PCCB) was available as an option and provided 13.8-inch-diameter front rotors and six-piston monoblocs. Pinky Lai's rear wing rose from the body rear deck at 75 mph. As with every other vehicle in Porsche's lineup, countless options were available through Porsche

Individual to personalize the car to any taste. Specifications and performance on both cars changed slightly for 2007, with the addition of VarioCam Plus variable valve timing. This took horsepower for the Cayman up to 245 and brought acceleration from 0 to 60 to 6.1 seconds with a top speed of 160 mph. The S remained unchanged, as did both models through 2008 except for the introduction of new colors and new folding bucket seats.

Rear suspension ....Independent, spring strut wheel guidance, wheels suspended on track control and longitudinal arms, spring struts with twin-sleeve gas-pressure shock absorbers. Optional PASM.

General

Wheelbase, mm/inches ....2,415 / 95.2
Track:
  Front, mm/inches:
    2006–2009 S....................................1,486 / 58.5
    2007–2008 ....1,490 / 58.7
    2009...1,491 / 58.7
  Rear, mm/inches:
    2007–2009 ....1,534 / 60.4
    2006–2009 S....................................1,528 / 60.2
Brakes .... Power-assisted, dual-circuit four-piston aluminum alloy monoblock fixed caliper anti-lock braking system.
  2006–2009 S..................Optional Porsche Ceramic Composite Brakes (PCCB)
Tire size: front, rear:
  2006–2009 ....205/55ZR17, 235/50ZR17
  2006–2009 S..................235/40ZR18, 265/40ZR18
Wheels:
  2007–2008 ....6.5Jx17, 8Jx17
  2009 .... 7Jx17, 8Jx17
  2006–2009 S.................................... 8Jx19, 9Jx18
Weight:
  2006 S.....................2,965 manual, 3,053 Tiptronic
  2007 ....2,877 manual, 3,009 Tiptronic
  2007 S.....................2,955 manual, 3,087 Tiptronic
  2008 ....2,866 manual, 2,998 Tiptronic
  2008 S.....................2,976 manual, 3,064 Tiptronic
  2009 ....2,932 manual, 2,998 PDK
  2009 S...........................2,976 manual, 3,031 PDK

For 2009, Porsche introduced direct fuel injection and new engines for both the Cayman and the S. Cayman displacement grew to 2.9 liters, and output increased to 265 horsepower. For the S, the 3.4-liter engine output increased to 320 horsepower. *Photo courtesy Porsche Cars North America*

For 2009, engines adopted direct fuel injection. The new Cayman powerplant displaced 2.9 liters, and output increased to 265 horsepower. This was sufficient to accelerate the car from 0 to 60 in 5.5 seconds, or 5.4 seconds with the new seven-speed, double-clutch PDK gearbox. Porsche quoted top speed as 165 mph for the manual, 163 for the PDK.

The Cayman S 3.4-liter engine, equipped with direct fuel injection, developed 320 horsepower. This 25-horsepower jump propelled the car to a top speed of 172 for the six-speed manual, 171 for the PDK. While these top speeds were slower than the previous incarnation, acceleration times dropped by a significant 1/2 second, to 4.9 seconds for the manual and a tenth quicker, 4.8, for the PDK.

New front and rear body panels on base and S models featured larger halogen head-lights, integrated direction indicators, and new LED rear lights. A new CD radio with MP3-compatible CD player and six-CD changer moved into the cockpit. Optional active seat ventilation kept backsides comfortable in hot or cold weather.

"We've been around a few years in the philosophy and design of the Porsche car," Pinky Lai said. "The customers never expect any revolution from us. We are not supposed to offer them a revolution in design. That is rule number one. What they expect is something new, and appealing. But it has to say—without looking at the badge—that this is the New Porsche or in the Porsche family."

Chapter 21

Panamera Gran Turismo Sedan

2010

It was all about targets: performance, package, and price. It was a philosophy that served Porsche well with its Carrera GT and the controversial Cayenne sport utility. Set benchmarks, drive competitors, move the benchmarks, revisit the heritage, peer into the future, revisit the competitors, move the benchmarks.

When Porsche invented the Carrera GT, no one had successfully taken a race car and mass-produced it for the street. Competitors were talking about it, but Wendelin Wiedeking, Herbert Ampferer, and Michael Hölscher held their engineers' and designers' feet to the fire. When the counting was done, Porsche had manufactured 1,270 of the 205 mph Le Mans-prototype-derived automobiles, nearly twice as many cars as Ferrari had produced counting the 400 Enzo and 349 F50 models combined.

When Wiedeking authorized the Cayenne, development chief Horst Marchardt and program director Klaus-Gerhard Wolpert turned on the heat again. Porsche's sport utility proved to be as capable as a medical support vehicle on track in a variety of racing series as it was cavorting on shifting sand dunes in the Middle East or the Far West.

Marchardt's successor, Wolfgang Dürheimer, had directed the development and the identity of the current 911, the Typ 997. He summed up Porsche's responsibility succinctly: "It takes a lot of passion and heart and feeling and craftsmanship. . . . The job we try

to conduct in Weissach is to do it perfect. Full stop. If it isn't you need to do it again. This is the search for constant perfection."

If the sports car and the SUV worlds were crowded, consider the universe of high-performance/high-luxury sedans: Bentley, BMW, Maserati, and Mercedes-Benz. Aston-Martin was coming, resurrecting a name from its own heritage, Lagonda. Porsche could do performance. That was a given. But how would it measure up in the luxury league?

"Initially, our performance and luxury benchmarks were the M-Five, Maserati Quattroporte, and Mercedes CLS," Dürheimer explained to *CAR* magazine's Phil McNamara early in 2009. "We realized we could outperform them, so we decided to aim for the S-class and the 7-Series." To accomplish that, he took away the Porsches his Panamera team members normally had used as "company" cars. He made them drive the competition for three years "to understand the levels of noise, comfort, and luxury in these cars." He admitted to McNamara that comfort and luxury were the challenge for him and his team. "To us, sporting comes naturally— our lockers are crammed with ideas. But not when it comes to comfort."

To reduce noise, lessen vibration, and modulate harshness (the treacherous NVH trio that could make a drive in a performance car sound like a torture session in a tin can filled with marbles), engineers mixed aluminum, magnesium, and graduated thicknesses of steel to develop the car body

Panamera 4S
Porsche's newest model, the four-passenger/
five-door Panamera, met U.S. customers first
at Monterey, California, in August 2009 when
Porsche celebrated its selection as featured
marque at the historic car races. The 4S used a
normally aspirated, 4.8-liter V-8 developing 400
horsepower. Performance was 5.0 seconds to
62 mph with a top speed of 175. *Photo courtesy
Porsche Cars North America*

structure. The suspension design—of course,
a fully independent system—incorporating
three-stage adaptive air springs helped
isolate road noise and vibrations. Acoustic
testing pointed out tendencies for body
panels or structure to broadcast road noise
into the interior.

The physical appearance of the car
provoked much consternation as first spy
photos and later official Porsche images
showed its silhouette and its somewhat
bulbous rear forms. It was large, measuring
195.7 inches overall, 55.8 inches high, and
76 inches wide. (For comparison, the 997
S coupe was 175.8 inches long, 51.2 inches
tall, and 71.2 inches wide. The M-B CLS63
AMG was 193.0 inches overall, 54.7 inches
tall, and 73.7 wide.) Creating the next car to
fit Porsche's DNA was always, as designer
Grant Larson explained it, a big challenge.
Couple that with input from a chairman who
always was an active participant, and then
the lines and shapes of the car make clearer
sense. While the seat model for Mercedes-
Benz CLS sedans may have been Napoleon
Bonaparte, Wendelin Wiedeking was a

bigger man. He wanted to sit comfortably
in the rear seat, either of them. He wanted
the car to accommodate full-size luggage for
all four occupants, accessible through a vast
hatchback rear door. To provide someone of
his height adequate head and leg room as
well as a suitable rear trunk, the car roofline
rose and the wheelbase stretched. Yet other
compromises occurred under the skin. To
provide comfortable and luxurious—those
two challenges again—seating for rear seat
occupants, engineers lowered seat height. To
do that, they moved the fuel tank rearward.
This provided a pair of benefits: it kept the
center of gravity low, and it participated
in achieving a 52 percent front/48 percent
rear weight bias despite the heft of the front
engine and transmission.

The result, from photos and from
passenger reports, was a success. Engineers
and interior designers replicated the look
and feel of a 911 from the driver's seat. "A
blindfolded Nine-Eleven owner," Dürheimer
explained, "can get into the Panamera and
know exactly the position of the steering
wheel, the pedals, the gear shifter. He'll
feel the seat's lateral support. The engine
responds instantly, and the sound is typical
Porsche, then he makes that first turn, feels
the direct steering, and knows it can only be
a Porsche."

Panamera Turbo
Porsche's 4.8-liter, twin-turbocharged V-8
developed 500 horsepower for the all-wheel-
drive turbo sports sedan. The company quoted
acceleration from 0 to 62 mph at 4.2 seconds
and reported the top speed was 188 mph.
Photo courtesy Porsche Cars North America

Panamera S, Panamera 4S (2010)

Engine

Design.............................Water-cooled aluminum V-8

Bore & Stroke, mm/inches:

   S..96.0x83.0 / 3.78x3.27

   4S......................................96.0x83.0 / 3.78x3.27

Displacement, cc/cid:

   S...4,806 / 293.3

   4S...4,806 / 293.3

Valve operation ....Dual overhead camshafts, four
valves per cylinder, VarioCam
Plus variable valve timing system

Compression ratio:

   S..12.5:1

   4S...12.5:1

Fuel feed .... Direct Fuel Injection

HP (SAE net) (mfr):

   S...400 at 6,500

   4S...400 at 6,500

Chassis & Drivetrain

Frame.........................Monocoque of steel, aluminum
and magnesium

Component layout........Front engine, rear-wheel drive

Transmission.........Porsche Doppelkupplungsgetriebe
PDK seven-speed double clutch
dual-function transmission

Axle ratio:

   S...3.55:1

   4S...3.55:1

Front suspension .... Independent, aluminum
double-wishbone axle, steel suspension.
Porsche Active Suspension Management (PASM)
electronically controlled shock absorber system
with three manually activated control maps.

Rear suspension ....Aluminum multi-link on
subframe. steel suspension. Porsche
Active Suspension Management (PASM)
electronically controlled shock absorber system
with three manually activated control maps.

General

Wheelbase: mm/inches

   S...2,920 / 115.0

   4S...2,920 / 115.0

Track:

   front, mm/inches:

     S...1,658 / 65.3

     4S...1,658 / 65.3

   rear, mm/inches:

     S...1,662 / 65.4

     4S...1,662 / 65.4

Brakes...........................Power-assisted dual-circuit.
Porsche Stability Management (PSM),
Brake Assistant, ABS, with six-piston (front)
and four-piston (rear) aluminum monoblock
calipers with grooved, inner-vented rotors.

Tire size: front, rear

   S....................................245/50ZR18, 275/45ZR18

   4S..................................245/50ZR18, 275/45ZR18

Wheels: front, rear

   S...8Jx18, 9Jx18

   4S...8Jx18, 9Jx18

Weight:

   S.. 3,968 Tiptronic only

   4S.. 4,101 Tiptronic only

Instant engine response was not just a figure of speech. Porsche engineers developed a stop/start capability made possible by the new direct fuel injection technology. As the driver reached the stop sign or light, the engine shut off, saving fuel and eliminating exhaust emissions at idle. When the light changed or the intersection cleared, depressing the gas pedal brought the engine back to life instantly. Because the direct fuel injection system pulsed a precise mist of gasoline into the cylinder at the instant the starter bumped the crankshaft, ignition occurred within hundredths of a second. Depending on the E-gas pedal position, the PDK transmission selected either second gear for a smooth start or first for harder acceleration.

The engine/gearbox combination—PDK only for the United States in the first year—offered plenty of acceleration. The 400 SAE net horsepower, 4.8-liter, V-8 Panamera S accelerated from engine-off standstill to 62 mph in 5 seconds. (By comparison, the 400-horsepower, 4.2-liter, normally aspirated Maserati

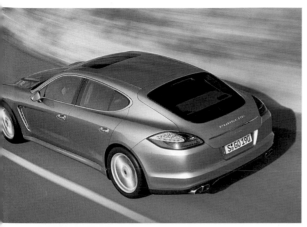

Panamera Turbo

Many observers criticized the appearance of the rear of the car. Porsche's director at the time, Wendelin Wiedeking, demanded that the sedan provide adequate seating room for tall adults, a factor that raised its roofline higher than other sport sedans in the marketplace. This decision made for much greater rear seat comfort. *Photo courtesy Porsche Cars North America*

Panamera 4S

In its introductory year, Porsche planned only to offer the Panamera with the seven-speed PDK transmission in the S, 4S, and Turbo models. The company planned a range of subsequent introductions for a V-6 version with an optional six-speed manual gearbox, as well as a hybrid and a Turbo S model. *Photo courtesy Porsche Cars North America*

Panamera 4S

The cabin-length center console—high at the dashboard—cleverly gave drivers the sensation of driving in a more intimate space. Several types of seats were offered. Front "comfort" seats in the Panamera S and 4S used motors to accommodate eight adjustments. Rear leg room and head room was generous. *Photo courtesy Porsche Cars North America*

Quattroporte S reached 62 mph in 5.5 seconds.) The 500-horsepower Panamera Turbo hit 62 mph in just 4.2 seconds. (The MB-CLS63 AMG with 507 horsepower reached 60 in 4.3 seconds; the 500-horsepower BMW M5 got to 62 mph in 4.7 seconds.) Such acceleration in other cars comes with—if not gas guzzler taxes—severe impact on the gas guzzler's pocketbook. Not so the Panamera. The 165 mph Turbo returned (on the more sedate EPA mileage loop) 23.2 mpg, 5.2 mpg better on the highway than Mercedes-Benz's comparable CLS63 AMG sedan, which reached 60 mph in 4.3 seconds and was governed to a top speed of 155 mph. (BMW's M5 rated 17 mpg on the highway.) The normally aspirated Panamera S delivered 26.2 mpg. (The base Maserati sedan rated 18 mpg on the highway.) For 2010, Porsche planned to introduce a gasoline V-6 with 300 horsepower, as well as its innovative single-electric motor hybrid that mated a 52-horsepower electric motor to a 333-horsepower 3-liter V-6.

Virtually every feature of the Panamera translated from ideas, concepts, computer designs, and blueprints into exceptional performance, fuel economy, interior comfort, and spaciousness. (Wiedeking sent suspension engineers back to the test

Panamera 4S
The rear hatch offered effortless access to the standard 15.7-cubic-foot rear storage (in the S and 4S; the Turbo provided 15.3 cubic feet). Folding down both rear seats opened up 44.6 cubic feet of cargo space. *Photo courtesy Porsche Cars North America*

Panamera Turbo
This five-door sport sedan measured 195.7 inches long on its wheelbase of 115.0 inches. It stood 55.8 inches tall and 76.0 inches wide. The S weighed 3,968 pounds, the 4S was 4,101, and the Turbo weighed 4,343 pounds. *Photo courtesy Porsche Cars North America*

Panamera Turbo (2010)

Engine

Design.............................Water-cooled aluminum V-8
Twin turbochargers
Bore & Stroke, mm/inches....... 96.0x83.0 / 3.78x3.27
Displacement, cc/cid.............................4,806 / 293.3
Valve operation ....Dual overhead camshafts,
four valves per cylinder, VarioCam
Plus variable valve timing system
Compression ratio..10.5:1
Fuel feed .... Direct Fuel Injection
HP (SAE net) (mfr)..................................500 at 6,000

Chassis & Drivetrain

Frame.......................Monocoque of steel, aluminum
and magnesium
Component layout........Front engine, rear-wheel drive
Transmission.........Porsche Doppelkupplungsgetriebe
PDK seven-speed double clutch
dual-function transmission
Axle ratio (manual/Tiptronic)............................3.15:1
Front suspension .... Independent, aluminum
double-track control arms and, tie bars;
conical stump springs, dual-sleeve
gas-filled shock absorbers, PASM

Rear suspension ....Aluminum multi-link on
subframe. Coil springs. Dual-sleeve
gas-filled shock abosrbers, PASM

General

Wheelbase, mm/inches..........................2,920 / 115.0
Track:
front, mm/inches..................................1,656 / 65.2
Rear, mm/inches ....1,646 / 64.8
Brakes............... Power-assisted dual-circuit. Porsche
Stability Management (PSM), Brake Assistant,
ABS, with six-piston (front) and four-piston
(rear) aluminum monoblock calipers with
grooved, inner-vented rotors.
Tire size:
front, rear 255/45ZR19, 285/40ZR19
Wheels:
front, rear 9Jx19, 10Jx19
Weight.. 4,343 Tiptronic only

benches when rear-seat ride harshness made it difficult for him to handwrite memos.) Materials used to cover interior surfaces felt luxurious. Porsche introduced the models in the United States in October 2009, at $89,800 for the Panamera S, $93,800 for the all-wheel-drive Panamera 4S, and $132,600 for the all-wheel-drive Panamera Turbo.

"The great thing about this car," Dr. Michael Steiner, head of the project, told *CAR* magazine writer Steve Moody, was "that we started with a blank sheet of paper. We didn't

need to fit it in between other models in our range. We just asked ourselves what we wanted a Porsche GT to be."

Two decades earlier, Ferry Porsche confessed to then chairman Peter Schutz that—four decades before that—he had looked around the automotive world at what was available. When he asked himself what he wanted a sports car to be, he developed the 356. Heritage was never very far from the surface at Porsche.

Index